Touching Bases with Our Memories

Touching Bases with Our Memories

The Players Who Made the Minnesota Twins
1961 to 2001

Dean Urdahl

North Star Press of St. Cloud, Inc.

Sources:

For the story on Rod Carew, I consulted his book, *Carew,* by Rod Carew, with Ira Berkow, Simon and Schuster, New York, 1979, pp. 12, 13, 17, 18, and 20-21. For most biographical sketches I reviewed *The Baseball Online Library* from the *CBS SportsLine* website. I also used *Minnesota Twins' Yearbooks* from 1961, 1962, and 1963 and the *Twins" 2000 Media Guide*. Most of the information on these pages was derived from interviews with the players and personalities themselves.

ISBN: 0-87839-162-2

First Edition: April 2001

All photos courtesy Minnesota Twins Baseball Club, Minneapolis, Minnesota.

Cover photo: 1987 World Series mob on the mound

Photo page 329 courtesy Dean Urdahl

Stat Chart Design: Chad Urdahl

Design: Seal Dwyer

Printed in the United States of America
by Versa Press, Inc., East Peoria, Illinois

Published by

North Star Press of St. Cloud, Inc.

PO Box 451

St. Cloud, Minnesota 56302

This book is dedicated to my editor, partner, and best friend.
My wife Karen.

Table of Contents

Foreword

I'm a teacher of seventh graders. I once asked some of my students who their heroes were. They listed sports personalities and rock stars. Then I asked them to imagine what it would be like, thirty years into the future, to call their heroes on the phone and talk to them about their lives. They thought that would be "kind of cool."

It was. That's what I did for this book. I talked to some of my baseball heroes from my childhood, and also to great players from later years, when I had grown too old to have heroes.

Minnesota Twins baseball has a great legacy. I want to remind fans of the careers and stories of these past and near-present Twins baseball players.

That was my original intent, and I think the book accomplishes that. But as I wrote their stories, I realized something else. I was actually writing a history of the Twins. As the players recounted their careers, the big moments, games, series, and seasons of Minnesota Twins baseball were mostly all there.

The Twins have played forty seasons. During that time, more than 500 players have taken the field for Minnesota. Twenty-three are now deceased. I decided to highlight players from each decade of major-league baseball in Minnesota. I also decided not to write exclusively about the "stars," so this book includes a mixture.

Yes, Oliva, Killebrew, Puckett, Carew, Winfield, Molitor, and Hrbek are here. But some of the average players—the role players, if you will—are also included. Some of the best stories come from them.

The criteria for including a player were simple: he had to be alive, he had to have played for the Minnesota Twins, and he could not be currently playing major-league baseball.

An obvious question is why some people are in the book and others are not. First, I had a number in mind when I started, forty, although it was flexible. I didn't think it possible to contact all former Twins, so I wanted a representative number.

Then, when I began to contact people on my original list, I found some players had moved and their phone numbers were disconnected or unlisted. The Minnesota Twins office was helpful, but it didn't have all the current numbers I needed.

Players who had remained in contact with others provided me with many phone numbers. For example, I located Bill Pleis' father, who gave me his son's number; in turn, Bill gave me Camilo Pascual's number, and Camilo gave me Pedro Ramos' number.

Yes, there are other players I really wanted to include in this book, but I was unable to locate them. The length of the stories was, of course, influenced by how talkative the players were.

Of the forty-seven Twins players included in the book, I personally interviewed forty-three over the telephone. Of the other four, Jim Kaat e-mailed me, while Rod Carew and Dave Winfield answered my questions through their agents. I received an e-mail from Paul Molitor through the Twins.

I found the players to be gracious and often generous with their time. They were great! Many really loved to talk about baseball and tell their stories. I have related reminiscences in the players' own words as often as possible.

I might add that, over the course of time, some memories had grown a little fuzzy when compared to fact. I especially tried to verify game descriptions. But these are their stories. Only one of the fifty-plus people I contacted refused to be interviewed.

Some people deserve special thanks for their help. Minnesotan Mike Kingery, not a Twin, but a friend who played major-league baseball for many years, helped with a couple of contacts. Frank Quilici and Frank Kostro were very helpful in giving me phone numbers.

I owe a debt of gratitude to Sean Harlin, Denise Johnson, and Dave St. Peter of the Minnesota Twins, without whose cooperation the whole project would have been impossible.

My wife, Karen, has been my editor, and our eldest son, Chad, my graphic designer. Their time and effort are deeply appreciated.

Most of all I'd like to thank the players. They gave us thrills for forty years. They set examples that parents were proud to have their kids follow. They are good people and great baseball players, whether they played twenty-five years or just half a season.

They will always be the Minnesota Twins.

A Brief History

The Minnesota Twins were born on October 26, 1960, when American League owners, meeting in New York, voted to allow owner Calvin Griffith to move his Washington Senators to Minnesota. At the same meeting, they approved expansion franchises for Los Angeles and Washington, D.C.

From 1961 through 1981, the Twins played at Metropolitan Stadium in Bloomington. Their tenure there saw three titles: an American League pennant in 1965, and Western Division titles in 1969 and 1970. The 1965 All-Star Game was played at the Met. Ending in a 6-5 win by the National League, the game featured a home run by Harmon Killebrew.

The Twins opened up their new ballpark in downtown Minneapolis, the Hubert H. Humphrey Metrodome, in 1982. Carl Pohlad purchased the Twins from Griffith in 1984 and ushered in a new era of Minnesota baseball.

1985 saw the second All-Star Game played in Minnesota. The National League won 6-1.

Two world championships followed: in 1987 and 1991 the Twins defeated the St. Louis Cardinals and the Atlanta Braves, respectively. Each series was decided four games to three. In 1992, the Twins became the first American League team to draw over three million fans, when 3,030,762 passed through the Metrodome turnstiles.

Twins fans have been treated to much more than the excitement of team championships. Individual accomplishments have also captivated Minnesota fans.

They were thrilled to watch Zoilo Versalles, Rod Carew, and Harmon Killebrew capture league MVP honors, with Killebrew driving in 140 runs and lofting balls deep beyond Met Stadium's fences. Twice he crashed forty-nine homers.

There was the excitement of Rod Carew's flirting with a .400 batting average before finishing at .388; Ken Landreaux's thirty-one-game hitting streak in 1980; Tony Oliva, Mickey Hatcher, and Todd Walker rapping nine consecutive hits; Carew's multiple steals of home; and Jim Kaat's twenty-five pitching victories in 1966.

Fans were there to marvel at Bert Blyleven's 258 strikeouts; the no-hitters of Jack Kralick, Dean Chance, Scott Erickson, and Eric Milton; the magic glove of Vic Power at first; Dave Winfield's and Paul Molitor's 3,000th hits; and just the way Kirby Puckett played the game.

Over 500 players have donned the Twins uniform. As we move into a new century, new players will build upon the legacy of those who came before and more history will be made.

Bernie Allen

Bats: Left
Throws: Right
Height: 6' 0"
Weight: 175 lbs.
Born: April 16, 1939, in Ohio

YEAR	TEAM	LG	AVG	G	AB	R	H	2B	3B	HR	RBI	BB	K	OBP	SLG
1962	*Min*	*AL*	*.269*	*159*	*573*	*79*	*154*	*27*	*7*	*12*	*64*	*62*	*82*	*.338*	*.403*
1963	*Min*	*AL*	*.240*	*139*	*421*	*52*	*101*	*20*	*1*	*9*	*43*	*38*	*52*	*.302*	*.356*
1964	*Min*	*AL*	*.214*	*74*	*243*	*28*	*52*	*8*	*1*	*6*	*20*	*33*	*30*	*.309*	*.329*
1965	*Min*	*AL*	*.231*	*19*	*39*	*2*	*9*	*2*	*0*	*0*	*6*	*6*	*8*	*.326*	*.282*
1966	*Min*	*AL*	*.238*	*101*	*319*	*34*	*76*	*18*	*1*	*5*	*30*	*26*	*40*	*.299*	*.348*
1967	*Was*	*AL*	*.193*	*87*	*254*	*13*	*49*	*5*	*1*	*3*	*18*	*18*	*43*	*.244*	*.256*
1968	*Was*	*AL*	*.241*	*120*	*373*	*31*	*90*	*12*	*4*	*6*	*40*	*28*	*35*	*.301*	*.343*
1969	*Was*	*AL*	*.247*	*122*	*365*	*33*	*90*	*17*	*4*	*9*	*45*	*50*	*35*	*.337*	*.389*
1970	*Was*	*AL*	*.234*	*104*	*261*	*31*	*61*	*7*	*1*	*8*	*29*	*43*	*21*	*.342*	*.360*
1971	*Was*	*AL*	*.266*	*97*	*229*	*18*	*61*	*11*	*1*	*4*	*22*	*33*	*27*	*.359*	*.376*
1972	*NYA*	*AL*	*.227*	*84*	*220*	*26*	*50*	*9*	*0*	*9*	*21*	*23*	*42*	*.296*	*.391*
1973	*NYA*	*AL*	*.228*	*17*	*57*	*5*	*13*	*3*	*0*	*0*	*4*	*5*	*5*	*.290*	*.281*
1973	*Mon*	*NL*	*.180*	*16*	*50*	*5*	*9*	*1*	*0*	*2*	*9*	*5*	*4*	*.255*	*.320*
			AVG	*G*	*AB*	*R*	*H*	*2B*	*3B*	*HR*	*RBI*	*BB*	*K*	*OBP*	*SLG*
			.239	*1,139*	*3,404*	*357*	*815*	*140*	*21*	*73*	*351*	*370*	*424*	*.314*	*.357*

The name Bernie Allen was well known to Minnesota sports fans even before he played baseball for the Twins. In fact, Gopher football followers knew about Allen before the Twins even existed.

Bernie quarterbacked the Purdue Boilermakers in 1960. The University of Minnesota football team won the Big 10 championship that year and was named the national champion. The only blemish on the Gophers' regular season record was a loss at the hands of the Allen-led Boilermakers of Purdue.

Bernie was an Ohio native, born in East Liverpool, where he also went to school. Allen attended Purdue on a football scholarship. But he played football as a means of getting through college. It wasn't his favorite sport.

"Growing up, I played all sports in their season, football, basketball, baseball. I always liked baseball the best. I was a Cleveland Indian fan. I liked Al Rosen, Larry Dobey, and their pitchers, Bob Feller, Bob Lemon, Early Wynn, Mike Garcia."

Bernie played football and baseball both for three years at Purdue. Freshmen were ineligible for varsity competition at the time. After graduation from college, Allen signed with the Twins.

The former quarterback would have been drafted to play football, but he told callers not to waste a pick on him. He was going to play baseball. Bernie did sign a contract as a free agent with the Boston Patriots at the urging of their owner, baseball great Dom DiMaggio. But he did not intend to play football for them unless baseball didn't work out.

Allen reported to the Twins farm club in Class A Charlotte, North Carolina. He played eighty games for them in 1961 and made the Twins squad in 1962. The Twins released second baseman Billy Martin to scout and coach for them, and Bernie became the regular second sacker.

Bernie had an impressive first season. He batted .269, smacking twelve homers and driving in sixty-four runs. Allen had the Twins' longest hitting streak in 1962, thirteen games. A left-handed batter, he punished southpaw pitchers at a .305 clip.

His fielding was even more impressive. Over one twenty-nine-game span Bernie successfully handled 138 consecutive fielding chances. He shone in turning the double play and led American League second basemen in making the pivot his first two years.

"One thing I could do was turn a double play. Don't ask me why, I just could. I think my experience as a quarterback helped me out," Bernie said.

A second baseman has to withstand the punishment of hard-charging base runners trying to break up double plays. He got hit hard only once. But it dramatically changed his career.

On June 13, 1964, "Don Zimmer came in and threw a cross-body block. That's the way it was played back then. If you did it today, they'd throw you out of the game. But I don't blame him.

"My shortstop was hot doggin' a little bit and gave me a lollipop throw. I was waitin' on the throw. I wasn't even trying to make a double play, I was stretched out like a first baseman would. Zimmer came in. It was on a hit-and-run. Just one of those things."

The initial diagnosis was stretched ligaments. Bernie was out until August 4, when he tried to come back and play. But his knee had not responded to treatment. He was carried off the field three more times and hit only .214.

After the season, in late October, Bernie sought a second opinion independent of Twins' doctors. An orthopedic surgeon in Oklahoma City found that two of Allen's ligaments were torn, a medial collateral and anterior cruciate. He became an experimental model for the doctor, who took hamstring muscle from the back of Bernie's leg and used it for ligaments.

"I was told I'd never play baseball again. I feel very fortunate that I ended up playing nine more years. But to be truthful, in the first two years after the operation, I couldn't tell where my foot was comin' down. I couldn't feel anything."

Most of the 1965 season was spent in rehabilitation. Bernie got into just nineteen games of the Twins' first World Series season. He received a share of the championship payoff but wasn't on the Series roster and didn't get a ring.

Calvin Griffith was upset that Allen had gone to Oklahoma City for his medical care. At first he refused to pay for it because Twins' doctors hadn't operated. Calvin eventually paid, but he cut Allen's contract by $2,000, about the same amount as the cost of the operation. It was also Calvin who decided who got rings after the Series; Bernie was left out.

Allen bounced back with a decent year in 1966, hitting .238. After the season, he was traded to the Washington Senators, where he played for five years, mostly in a platoon capacity.

Ted Williams managed the Senators during Bernie's final three years. "He was a great ballplayer and a unique personality," Allen remembered of his manager. Bernie was traded to the New York Yankees for the 1972 season and played there for most of two years. He finished his career playing the last six weeks of 1973 with the Montreal Expos.

"I knew it was my last year. My knee was hurting, and I lost the will to do what you have to do to stay up there.

"People ask me if I was a good ballplayer," Allen chuckled. "I say no, but I was a helluva actor. I fooled 'em for nine more years after I got hurt.

"One thing about the Twins organization in the early to mid-sixties. They were all good guys. Rich Rollins was my roommate for five years. We have the same birthday, along with Gerry Roggenburk. We were all from Ohio and all signed by Floyd Baker."

After he stopped playing, Bernie was in the sporting goods business for a while. Then he went into industrial sales traveling the Midwest. He retired from that in the summer of 1999.

"My boyhood dream was to play major-league baseball," Bernie explained. "I have no regrets about not playing football. I was living my dream out by playing in the big leagues.

"It took me awhile my rookie year, especially playing against the Yankees, Mantle, Maris, Ford, Berra and all those guys, to accept I was there.

"I'd think, 'Am I really here playing against these guys?' They'd say, 'Hello, Bernie,' and I'd think, 'My God, he knows my name.' I was shocked. I was in awe.

"I had a hard time believing I was playing against them. I'd just seen them on TV on the World Series. That's the only time baseball was on except for Saturday afternoon."

What did Bernie like most about major-league baseball? "The competition, knowing that you're playing against the best. And, another thing about that Twins team, we're still good friends.

"We see each other at golf outings quite a bit. I always enjoyed playing for the Twins, the players and the fans were great."

Bernie and his second wife live in Carmel, Indiana. He has four grown children—three daughters and a son—and seven grandchildren.

Earl Battey

Bats: Right
Throws: Right
Height: 6' 1"
Weight: 205 lbs.
Born: January 5, 1935, in California

YEAR	TEAM	LG	AVG	G	AB	R	H	2B	3B	HR	RBI	BB	K	OBP	SLG
1955	Chi	AL	.286	5	7	1	2	0	0	0	0	1	1	.444	.286
1956	Chi	AL	.250	4	4	1	1	0	0	0	0	1	1	.400	.250
1957	Chi	AL	.174	48	115	12	20	2	3	3	6	11	38	.246	.322
1958	Chi	AL	.226	68	168	24	38	8	0	8	26	24	34	.325	.417
1959	Chi	AL	.219	26	64	9	14	1	2	2	7	8	13	.306	.391
1960	Was	AL	.270	137	466	49	126	24	2	15	60	48	68	.346	.427
1961	Min	AL	.302	133	460	70	139	24	1	17	55	53	66	.377	.470
1962	Min	AL	.280	148	522	58	146	20	3	11	57	57	48	.348	.393
1963	Min	AL	.285	147	508	64	145	17	1	26	84	61	75	.369	.476
1964	Min	AL	.272	131	405	33	110	17	1	12	52	51	49	.348	.407
1965	Min	AL	.297	131	394	36	117	22	2	6	60	50	23	.375	.409
1966	Min	AL	.255	115	364	30	93	12	1	4	34	43	30	.337	.327
1967	Min	AL	.165	48	109	6	18	3	1	0	8	13	24	.254	.211
			AVG	G	AB	R	H	2B	3B	HR	RBI	BB	K	OBP	SLG
			.270	1,141	3,586	393	969	150	17	104	449	421	470	.349	.409

The California kid dreamed of being a basketball player while growing up in the Los Angeles neighborhood of Watts. Earl Battey didn't idolize any major-league baseball players. Basketball was his first love.

But his 6' 1" height and 205-pound frame were more suited to another sport in which Earl excelled: baseball. The Chicago White Sox inked a contract with Battey in 1953 and sent him to Colorado Springs. The next year he played for Waterloo, Iowa.

Battey spent most of the 1955 season with Charleston, West Virginia. He was twenty when he made his major-league debut with the White Sox on September 10 of that year.

Battey returned to the minors for all but four games in 1956. Over the next three years, he divided time between the Sox and minor-league stints with Toronto and Los Angeles. Earl didn't bat more than 168 times in any season with the White Sox.

After appearing in only twenty-six games in 1959, he was traded to the Washington Senators. The Harlem Globetrotters had expressed interest in having Earl join them, but baseball rules at that time prohibited players from engaging in activities that could be viewed as injurious to their baseball careers.

Battey recorded an excellent 1960 season with the Senators. He batted 466 times and hit .270. Recognized as a defensive standout throughout the league, he won the Gold Glove as best-fielding catcher. It was the franchise's last year in the nation's capital before the team moved to Minnesota.

With Battey's arrival, fans in the Upper Midwest were treated to the best all-around catcher in Twins' history. Earl moved like a cat behind the plate. His lightning-quick throwing release gunned down attempted base-stealers and picked off many who wandered too far off base.

The year 1961 was a breakout year for a stellar career. Battey hit .302 with seventeen home runs. From 1961 through 1966, he played in 805 of the Twins' first 970 games. Battey was named to five All-Star games and earned two more Gold Gloves in 1961 and 1962. In 1962 he led all major-league catchers with a .280 batting average while picking thirteen runners off the bases and throwing out twenty-four would-be base stealers.

In 1963 Battey hit twenty-six home runs, more than any other Twins catcher, and hit .285 while driving in eighty-four runs. He did all of this despite a series of nagging injuries. Earl's knee bothered him, he dislocated his fingers several times, he had a goiter problem, and twice he suffered broken cheekbones from pitches. Once he was hospitalized after a beaning.

After those facial injuries, Earl and Twins' trainer Doc (George) Lentz created the first protective-flap batting helmet, which Battey wore to ward off more damage.

Earl's toughness was never more evident than during the 1965 World Series. In Game 3 at Dodger Stadium, he ran into a neck-high crossbar while attempting to catch a foul ball. Battey played the rest of the series even though he could hardly speak or turn his head.

Battey loved the job of catcher. It provided him an opportunity to be in control of the game. He called it "the thinking man's position." He doesn't miss the doubleheaders, however.

One game in particular stands out in Battey's memory: left-hander Jack Kralick's no-hitter of August 26, 1962.

"I called almost all the pitches that day," Earl remembered during a phone interview for this book. "Kralick hardly shook me off. He had a good slider and a knuckleball. I started thinking 'no-hitter' about the seventh inning. What made me focus in on it was that we were playing Kansas City.

"They had a lot of good first-ball hitters, and so I had to think in advance not just the current situation, but what we'd do if we got behind in the count. Because if a guy's a first-ball hitter and you get him 2-0, he's still a first-ball hitter."

Earl felt fortunate to have caught some of the great pitchers of the 1950s and 1960s. Early Wynn, a Hall of Fame 300-game winner, was caught by Battey while he was a White Sox, as was Billy Pierce. For the Twins, Camilo Pascual, Dave Boswell, Mudcat Grant, Jim Kaat, and Jim Perry had impressive years under the guidance of catcher Battey.

When working with pitchers, a catcher also works with the pitching coach. One of the Twins' best but most controversial, was Johnny Sain, who coached from 1965 to 1966.

"I always worked closely with him," Battey remarked. "I listened to him go over things with the pitchers and correct flaws in their delivery. I would go out and talk to pitchers and just remind them of something that Johnny Sain was trying to get them to do.

"He had a terrific pitching mind. Johnny was unique. He developed a contraption that taught pitchers how to spin the ball. Before you get a ball to break, you have to get the right spin on it. When pitchers weren't pitching, he had them constantly working on ball rotation. Johnny's device was like an ice pick through the ball with a handle, and you could simulate spin with it. It's what the guys worked on when they were in the bullpen or on the bench.

"Johnny got pitchers to buy into his philosophy. He could turn good pitchers into great ones."

But John Sain rubbed some people the wrong way. Possibly, according to Battey, it was because he separated the pitchers from the position players, except for catchers. After only a couple of years, Sain was let go from the Twins' coaching ranks.

It fell upon catchers as well as coaches to work on pitchers' flaws. Battey remembers advice he gave to Pedro Ramos. "I used to tell him that he'd telegraph his curve ball. I said to him, 'If you're gonna keep throwing it like that, I won't need any signals. If you can't fool the catcher, how are you gonna fool the batter?'"

The game has changed, Battey noted, especially in how games are called and how pitchers are handled.

"Now the bench calls the pitches and not the catcher," Earl commented. "We used to pace a pitcher to go nine innings. Now they tell them to go as hard as they can for as long as they can, and then a reliever will come in. Baseball is now much more specialized: starter, middle relief, closer."

Battey is quick to give others credit for his career. When Earl picked off thirteen runners in 1962, Rich Rollins played third base and the excellent-fielding Vic Power was at first.

"Rollins was excellent at decoying base runners," Earl said, "and Power was a tremendous fielder."

The years of playing through nagging injuries finally caught up with Battey in 1967. After hitting just .165 in only forty-eight games, he retired from baseball at the age of thirty-three. His career batting average was .270. No Twins catcher has ever hit more home runs or driven in more runs or fielded like Earl Battey.

Following his baseball career, Battey worked with disturbed youth at Children's Village in upstate New York. In 1980, at the age of forty-five, he moved to Florida and entered college, earning a degree as a special education teacher.

Earl taught and coached eighteen years in Ocala, Florida. He retired from teaching in 2000 and continues to live in Ocala with his wife, Sonia. He has two children in Florida and three others in California.

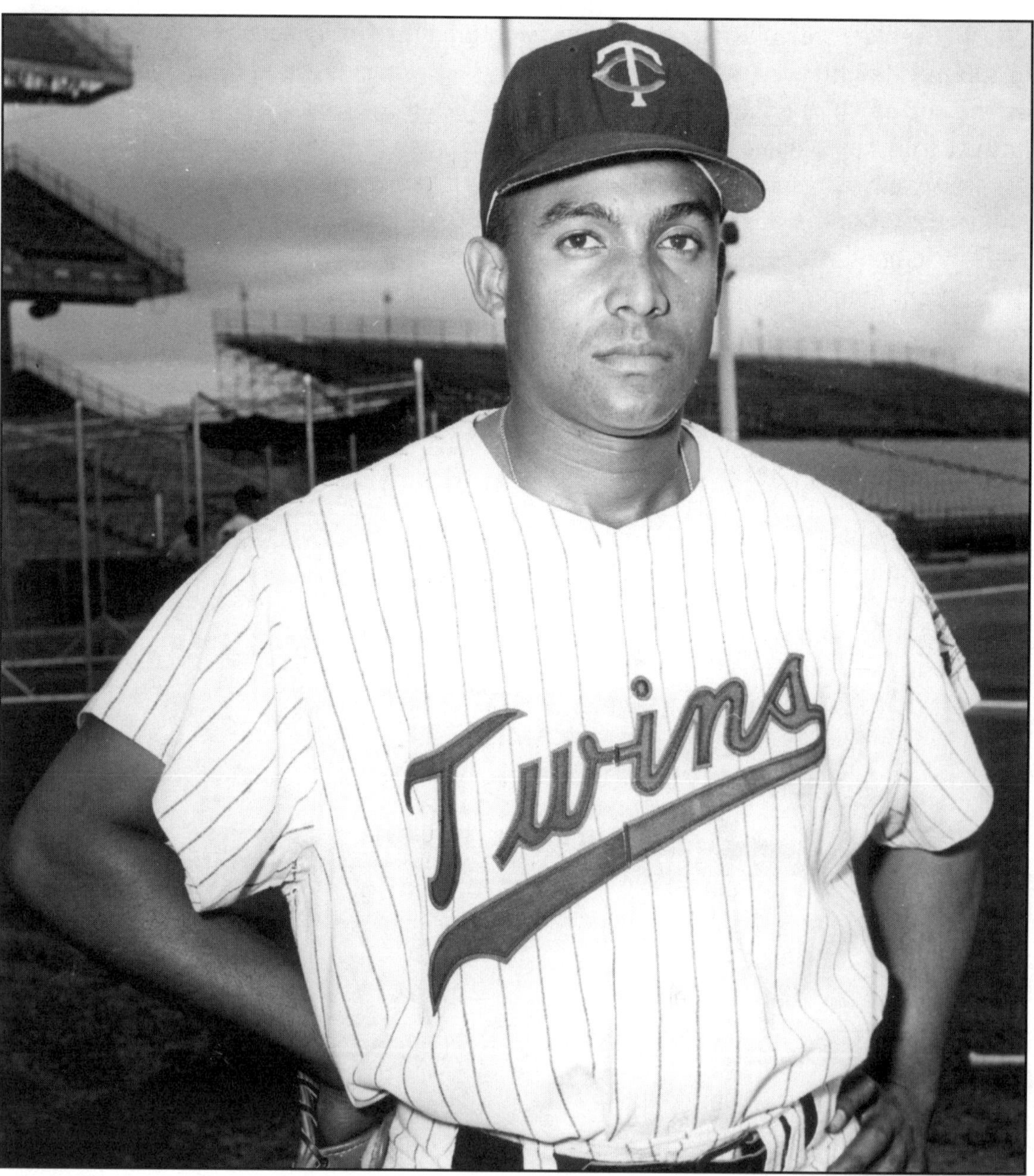
Twins

Julio Becquer

Bats: Left
Throws: Left
Height: 5' 11"
Weight: 178 lbs.
Born: December 20, 1931, in Cuba

YEAR	TEAM	LG	AVG	G	AB	R	H	2B	3B	HR	RBI	BB	K	OBP	SLG
1955	Was	AL	.214	10	14	1	3	0	0	0	1	0	1	.214	.214
1957	Was	AL	.226	105	186	14	42	6	2	2	22	10	29	.269	.312
1958	Was	AL	.238	86	164	10	39	3	0	0	12	8	21	.270	.256
1959	Was	AL	.268	108	220	20	59	12	5	1	26	8	17	.296	.382
1960	Was	AL	.252	110	298	41	75	15	7	4	35	12	35	.282	.389
1961	LAA	AL	.000	11	8	0	0	0	0	0	0	1	5	.111	.000
1961	Min	AL	.238	57	84	13	20	1	2	5	18	2	12	.253	.476
1963	Min	AL	--------	1	0	1	0	0	0	0	0	0	0	--------	--------
			AVG	G	AB	R	H	2B	3B	HR	RBI	BB	K	OBP	SLG
			.244	488	974	100	238	37	16	12	114	41	120	.276	.352

The sun shone brightly on the emerald-green grass of Metropolitan Stadium on July 4, 1961. The hometown Minnesota Twins trailed the Chicago White Sox in the first game of a doubleheader.

It was 4-2 in the bottom of the ninth. The large crowd grew hopeful as the Twins loaded the bases. But there were two outs when a left-handed Cuban was announced as a pinch hitter.

Julio Becquer dug in against the Sox's Warren Hacker. He lined the first pitch deep to right into the bleachers for a grand-slam homer. The Twins fans left Met Stadium savoring a 6-4 victory.

Pinch-hitting was a big part of the Man-from-Havana's career. Julio had sixty-three career pinch-hits and was the American League's top pinch hitter in 1957 and 1959.

Growing up in baseball-crazy Cuba, Becquer admired the Cuban legend Minnie Minnoso and a great Cuban first baseman, Salazar. Julio signed in 1951, one of many future stars inked by expert scout Joe Cambria of the Washington Senators. Julio played in the Senators' farm system until making the big club late in 1955.

The next year, the slick-fielding, left-handed first baseman ended up back in the minors in Louisville, Kentucky. While there, he also played nineteen games at third base. He admitted that the throw from third to first was tougher for a lefty. But Julio was quick, agile and had an excellent arm.

Because of that, "I could cheat and play closer to the hole at short," he said.

Being a black Latino baseball player in the 1950s posed frequent challenges. Segregation and racism were especially prevalent during spring training, which was, of course, in the South.

Julio commented on race and baseball in the 1950s. "It was really tough, because we came here at the height of segregation, and I came to the South. Whites and blacks were separated at spring training in Orlando. We didn't stay together. We had to stay in separate quarters.

"We stayed in the black section of Orlando in a small hotel. It was clean but not the best facilities. White Latinos like Ramos and Pascual stayed with the whites.

"There was never any problem with the white players. I had great respect for Killebrew, Allison, and Kaat. They were great guys," Becquer said.

"Some of the other clubs didn't treat their Latin players as well. But fortunately for us, we were treated well by the Griffith family. We didn't have any trouble with Calvin. Calvin always made sure that everything was okay for us, even when we were segregated."

The Griffith organization was one of the pioneers in bringing Latin players to the major leagues. White Latinos played for the Senators in the late 1930s and 1940s.

Becquer stuck with the Senators as a pinch hitter and a defensive replacement from 1957 to 1960. There he had the misfortune to play behind two great first basemen, Roy Sievers and Harmon Killebrew. 1960 was Julio's most productive year. He hit .252 in 298 at-bats with four home runs and 35 RBIs.

Also that year, he was part of the first all-Cuban triple play. Whitey Herzog hit back to Pedro Ramos for one out, Ramos threw to Julio for the second out, and Becquer threw to Zoilo Versalles to complete the triple play.

Versalles played shortstop for the Twins from 1961 to 1967, earning American League MVP honors in 1965. Julio commented on his now-deceased friend. "People remember that Zoilo was a great player compared to other shortstops, but they forget that Zoilo had a lot of power for being a little guy. He hit a lot of home runs, over a hundred in his career. Zoilo's slugging percentage was incredible. He hit nineteen or twenty home runs one year and could really run the bases."

The Senators moved to Minnesota after the 1960 season, and the American League expanded to Los Angeles. The Angels took Becquer from the Twins' roster.

But Julio played in just eleven games for the Angels. Once again he was behind another star first baseman, this time slugger Ted Kluszewski. The Angels sold Becquer to the minor-league Buffalo, New York, team. On June 2, the Twins reacquired Julio, purchasing his contract from Buffalo.

In addition to his grand-slam heroics against the White Sox, Becquer remembered another big pinch-hit that 1961 season. He cracked a pinch-hit homer off Ryan Duren of the Yankees to beat them 4-3.

Julio's versatility was put to the test on September 9. In a blowout game against Kansas City, he took the mound for 1.1 innings. He surrendered three runs in his only Twins pitching appearance.

When asked what makes a good pinch hitter, Julio responded, "Just go up and swing the bat. A good pinch hitter has to be a good contact hitter. All pitchers were tough. On a given day, you just had to be ready."

It was back to the minors for Julio in 1962. The next year, the Twins brought him back for a short time so that he could qualify for his major-league pension.

"I was playing in Veracruz in the Mexican League," Julio recalled. "I needed seven days to qualify for my major league pension. Calvin bought my contract from Veracruz and brought me up for the end of the season."

Becquer feels indebted to the sport he loves. "Playing big-league baseball was like a dream," he said. "It was like hitting the lottery. It gave me the opportunity to come to the United States and always played a part in my life. It opened doors for my life.

"What you learn in baseball you apply to other things in life," Julio explained. "It helped teach the motivation and discipline that people need to be successful. The game has been very, very good to me."

After his major-league baseball career ended, Julio entered the retail business world, working for Dayton-Hudson Corporation for thirty years.

He has also continued to work for the Twins, doing baseball clinics for young players.

Julio lives in Minneapolis. He has two boys and a girl, as well as three grandsons and a granddaughter. The grandsons are ages fourteen and twelve. In addition to baseball, hockey has become a favorite sport in the Becquer family as the boys chase a puck on the ice.

Dave Boswell

Bats: Right
Throws: Right
Height: 6' 3"
Weight: 185 lbs.
Born: January 20, 1945, in Maryland

YEAR	TEAM	LG	ERA	W	L	Sv	G	IP	H	R	ER	BB	K	AVG. A
1964	Min	AL	4.24	2	0	0	4	23.1	21	11	11	12	25	.236
1965	Min	AL	3.40	6	5	0	27	106.0	77	43	40	46	85	.204
1966	Min	AL	3.14	12	5	0	28	169.1	120	66	59	65	173	.197
1967	Min	AL	3.27	14	12	0	37	222.2	162	84	81	107	204	.202
1968	Min	AL	3.32	10	13	0	34	190.0	148	79	70	87	143	.213
1969	Min	AL	3.23	20	12	0	39	256.1	215	105	92	99	190	.226
1970	Min	AL	6.42	3	7	0	18	68.2	80	55	49	44	45	.292
1971	Det	AL	6.23	0	0	0	3	4.1	3	3	3	6	3	.200
1971	Bal	AL	4.38	1	2	0	15	24.2	32	16	12	15	14	.305
			ERA	W	L	Sv	G	IP	H	R	ER	BB	K	AVG. A
			3.52	68	56	0	205	1,065.1	858	462	417	481	882	.219

Dave Boswell believed he was born to be a major-league baseball player. From when he first threw a baseball in his hometown of Baltimore, onlookers knew there was something special about his arm.

He starred for Calvert Hall High School in Baltimore, where many scouts, including the Twins' Ed Dunn, watched him pitch and play the outfield. All the teams offered small bonuses. Dave looked at what the Twins had in pitching and was excited about how they could hit the baseball. He wanted to go somewhere where he felt he could move up in a hurry.

Dave signed his pro contract on his high school graduation day in 1963. His dad insisted the contract provide that Dave go to an instructional league and be invited to major-league training camp his first year.

Dave's dad accompanied him to Orlando, Florida, for the Twins camp. Catcher Earl Battey recalled, "Mr. Boswell walked over to me with Dave. He said, 'Earl, this is my son. I'm giving him to you.'"

Boswell spent most of the time before the 1964 camp in the Florida Instructional League. Dave felt he had his best spring in 1964, but the Twins determined he needed more experience and shipped him to Bismarck in the Northern League. After three or four months, he moved up to AA Charlotte, North Carolina. Then the Twins brought him up at the end of the 1964 season.

He started four games and went 2-0 with a 4.24 ERA. Boswell showed a live arm to manager Sam Mele. He could throw ninety-five to ninety-seven miles per hour and had a wicked break on his curveball.

"People always talked about my curve," Boswell commented. "But my fastball was my best pitch."

One of his first games was against Boston. His first three pitches went for a double, another two-bagger, and a home run. Sam Mele went out to the hill for a conference.

"What's he got?" Mele asked catcher Battey.

"I don't know," Battey answered. "I haven't caught a pitch yet."

Dave was in the big leagues full time in 1965, facing menacing hitters like his boyhood heroes Mickey Mantle and Al Kaline. Kaline gave the young pitcher fits.

"If everybody batted off me the way Kaline did, I wouldn't have survived," Boswell said. "One game I pitched a three-hitter against the Tigers and then came back and threw a four-hitter. Kaline had six out of the seven hits. I said, 'Al, if you'd been sick, I'd be in the Hall of Fame.'"

Dave went 6-5 with a 3.40 ERA in 1965. Although respectable by most standards, it wasn't the kind of year he had hoped to have. He was sick a good part of the season, suffering from mononucleosis and pneumonia.

"I was overused, I believe," Boswell said. "After graduation I was down in the Instructional League, then bang, into spring training, then the '64 season. When the season was over, bang, I was down in the Instructional League again. I ended up the '65 season just wearing myself out."

Boswell did appear in Game 5 of the 1965 World Series against the Los Angeles Dodgers. He pitched 2.2 innings in relief of Jim Kaat, surrendering one run while striking out three.

Dave's career exploded the next year. In some ways he considered 1966 to be his most dominating season. He went 12-5 with his lowest ERA, 3.14. The most telling statistic was that opponents hit only .143 off him.

Boswell even developed a new pitch. While he was winding up to deliver, his right hand brushed his side, throwing off his grip. If he stopped his motion, it would be a ball, so he went through with the pitch. The ball took a crazy screw-ball-like dive into the batter for a strike.

Accusations of spitball were heard. But it was simply a new way to throw the ball. Dave held it with his middle finger and thumb, the finger gripping the ball tightly on one side, holding about one-third of the ball. His forefinger served as a guide, just touching the ball, as Dave rolled his thumb. Then he threw hard. The ball took strange twists and dropped about thirty inches.

Boswell admitted throwing a spitball once in his career. "It was to Mickey Mantle, he struck out on it. The ball went between the catcher's legs and Mantle got to first. I struck out four that inning."

Boswell, Dean Chance, and Jim Kaat made the record books in 1967 when, for the first time, three pitchers from the same team posted over 200 strikeouts each.

Those were the days when pitchers were expected to throw a lot of innings. Starters were even expected to relieve when called upon. Dave explained that he was expected to go as long as he could.

"You don't leave the game unless you were hurting the club. They'd say, 'Keep pitchin', we can't help ya until the ninth.' Pitchers are pacified today."

But Boswell had his most respect and admiration for the skipper who used him the most, Billy Martin. "He was the best manager I played for. No one wanted to win more than Billy. He was the only one who gave me more than thirty starts."

Boswell frequently had problems with blisters on his throwing hand. Occasionally he tried his own remedies. One night before he was due to start, Dave poured a little alum into an open blister, hoping to dry it up. More pain resulted.

Then he obtained a couple of surgical gloves. As he warmed up for a game against the Angels, he wore the rubber glove on his pitching hand and had no ill effects.

"The rubber gave me a better grip, it felt good," Boswell related.

He took the mound and threw his variety of pitches successfully as umpire Frank Umont watched. Dave's surgical glove was undetected.

"Jim Fregosi was the first hitter. I thought I had been warming up at the same speed I'd be throwin' in the game. When I threw the first pitch to Fregosi, ninety-five to ninety-seven miles an hour, the glove exploded in my hand. Air must have got into it when I threw. I looked down at my hand and it looked like a couple of rubbers hanging from my fingers.

"I tried to blow it off, I turned around, put the glove under my arm. The umpire was wonderin', 'What the heck's he doin'?'

"The ball was right down the middle. Earl Battey said, 'Wasn't that a strike?'

"Umont said, 'I don't know, what happened to his hand?'

"I proceeded to put the glove in my pocket and pitch."

For several reasons, 1969 was the highlight year in Boswell's career. The Twins won the Western Division, and he won twenty games. A dominating pitcher who went deep into games, Dave threw over 256 innings that season, the most in his career. But controversy marred his brilliant year.

Dave pitched and beat Detroit on August 5. The next day players passed time in the clubhouse before the game, playing cards and socializing. Pranks are part of player interaction. Boswell fell victim to one that day.

As Dave played cards, someone gave him a hotfoot by sticking a lit match into his right spike. The hotfoot actually burned into the leather of his baseball spike and gave Boswell a blister the size of a fifty-cent piece on his right foot.

In a bit of irony, Dave wore size thirteen street shoes, but he preferred much tighter cleats, size ten or eleven, believing that tight spikes would help him avoid foot blisters.

Boswell was incensed by the results of the prank. He could hardly walk when he went to George Lentz, the trainer. Lentz told him to skip the pre-game pitchers' conditioning run.

"Then the pitching coach, Art Fowler, made some comment to me about not running. Martin had complained to him that I wasn't doing the workout. I guess he didn't know I was hurt," Boswell said in a phone interview for this book. "It bothered me when Art cussed at me, and I said something back. Billy came and told me to go back to the hotel."

Boswell continued his account of how the prank exploded into fisticuffs. He said he spent most of the evening in the Lindall A.C., a restaurant/bar/club near the hotel. When the game was over, Billy Martin, Bob Allison, and Art Fowler entered the bar. Upon spying Boswell, Fowler walked out the door into an alley.

Boswell, wanting to make peace, followed Art outside. Allison, misunderstanding Dave's intention, blocked the pitcher's path to his departing pitching coach.

"We'll talk tomorrow!" Fowler yelled.

As Boswell continued after Art, Allison grabbed him. A mini-brawl ensued, during which big Bob was knocked unconscious with a blackened eye. Others, including Martin, ripped into the pitcher.

Dave wound up in the hospital with fifty stitches. Martin had to have wounds on his hand sewn up as well. Boswell missed a couple of starts.

"It was funny how the Twins called me back," Dave related. "I was fishing and listening to the radio when Martin came on and said, 'Wherever you are, Dave, we need you at the ballpark.'

"It's all a forgotten memory. Billy was my best manager. We were all friends. Funny thing is, I later found out it was Billy that gave me the hotfoot."

The fight in Detroit wasn't the only blemish on a great season. While pitching in the League Championship Series against the Orioles, Dave severely hurt his arm.

It was Game 2. The Twins had lost the first game in twelve innings, 4-3. This game was scoreless after ten innings. But in the bottom of the tenth, Dave knew something had gone wrong.

"I threw a 3-2 slider to Frank Robinson, and I felt something let go in the back of my arm. I knew it was hurt bad, but I came out for the eleventh.

"I walked Boog Powell, the first batter, and Brooks Robinson bunted him over. I got Mark Belanger; now there's two outs, and I've got Davey Johnson up there. Johnson gave me more trouble than most anybody on the Orioles.

"Billy Martin came out to talk to me and said, 'Don't give him nothin'.' I said, 'Are we gonna pitch to him or what?' He said, 'Yeah, there's two outs.'

"I got the first pitch outside, ball one. The next was a slider for a strike. Then I came up with a fastball behind him. I couldn't feel anything in my arm. Martin yelled, 'Put him on!' Then I got behind 2-1, so I walked him. I knew I was comin' out."

Billy Martin was thinking ahead. When Orioles catcher Elrod Hendricks was announced, the Twins skipper brought in his southpaw, Ron Perranoski, to pitch against the left-handed Hendricks.

The Orioles countered with Curt Moten, a righty who hit for Hendricks. If the game went to the thirteenth, then Clay Dalrymple, a sore-armed catcher, would have to enter the game for the Orioles. Billy hoped his pitching maneuver would result in his team's exploiting the Orioles catcher.

But Moten messed up Martin's strategy when he lined a sharp base hit to right. Tony Oliva made a strong throw to the plate. As catcher George Mitterwald braced himself from the onrushing Boog Powell, the ball took a sideways short-hop away from Mitterwald, and Powell scored the winning run.

On the plane home, Dave remarked to Frank Quilici, "I think I'm done." Frank tried to reassure his friend that his arm would heal.

The next game in Minnesota, Billy Martin played a hunch and started Bob Miller on the mound. The move soured as the Twins suffered an 11-2 defeat.

When Dave got home to Baltimore, he went to the hospital at Johns Hopkins. Doctors there discovered that the posterior deltoid muscle in his right arm had detached from the bone and that he had a tear in his rotator cuff as well.

"Put your right arm in a sling and hope it doesn't fall off," one doctor advised. Today, doctors probably could have fixed the arm and prolonged Dave's career. In 1969 there wasn't a lot they could do.

In 1970 the arm didn't come around, and Boswell won just three games. The Twins let him go. He signed with the Tigers for the start of the 1971 season. After he appeared in just three games for Detroit, they decided to send Boswell to the minors.

Dave asked for his release. Billy Martin, the Tiger's new manager, granted his request and the pitcher signed with Baltimore. Boswell finished the season, and his career, with the Orioles. He was in fifteen games for the eventual AL champions.

In 1972, Boswell's career was over.

His prediction on the plane ride home in 1969 was essentially right. Never again the same pitcher, Boswell won only another four games after being hurt. In 1973 his pro career was over.

It was a traumatic adjustment for a man not thirty. Baseball was his life.

"It meant everything. Ever since I was nine years [old] they knew I could throw a ball better than anyone else my age at that time. I was a honed instrument to be a ballplayer. I wouldn't even marry my wife until I made the big leagues," Boswell said.

"I couldn't accept the fact that they couldn't fix my arm. I was offered a job working downtown in Baltimore with the National Brewery. I would have been working in advertising and stuff.

"But I wanted to build up my arm and I asked if I could work in keg racking, throwing kegs around, powerhouse work. I worked five or six years for them. I'd work all day throwin' kegs, and then I'd go out back and throw a baseball at the wall. They asked me to stop doin' that because I was bustin' out the back of the wall."

After a merger, Dave went to work at various jobs for short periods, including one for Anchor Motor Freight. Then he took a position as a supervisor with Winner Distributing, a beer distributor. After twelve years, he retired.

For the last eight years he has worked for Grand Slam, teaching pitching lessons in the Baltimore area.

Dave and his wife, Lou, still live near Baltimore. Childhood sweethearts since the age of thirteen, they were married the day after the 1965 World Series ended. The groom was worried he might have to have a proxy stand in. They have been together for thirty-five years and have three children.

It was exciting being the wife of a major-league baseball player, Lou Boswell remembered.

"The travel was exciting, we went on one or two trips a year. The money was good," she said.

"But it was lonely, too, and there was a lot of stress. With some teams, the wives formed cliques. That's not the way it was in Minnesota. We all had fashion shows, church Bible studies, and went on pontoon boats fishing. We didn't have 'elites' like they did some places."

Does Dave have any regrets about his career? Maybe that he pitched instead of playing outfield. He did sign as a pitcher-outfielder and had a career average of .202, which was good considering pitchers get very little time in the batting cage. He also had excellent speed and was used frequently by the Twins as a pinch runner.

Dave Boswell gave thrills to the fans of the mid-1960s and remembers Minnesota fondly. "It was they who gave me the thrills," he concluded.

DEAN CHANCE

Bats: Right
Throws: Right
Height: 6' 3"
Weight: 200 lbs.
Born: June 1, 1941, in Ohio

YEAR	TEAM	LG	ERA	W	L	Sv	G	IP	H	R	ER	BB	K	AVG. A
1961	LAA	AL	6.87	0	2	0	5	18.1	33	15	14	5	11	.413
1962	LAA	AL	2.96	14	10	8	50	206.2	195	83	68	66	127	.250
1963	LAA	AL	3.19	13	18	3	45	248.0	229	109	88	90	168	.243
1964	LAA	AL	1.65	20	9	4	46	278.1	194	56	51	86	207	.195
1965	Cal	AL	3.15	15	10	0	36	225.2	197	86	79	101	164	.238
1966	Cal	AL	3.08	12	17	1	41	259.2	206	113	89	114	180	.222
1967	Min	AL	2.73	20	14	1	41	283.2	244	109	86	68	220	.229
1968	Min	AL	2.53	16	16	1	43	292.0	224	96	82	63	234	.211
1969	Min	AL	2.95	5	4	0	20	88.1	76	39	29	35	50	.233
1970	Cle	AL	4.24	9	8	4	45	155.0	172	80	73	59	109	.287
1970	NYN	NL	13.50	0	1	1	3	2.0	3	3	3	2	0	.500
1971	Det	AL	3.51	4	6	0	31	89.2	91	43	35	50	64	.265
			ERA	W	L	Sv	G	IP	H	R	ER	BB	K	AVG. A
			2.92	128	115	23	406	2,147.1	1,864	832	697	739	1,534	.234

Few pitchers were as dominating as Dean Chance was in his prime. In 1964, pitching for the Los Angeles Angels, Chance was 20-9 with a 1.65 ERA. He led the American League with fifteen complete games and eleven shutouts.

Chance also relieved eleven times and saved four games in an era when pitchers had to actually face the tying run to be credited with saves. He often threw on three days' rest and blew away other teams' best hitters with a lively, naturally sinking fastball.

Dean also led the league in innings pitched while striking out 207 hitters. He won the Cy Young Award in 1964, when only one hurler in the major leagues received it.

Chance grew up in Ohio and attended Northwestern High School in Wayne County, graduating in 1959. He was signed by Baltimore and then picked by a new expansion team, the Los Angeles Angels, in the winter draft of 1961.

Chance pitched as a rookie for the Angels in 1962. As an occasional starter, he had a 14-10 record and a 2.96 ERA. He was a regular member of the starting rotation in 1963, but the weak-hitting Angels left him with a 13-18 mark.

The L.A. Angels of the early 1960s didn't score many runs. Chance lost thirteen times when the Angels were shut out. In one game, Dean blanked the Yankees for fourteen innings. The Angels lost 2-0 after he left the game.

In his Cy Young season, Chance proved he didn't need many runs to win. Six times he recorded 1-0 victories that year, setting a major-league record. His twentieth win came on September 25, 1964, fittingly a 1-0 victory over Jim Kaat and the Twins. Chance beat Kaat 1-0 three times in his career.

Chance was thankful to pitch in spacious Dodger Stadium. "I remember a night game there when Harmon Killebrew hit a fastball deep to right-center. I thought it was gone. In a day game it would have been, but that night it was caught against the fence. There's a reason that five Cy Young winners in a row pitched in that park."

After two more years in Los Angeles struggling to pitch well for a poor team, Chance welcomed the trade that sent him to Minnesota for Jimmie Hall, Don Mincher, and Pete Cimino.

"Having to pitch in close games meant a lot of wear and tear on my arm," Chance explained.

Chance described his pitching motion as "just a natural motion. I liked to turn my back to home plate. I extended my arm, I don't know if anybody ever extended their arm more than I did. It was just my natural way, ya gotta throw your natural way or you'll hurt yourself."

After he took the sign, Chance totally turned his back on the catcher, not looking at him again until he ended the delivery. In addition to the fastball, Dean had a good slider on which he changed speeds.

The year he joined the Twins, 1967, was a big rebound year for Chance. He won the American League Comeback Player of the Year Award. Dean was 20-14 for the Twins and threw two no-hitters. One went five innings, shortened by rain; the other was a 2-1 handcuffing of the Cleveland Indians.

But, even with the powerful Twins, power outages occurred. Dean recalled, "I remember losing on my birthday 1-0 to the White Sox. I had a no-hitter for eight innings."

His biggest disappointment in baseball came on the last weekend of the 1967 season. The Twins went to Boston with a one-game lead over the Red Sox. One win would give them the American League title. Jim Kaat lost the first game. Dean took the hill on the final day of the season, needing a win to clinch the pennant. He lost 5-4.

When he recalls his personal highlights, the first time he won twenty games as an Angel comes to mind. "It's every kid's goal to win twenty games. When the ball came down and little Albie Pearson caught it, it was a great thrill.

"Another was the first All-Star Game I started. I struck out the first two hitters, Clemente and Groat. That was a thrill in New York. The Cy Young was also special."

Chance continued, "My big break was getting to go to the Angels, because if you don't get a chance to pitch, you don't know what you can do. I was thankful my manager gave me the ball and let me go out and start."

He had two one-hitters with the Angels, including one in which Zoilo Versalles of the Twins got the only hit, an infield roller, in the eighth inning.

Chance had another strong year for the Twins in 1968 with six shutouts and sixteen wins. But he also lost sixteen games, and Calvin Griffith tried to trim his $60,000 salary to $51,000.

Dean held out, reported to spring training late and hurt his arm. He was 5-4 for the 1969 Twins and was never again the same.

Pitching for the Indians and Mets, he won another thirteen games but no longer dominated. He retired in 1971 at the age of thirty-one.

He had won 128 and lost 115 with a 2.92 ERA, pitching with a motion that put strain on his arm, and lost about fifteen games in relief. Often pitching late in games against the opposition's best hitters, Chance twice led the league in innings pitched. And, for a period, he shined as baseball's best.

"When I couldn't do physically what my mind told me to do, I just got out," he said.

Chance appreciated his managers. "They are different. As far as baseball knowledge, the tops was Billy Martin. He was like a gambler. His instincts for baseball were absolutely phenomenal.

"Alvin Dark was a tremendous baseball man. Bill Rigney gave me the ball with the Angels, but he could wear a bullpen out.

"Another highlight is that you meet a lot of great, nice people in sports, including writers like Jim Murray and Sid Hartman."

Dean recognizes the changes in baseball, from the way pitchers are used, to the huge impact of corporations and television.

"Commercialism has changed the game. They have smaller ballparks today with signs all over and charge more. Minnesota needs a new ballpark. But it should have a retractable roof," Chance said.

"I pitched in Metropolitan Stadium when it was twenty-nine degrees. Fritz Peterson was the opposing pitcher and he couldn't throw a strike. Minnesota is a great place, and the last made park should be the best."

Chance would like to see right done by another of his Minnesota connections. "Tony Oliva belongs in the Hall of Fame," he stated emphatically. "He was the toughest hitter I faced; ask any right-handed pitcher."

Since leaving baseball, Chance has kept land in Ohio and worked in boxing. He is the president of the International Boxing Association. He used to manage Ernie Shavers and had Ray Anderson when he was in Minnesota in 1969. He also spent some time in the carnival amusement business.

The former Cy Young winner is satisfied with his career. "First ya wanna make it to the majors, then just get enough time in for a pension. I got the maximum in, ten years. I get as much from my pension as I ever made playing, about $60,000 a year. So what's the matter with that? I got a lot of great memories and ended up with some decent stats."

Chance lives on a farm near Wooster, Ohio. He has a thirty-eight-year-old son who also resides in Ohio.

Twins

Paul Giel

Bats: Right
Throws: Right
Height: 5' 11"
Weight: 185 lbs.
Born: September 29, 1932, in Minnesota

YEAR	TEAM	LG	ERA	W	L	Sv	G	IP	H	R	ER	BB	K	AVG. A
1954	NYG	NL	8.31	0	0	0	6	4.1	8	4	4	2	4	.421
1955	NYG	NL	3.39	4	4	0	34	82.1	70	36	31	50	47	.233
1958	SF	NL	4.70	4	5	0	29	92.0	89	56	48	55	55	.259
1959	Pit	NL	14.09	0	0	0	4	7.2	17	12	12	6	3	.472
1960	Pit	NL	5.73	2	0	0	16	33.0	35	25	21	15	21	.276
1961	Min	AL	9.78	1	0	0	12	19.1	24	27	21	17	14	.289
1961	KCA	AL	37.80	0	0	0	1	1.2	6	7	7	3	1	.600
			ERA	W	L	Sv	G	IP	H	R	ER	BB	K	AVG. A
			5.39	11	9	0	102	240.1	249	167	144	148	145	.271

Paul Giel is a Minnesota sports legend. Out of Winona High School in 1950, Giel attended the University of Minnesota, where he excelled in football and baseball. He was drafted by the Chicago Bears following his illustrious Gopher football career. Giel chose instead to pursue baseball at the professional level, a path that brought him to the Twins for a short time.

Paul knew he could play baseball at the university. However, "I didn't know about my football, because when you see guys like Bud Grant and Billy Bye and Leo Nomilini, when you're a seventeen-year-old kid looking at a Gopher football game from the bleachers, you wonder if you can do it."

Giel didn't need to doubt himself. He played football in 1951, 1952, and 1953 for Coach Wes Fesler and gained national prominence. The famous Bernie Bierman coached the Gophers when Paul was a freshman, but first-year players weren't eligible to play back then. In 1952, 1953, and 1954 Giel played baseball as well.

Paul came to the "U" as a quarterback and was switched to left halfback. In the huddle, he still called the plays. While neither real big nor remarkably fast, Giel had a knack for playing smart football with a shifty running style that made opponents miss him.

Giel earned All-American honors at Minnesota. In the balloting for the prestigious Heisman Trophy, he finished second to Johnny Lattner of Notre Dame. But a 4-3-2 season was the best finish for any of Paul's teams. The most memorable game: a 22-0 drubbing of Michigan in the Little Brown Jug game, his senior year. Paul remembers it as the best game of his college football career.

Another of Giel's biggest thrills was being twice named as Most Valuable Player in the Big Ten Conference, a feat not duplicated until Archie Griffen did it with Ohio State in the mid-1970s.

Despite liking and excelling at football, Giel had always dreamed of playing pro baseball. After his sophomore year in high school, he journeyed to Wrigley Field to watch the Cubs take on the Giants.

During high-school, Giel's American Legion baseball team made it to Minnesota's state tournament finals. Paul pitched well and struck out twenty, but his team lost. He still regards that defeat as one of the biggest disappointments of his life.

Another legend was coaching baseball at Minnesota when Giel arrived. He was Dick Siebert. But Minnesota's baseball teams were also mediocre during Paul's tenure, usually finishing around .500. Giel went 5-0 his sophomore season and led the Big Ten in ERA and fewest walks.

Semi-pro baseball was big in Minnesota in the 1950s. Siebert spent time in the summer coaching the Litchfield Optimists. In 1954, after his senior year, Giel—at Siebert's urging—went to Litchfield to pitch against the Willmar Rails.

Later that summer the New York Giants signed Paul to a bonus contract. In the early 1950s the owners had an agreement called the bonus rule: If a player signed for over $30,000, he had to be kept at the major-league level for two years.

The Giants won the pennant in 1954 and went on to sweep the World Series in four games. But Paul didn't play in the postseason. In fact, although he was on the roster all year, Giel appeared in just six games that season.

Paul remembered his first season, "About all I did was throw batting practice. I'd pitch an inning or two when the Giants were way behind; they called it 'mop up.'"

A more productive year, 1955, for the right-hander from Winona, he pitched over eighty-two innings and was 4-4 with a 3.39 ERA. Then, Giel had to fulfill his ROTC obligation. He left for the military during the 1956 and 1957 seasons.

When he returned to baseball, the Giants had moved to San Francisco, where Paul joined them for the 1958 campaign. He had another decent year for the Giants, but for the 1959 season he was sold to the Pittsburgh Pirates.

For the next two years, Giel divided his time between the Pirates and their minor-league affiliates at Columbus, Ohio, and Salt Lake City, Utah. Unfortunately, after being with the Pirates over half of the 1960 season, he was sent to the minors in July. The Pirates won the World Series that fall, against the New York Yankees, four games to three, on Bill Mazeroski's dramatic ninth-inning home run.

After the season Giel evaluated his career. "I was going to get out of baseball. I had a family and I wasn't producing the way I thought I should. I was lacking some confidence," he recalled.

"I would have retired then, but I got a call from Calvin Griffith asking me to become a Twin. I thought, well, I'll give it another try in my own backyard, so I was there until June.

"Then I was traded to Kansas City, along with Reno Bertoia, for Bill Tuttle. I reported for one game, second-guessing myself, and then decided, no, it's time for me to hang 'em up."

Giel earned one victory for the Twins, but the most memorable afternoon of that short career came on May 9, 1961. Jim Gentile, Baltimore's slugger, had ripped a grand slam off Pedro Ramos in the first inning. He duplicated the feat against Giel in the second. No major-league player had ever hit grand slams in back-to-back innings. It was an inauspicious way for Paul's name to appear in the record book.

The most memorable game of Giel's major-league career was his first victory. It came during the 1955 season for the Giants. Paul pitched three innings of relief, and the Giants came from behind to win on a home run by Dusty Rhodes.

"To win a game in the major leagues was my dream, to be in the major leagues is a dream. Leo Durocher was the manager, Willie Mays was the center fielder. It was even better to win the game in Wrigley Field, where I had seen my first major-league game. That was a thrill," said Giel.

Some have questioned over the years whether he made the right choice in choosing baseball over football. To Giel, there was no real choice.

"Not for one minute did I regret choosing baseball over football. It wasn't the physical part of it, but baseball was so far ahead of pro football as far as salary, fringe benefits, and longevity," he explained.

"Also, if you didn't make it right away at the top in baseball, there was someplace to go. I went down to Phoenix. I've been to Salt Lake City and Columbus, Ohio. As far as AAA ball, I had a chance to work myself back up.

"But in football, if you got hurt or just didn't cut it, you're gone. Maybe I could have jumped into the Canadian Football League. I could have played with the Winnipeg Blue Bombers; they had territorial rights on me, and the Chicago Bears had drafted me. But I had no regrets whatsoever in my decision."

From baseball Paul went to work for the Minnesota Vikings in public relations and promotions. He left the Vikings in 1963 to take a job as sports director with WCCO Radio.

In January 1971, the University of Minnesota's Board of Regents accepted a recommendation to name Giel as Athletics Director of the university, a position he held until July 1988.

Upon leaving the university, Giel went to work for the Minneapolis Heart Institute Foundation, located on the Abbot Northwestern Hospital campus. Paul calls it the most satisfying work he's done.

"I've had heart problems. These people took good care of me and kept me going. I want to help people through my fundraising and help people because I've had heart disease. I take phone calls and talk to people about their problems and concerns.

"It's nice to be able to help somebody else when you can truly say, 'I know how you feel, I know what you're going through.'"

Regarding his days at the university, Giel said what gave him a lot of pleasure was that "I never had to cut a sport. We kept the big revenue sports going and never had to cut a so-called 'non-revenue sport.'

"They all became stronger. When he was twenty-six, I hired John Anderson, the baseball coach. I hired Fred Rothlesberger with gymnastics. I hired Jim Dutcher, a real solid citizen. I hired Clem Haskins; Clem Haskins is a good coach, a good person who got caught up in the pressures to win.

"We won three NCAA hockey championships with Herb Brooks, who I hired, and who coached the 1980 U.S. Olympic Gold Medal team with mostly Minnesota kids," Giel said.

"I inherited a $500,000 deficit. We erased that and built up some reserves. If you look at the University of Minnesota's men's athletic department, you can say that, other than not going to the Rose Bowl, it's a very good program.

"I helped keep the program alive, and we've been very competitive."

But in the total picture, Paul Giel believes that his current position with the Heart Foundation is the most meaningful.

"It's more important than wins and losses in athletics to help keep people alive by trying to find the kind of money that enables our researchers to find better ways to fight heart disease," he said.

Paul lives in Minnetonka with his wife, Nancy. They raised three children: Paul, Jr., Gerilynn, and Tom.

In summation, Paul Giel said, "I've been a pretty lucky guy. Going to the university, having a chance to go to major-league baseball, qualifying for the major-league baseball players' pension plan. My days at 'CCO were lots of fun, working with guys like Ray Christensen. I covered some Super Bowls; I covered the Green Bay-Dallas championship game for CBS, when Starr snuck over on a frozen field.

"I've just been doggoned lucky. I have a good family, I enjoyed my years working at the university, and I like what I'm doing now."

Jim "Mudcat" Grant

Bats: Right
Throws: Right
Height: 6' 1"
Weight: 186 lbs.
Born: August 13, 1935, in Florida

YEAR	TEAM	LG	ERA	W	L	Sv	G	IP	H	R	ER	BB	K	AVG. A
1958	Cle	AL	3.84	10	11	4	44	204.0	173	93	87	104	111	.228
1959	Cle	AL	4.14	10	7	3	38	165.1	140	80	76	81	85	.232
1960	Cle	AL	4.40	9	8	0	33	159.2	147	88	78	78	75	.243
1961	Cle	AL	3.86	15	9	0	35	244.2	207	118	105	109	146	.227
1962	Cle	AL	4.27	7	10	0	26	149.2	128	75	71	81	90	.233
1963	Cle	AL	3.69	13	14	1	38	229.1	213	107	94	87	157	.243
1964	Cle	AL	5.95	3	4	0	13	62.0	82	41	41	25	43	.324
1964	Min	AL	2.82	11	9	1	26	166.0	162	73	52	36	75	.248
1965	Min	AL	3.30	21	7	0	41	270.1	252	107	99	61	142	.247
1966	Min	AL	3.25	13	13	0	35	249.0	248	104	90	49	110	.260
1967	Min	AL	4.72	5	6	0	27	95.1	121	56	50	17	50	.315
1968	LA	NL	2.09	6	4	3	37	94.2	77	29	22	19	35	.226
1969	Mon	NL	4.80	1	6	0	11	50.2	64	33	27	14	20	.299
1969	StL	NL	4.12	7	5	7	30	63.1	62	31	29	22	35	.252
1970	Oak	AL	1.82	6	2	24	72	123.1	104	26	25	30	54	.235
1970	Pit	NL	2.25	2	1	0	8	12.0	8	3	3	2	4	.190
1971	Pit	NL	3.60	5	3	7	42	75.0	79	32	30	28	22	.274
1971	Oak	AL	1.98	1	0	3	15	27.1	25	9	6	6	13	.243
			3.63	145	119	53	571	2,441.2	2,292	1,105	985	849	1,267	.248

The young man, a year out of high school, was toiling on a rooftop in the hot Florida sun. Jim Grant of Lacoochee, Florida, had graduated from Dade City High School in 1953.

He had briefly considered going to college and becoming an English teacher until he discovered what teachers were paid. After that he was hoping to pursue another love, baseball.

He planned to go to a baseball tryout camp and was passing the time staying at an uncle's house and working. In the 1950s, with no draft for players, "Bird Dog" scouts watched for talented players and brought them to camp.

As Jim rapped shingles into the roof that spring day of 1954, he spied a car driving nearby.

"The car looked familiar," Jim recalled. "Soon it came by the house. It was my old high school baseball coach.

"I yelled out, 'Coach!'

"He stopped and said, 'Come on down off o' that roof. They're lookin' for you.'

"I came down. I thought maybe he was talkin' about the police," Grant joked.

"He said, 'The Cleveland Indians, they came by my office. Let's go.'"

Jim and his coach stopped by Bethune-Cookman College and picked up another coach before heading for the Indians spring training camp.

The Indianapolis Indians, a *AAA* team, were training at the time. Jim and the two coaches watched the team work out for a while. When the drills were finished, Jim's coach walked with Grant over to Mike McNalley, the camp director. McNalley told Jim he had a scouting report on him and that they planned to bring him in for a rookie camp in three weeks.

As they talked, they were joined by Hank Greenberg, a former Detroit Tigers slugger who was working for the Indians. McNalley explained who Jim Grant was and said that they had planned to bring him in with the rookies. Greenberg suggested that Grant just stay in the players' barracks and hang out with the team until the rookie camp.

"That's how it all started," Grant related. "I became a gopher for the AAA team. They'd play poker at night, and I'd get sandwiches and beer for them. They would tip me. I was making more in a week with them than I did in a month when I signed my contract."

At camp, people thought Jim was from Mississippi, so they called him "Mississippi Mud" or "Mudcat." It was the origin of his famous nickname.

"The last week of spring training, I signed a contract and went to Fargo, North Dakota, in the Northern League, Class C. I couldn't go to Tifton, Georgia, where they had their Class D team. They didn't allow Afro-Americans in the Georgia/Florida League."

Grant became the Rookie of the Year in the Northern League that year, winning twenty-one games. He was the first African-American to win twenty games in the minor leagues.

In 1955 Jim advanced to Class B at Keokuk, Iowa. He was 19-3 that season. The following year, Grant moved up again, this time to Class A in Reading, Pennsylvania.

"It was a pivotal year for me. I had done pretty good and worked hard and remembered my manners," Grant recalled.

"I was getting pretty confident and thought I should be in the big leagues. I had argued with the organization when I was 11-3 at the All-Star break.

"I kind of thought that I knew it all. I was 11-3, and no one could tell me anything. I said some things to my manager that even my mother didn't approve of. I won one game the second half of the season. It was one of the best things that ever happened to me. It proved to a little Southern kid that he didn't know everything," said Mudcat.

"The next year they couldn't send me to Mobile in the Southern Association, because Afro-Americans couldn't play there, either. I went to winter ball in Colombia, South America, and did pretty good there."

Because of his success in winter ball, the Indians gave Grant a chance to make their AAA club. In 1957 spring training, Mudcat Grant pitched against some major league teams.

"I did pretty good, and they sent me to Triple A in San Diego," he said.

Ironically, whenever Jim was denied a chance to play because of racism, he advanced beyond where he would have been.

In San Diego, they actually took Grant off the mound and were going to make a shortstop out of him. Then the parent Cleveland club was decimated by injuries to its pitching staff. Herb Score got hit by a line drive; Bob Lemon had an operation; Early Wynn developed gout and lumbago; and Mike Garcia had a disc problem. Grant was returned to the hill.

Mudcat Grant began his fourteen-year major-league career in 1958. He was 10-11 in his rookie year, the first of six-plus seasons with the Indians. Cleveland traded Grant to the Minnesota Twins for George Banks and Lee Stange on June 15, 1964.

Grant had an unusual motion. He would tap the mound with his foot before releasing the ball. His Twins catcher, Earl Battey, laughingly accused him of pitching from sixty feet, not sixty feet six inches, because he gradually moved forward when tapping.

"I had a little bit different motion. I'd tap the mound a bit. I threw three-quarter. But I could throw strikes. I didn't have a curveball, but I had a good fastball and a sinker. I had a change-up. I had most of the pitches that you're supposed to have," Grant said.

"I could throw the ball into areas where it wouldn't hurt me too much. I learned how to pitch my first three years in the big leagues.

"Pitching was a matter of game plan. There used to be a saying, 'Make the hitter hit the ball with something on it.' It's not the speed of the ball; it's where the ball is. You have to remember what the hitter did the last time he was at the plate.

"The art of pitching was setting up hitters. Back in those days pitchers had their pitch and hitters had their pitch. That's why I had to pitch inside," Mudcat continued.

"The outside corner of the plate was the pitcher's. The other spots were the hitter's. If you didn't pitch inside, the outside corner didn't mean anything because the hitters would go out there and get it.

"Pitching inside was a type of intimidation. I was sayin', 'This game is fair, I don't want you goin' out there and messin' with my pitch.' If I got it over the middle of the plate, I was in trouble because that's the hitter's pitch.

"It's a game of thoughts and patterns," he concluded.

The World Series year of 1965 was Grant's big season. He went 21-7, leading the American League in victories, winning percentage, and shutouts (six).

He won two games and lost one in the series against the Dodgers. He helped himself in his 5-1 triumph in Game 6 when he jacked a three-run homer.

Of what is Jim most proud? "The night I signed my first major-league contract, and became the first Afro-American to win twenty games in the American League."

He was also the first African-American to win a World Series game or lead the league in winning percentage. Unfortunately, there was only one pitching champion, only one Cy Young Award each year. It went to Sandy Koufax in 1965.

Grant was 13-13 the next year. Then he dropped to 5-6 in 1967.

Jim said, "I had developed a bad relationship with the ball club. Mr. Griffith didn't want to pay. What started out as a beautiful thing ended on a sour note. I wasn't starting games, and they had other pitchers that they preferred over me."

Grant and Zoilo Versalles were traded to the Los Angeles Dodgers for Bob Miller, Ron Perranoski, and John Roseboro prior to the 1968 season. Mudcat was a relief pitcher for most of his remaining career.

Grant recorded the Montreal Expos' first victory in 1969. He finished up his career with stints at St. Louis, Oakland, and Pittsburgh. He retired from major-league ball after the 1971 season with 145 wins and 119 losses.

Always an entrepreneur, Jim tried his hand at various businesses. He worked in areas of entertainment, motivation, and speaking. For ten years, he worked as a broadcaster with the Indians, A's, and Dodgers. Grant was the first African-American baseball analyst.

Grant was the lead singer of a group called "Mudcat and the Kittens" in the 1960s. While the kittens are gone, Jim has continued with his singing. He makes public appearances and has put together a Black golf tour.

Grant started an organization called Slugout, a baseball clinic for six- to sixteen-year olds. They bring in the kids to play baseball, but the three-day clinic also stresses improving as students and drug awareness. The importance of education is a cornerstone of Mudcat's program and beliefs.

Jim works at his various ventures, golfs, and attends some fantasy baseball camps. He lives in Los Angeles with his wife, Trudy. The Grants have four grown children and fourteen grandchildren.

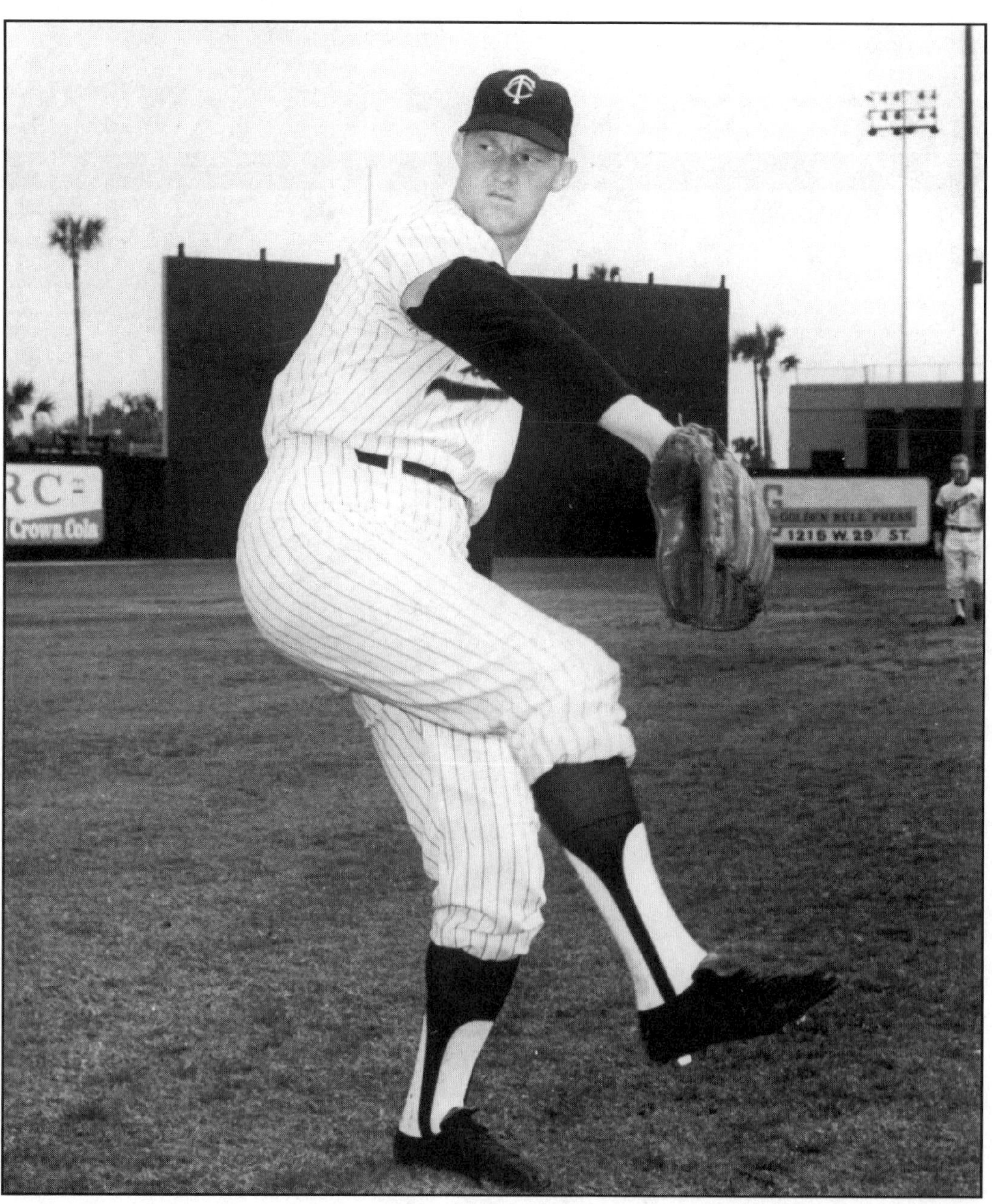
Crown Cola
GOLDEN RULE PRESS
1215 W. 29 ST.

Jim Kaat

Bats: Left
Throws: Left
Height: 6' 4"
Weight: 205 lbs.
Born: November 7, 1938, in Michigan

YEAR	TEAM	LG	ERA	W	L	Sv	G	IP	H	R	ER	BB	K	AVG. A
1959	Was	AL	12.60	0	2	0	3	5.0	7	9	7	4	2	.350
1960	Was	AL	5.58	1	5	0	13	50.0	48	39	31	31	25	.255
1961	Min	AL	3.90	9	17	0	36	200.2	188	105	87	82	122	.248
1962	Min	AL	3.14	18	14	1	39	269.0	243	106	94	75	173	.243
1963	Min	AL	4.19	10	10	1	31	178.1	195	96	83	38	105	.274
1964	Min	AL	3.22	17	11	1	36	243.0	231	100	87	60	171	.251
1965	Min	AL	2.83	18	11	2	45	264.1	267	121	83	63	154	.258
1966	Min	AL	2.75	25	13	0	41	304.2	271	114	93	55	205	.235
1967	Min	AL	3.04	16	13	0	42	263.1	269	110	89	42	211	.260
1968	Min	AL	2.94	14	12	0	30	208.0	192	78	68	40	130	.243
1969	Min	AL	3.49	14	13	1	40	242.1	252	114	94	75	139	.265
1970	Min	AL	3.56	14	10	0	45	230.1	244	110	91	58	120	.273
1971	Min	AL	3.32	13	14	0	39	260.1	275	104	96	47	137	.268
1972	Min	AL	2.06	10	2	0	15	113.1	94	36	26	20	64	.227
1973	Min	AL	4.41	11	12	0	29	181.2	206	101	89	39	93	.282
1973	ChA	AL	4.22	4	1	0	7	42.2	44	23	20	4	16	.260
1974	ChA	AL	2.92	21	13	0	42	277.1	263	106	90	63	142	.250
1975	ChA	AL	3.11	20	14	0	43	303.2	321	121	105	77	142	.274
1976	Phi	NL	3.48	12	14	0	38	227.2	241	95	88	32	83	.274
1977	Phi	NL	5.39	6	11	0	35	160.1	211	100	96	40	55	.320
1978	Phi	NL	4.10	8	5	0	26	140.1	150	67	64	32	48	.280
1979	Phi	NL	4.32	1	0	0	3	8.1	9	4	4	5	2	.281
1979	NYA	AL	3.86	2	3	2	40	58.1	64	29	25	14	23	.287
1980	NYA	AL	7.20	0	1	0	4	5.0	8	5	4	4	1	.381
1980	StL	NL	3.82	8	7	4	49	129.2	140	61	55	33	36	.281
1981	StL	NL	3.40	6	6	4	41	53.0	60	25	20	17	8	.299
1982	StL	NL	4.08	5	3	2	62	75.0	79	40	34	23	35	.276
1983	StL	NL	3.89	0	0	0	24	34.2	48	19	15	10	19	.327
YEAR	TEAM	LG	ERA	W	L	Sv	G	IP	H	R	ER	BB	K	AVG. A
			3.45	283	237	18	898	4,530.1	4,620	2,038	1,738	1,083	2,461	.264

Jim Kaat was one of the greatest all-around athletes ever to wear a Twins uniform. For thirteen years, he was an ace of the Twins' staff. He pitched twenty-five years in the big leagues, won sixteen consecutive Gold Gloves, had fifteen double-digit victory seasons, hit sixteen home runs, and often used his exceptional speed as a pinch runner.

Jim's big-league career spanned from 1959 to 1983. He had the unique distinction of pitching to both Ted Williams and Daryl Strawberry.

"Kitty" Kaat hails from Zeeland, Michigan, where he attended Hope College. While in college, he was scouted by Dick Wiencek of the Senators, who inked him to a contract in 1957.

The 6' 4" lefty was sent to Superior for fourteen games in the 1957 season. Then he moved up to Missoula the following year, where he went 16-9. Kaat spent most of 1959 in Chattanooga but did get called up to Washington for three games late in the year.

Jim split 1960 between Charleston, West Virginia, and the Senators. He appeared in thirteen games for Washington, getting his first big-league victory while losing five. In 1961 he made the Twins out of spring training and began his long consecutive streak of major-league service.

After going 9-17 in his first full year, Kaat won at least ten games every year he pitched for the Twins. In 1965, he won eighteen games for the A.L. Champion club. Kitty also racked up a win against the Dodgers in the World Series.

"The highlight of my Twins career was winning the 1965 American League pennant and going to the World Series for the first time," Kaat related.

"There were several individual moments that stood out that year. I pitched the pennant clincher against Washington on September 26, and Game 2 of the World Series against Sandy Koufax.

"There was game two of a doubleheader against the Yankees just before the All-Star break. We had a three-game lead, a loss would cut it to two games, a win would mean a four-game lead over New York. I wasn't pitching that game.

"Harmon Killebrew hit a home run off Pete Mikkelsen in the bottom of the ninth to win it. In my opinion, it was the most important win of the year."

Jim's best year in baseball was 1966. He was 25-13 and led the league with forty-one starts, nineteen complete games, and 304 innings. The *Sporting News* selected Kaat as American League Pitcher of the Year. But in those years only one pitcher in all of baseball received the Cy Young Award. It was given to Sandy Koufax.

Jim credited a lot of his success to pitching coach John Sain. That coach left the Twins after the 1966 season.

Kaat continued his winning ways and looked to be on his way to another exceptional season in 1972. He was 10-2, "having the best year of my career up to that time," he felt. Then Jim broke his wrist sliding into second base on July 2 and was done for the season.

The lefty had a lively fastball, sharp curve, and smooth delivery. His catcher for most of the 1960s, Earl Battey, described Kaat this way: "He had a good sinking fastball and a good hard slider. He had exceptional control and great ball movement.

"Jim threw what we call a 'heavy' ball, which is a catcher's nightmare. He kept the ball fairly low, and that was back in the days of two-handed catchers," Battey continued.

"So when you catch a low ball you have to catch it palms up and it's hard to cushion. Jim's heavy ball with a sinking rotation would tear up my hands, but it was hard to hit."

In August 1973, Kaat was 11-12. He had pitched a one-hitter in California on July 1. But the Twins put Jim on waivers to be sold or released.

Kaat explained, "When I came back I still didn't have the 'feel' of my screwball because of the wrist injury. I knew it would take time. I was thirty-four years old, and the organization thought I was done. Thirty-four was considered 'old' for a pitcher then.

"I told Bob Rodgers, our bullpen coach, that I knew I was on waivers but that my arm was starting to come back, and I thought I still had something left.

"When I was sold to Chicago in August, I was reunited with my favorite coach, Johnny Sain, and the White Sox made me feel wanted."

Kaat rebounded with twenty-one- and twenty-victory seasons, often using a quick-pitch delivery. He was transforming from a power pitcher to a finesse pitcher. But the White Sox traded the thirty-seven-year-old hurler to the Phillies for three players, the oldest of whom was twenty-four.

In Kaat's first three seasons in the National League, he was 26-30 and, in May 1979, Jim was sold to the Yankees. New York used Kaat mostly in relief. It was the first time he relieved more games than he started.

For most of the rest of his career Kaat worked out of the bullpen. He finished up his twenty-five years with the St. Louis Cardinals, pitching in relief in four games in the 1982 World Series against Milwaukee. Kaat was forty-four years old when he retired. How had he lasted so long?

"I always considered baseball a full-time deal," Kaat explained, "and I kept myself in good condition the year around. Also, being left-handed with good control and having the knack to adjust from being a fairly hard thrower into a 'finesse' pitcher."

Kaat earned a spot on three All-Star squads: 1962, 1966, and 1975.

Jim ranks either first or second in ten Twins pitching categories. Among them, he is the winningest all-time pitcher with 189. Kaat pitched 2,959.1 innings for the Twins and started 422 games.

There were a lot of positive things about baseball in Kaat's career. Jim stated that he "liked the competition and the friendships I made, being a part of a team at every level, major and minor leagues was a satisfying feeling."

Satisfaction also came from "having the dream of getting to the big leagues, having individual success, getting to the World Series, then finally being on a winning World Series team, the 1982 St. Louis Cardinals.

"I was happy to pitch twenty-five seasons in the majors, which, when my career ended, was a record. Tommy John eventually pitched in twenty-six seasons and Nolan Ryan in twenty-seven!"

Baseball, as with many other players, has been Kaat's life. He was a professional ball player for twenty-seven years, coached pitchers for the Cincinnati Reds for a year and one-half, broadcast Twins games for six years, and is currently doing Yankee broadcasts for Madison Square Garden Network. That's forty-four baseball seasons.

"It was fulfilling a boyhood dream," Kaat said of the sport he loves. "I wanted to be a major leaguer since I was seven or eight. My Dad was an avid fan and enjoyed my career as well. That was special to me."

But all is not bright in Jim Kaat's baseball future. He casts a sad eye on the future of the sport.

"I have lost a little passion for the game in recent years," Jim said. "The players are bigger, faster, more talented than we were at their age, but the quality and harmony or beauty of the game has diminished.

"The little things that were important to winning baseball are overlooked. With the miniscule strike zone and small parks, it has turned into adult T-ball. Don't be suckered into thinking if Alex Rodriquez approaches Hank Aaron's accomplishments that he should be mentioned in the same breath as Aaron.

"It's so much easier to hit now that you can't compare records of past eras to now. I' m disappointed in the leadership, or lack of it, the game has had in recent years.

"Frank Robinson is a good addition, but we miss Bill White. TV and cash are king, and the integrity and reason the game was created has gotten lost along the way. I'm ready to get out."

Jim and his wife, Mary Ann, live in Stuart, Florida. They have four married children and two grandchildren, with a third expected in August of 2001.

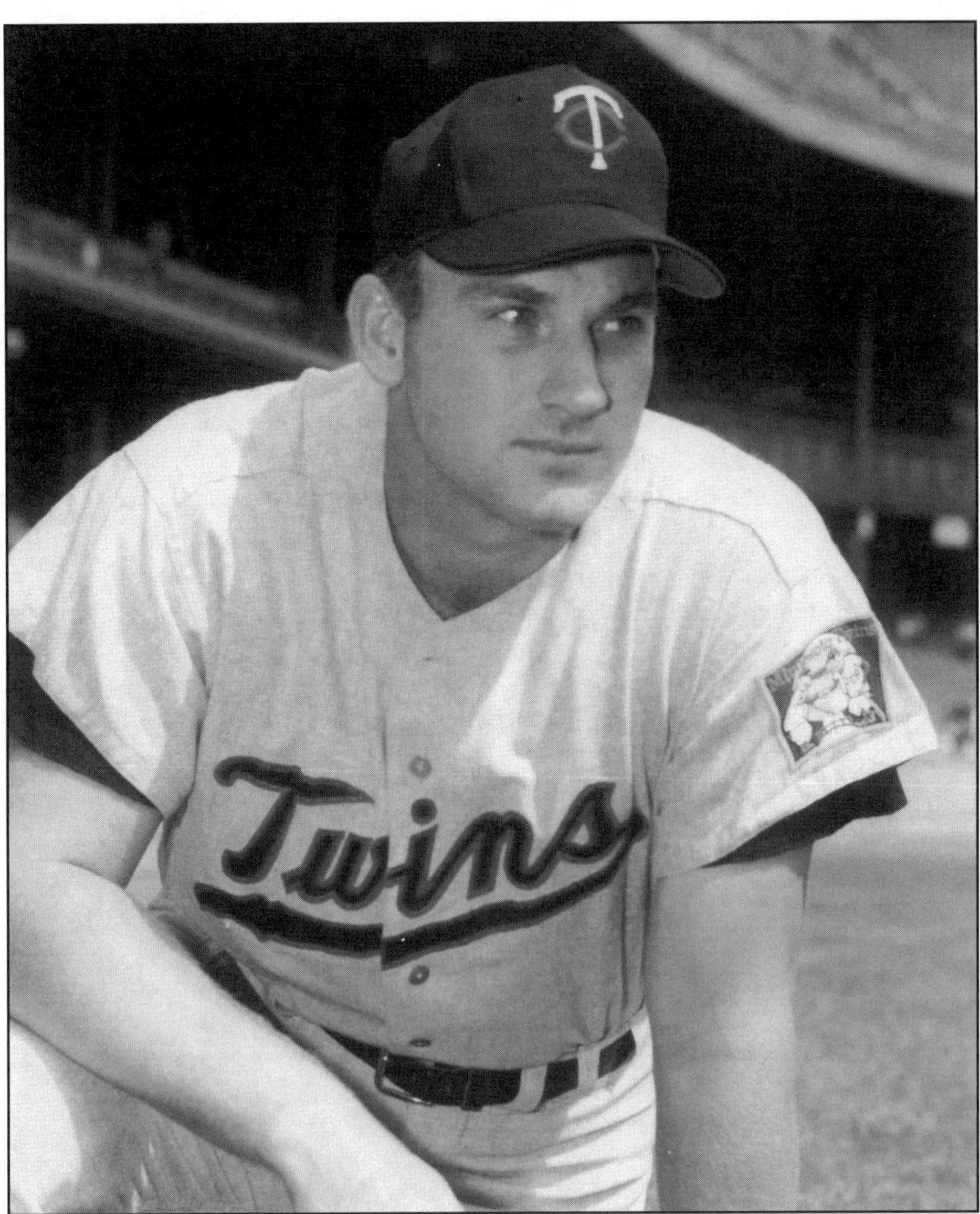
Twins

HARMON KILLEBREW

Bats: Right
Throws: Right
Height: 6' 0"
Weight: 195 lbs.
Born: June 29, 1936, in Idaho

YEAR	TEAM	LG	AVG	G	AB	R	H	2B	3B	HR	RBI	BB	K	OBP	SLG
1954	Was	AL	.308	9	13	1	4	1	0	0	3	2	3	.400	.385
1955	Was	AL	.200	38	80	12	16	1	0	4	7	9	31	.281	.363
1956	Was	AL	.222	44	99	10	22	2	0	5	13	10	39	.291	.394
1957	Was	AL	.290	9	31	4	9	2	0	2	5	2	8	.333	.548
1958	Was	AL	.194	13	31	2	6	0	0	0	2	0	12	.212	.194
1959	Was	AL	.242	153	546	98	132	20	2	42	105	90	116	.354	.516
1960	Was	AL	.276	124	442	84	122	19	1	31	80	71	106	.375	.534
1961	Min	AL	.288	150	541	94	156	20	7	46	122	107	109	.405	.606
1962	Min	AL	.243	155	552	85	134	21	1	48	126	106	142	.366	.545
1963	Min	AL	.258	142	515	88	133	18	0	45	96	72	105	.349	.555
1964	Min	AL	.270	158	577	95	156	11	1	49	111	93	135	.377	.548
1965	Min	AL	.269	113	401	78	108	16	1	25	75	72	69	.384	.501
1966	Min	AL	.281	162	569	89	160	27	1	39	110	103	98	.391	.538
1967	Min	AL	.269	163	547	105	147	24	1	44	113	131	111	.408	.558
1968	Min	AL	.210	100	295	40	62	7	2	17	40	70	70	.361	.420
1969	Min	AL	.276	162	555	106	153	20	2	49	140	145	84	.427	.584
1970	Min	AL	.271	157	527	96	143	20	1	41	113	128	84	.411	.546
1971	Min	AL	.254	147	500	61	127	19	1	28	119	114	96	.386	.464
1972	Min	AL	.231	139	433	53	100	13	2	26	74	94	91	.367	.450
1973	Min	AL	.242	69	248	29	60	9	1	5	32	41	59	.352	.347
1974	Min	AL	.222	122	333	28	74	7	0	13	54	45	61	.312	.360
1975	KC	AL	.199	106	312	25	62	13	0	14	44	54	70	.317	.375
			AVG	G	AB	R	H	2B	3B	HR	RBI	BB	K	OBP	SLG
			.258	2435	8174	1283	2086	290	24	573	1584	1559	1699	.376	.509

They called him the "Killer." Every time he dug in at the plate, the Minnesota Twins crowds at Metropolitan Stadium became rife with anticipation. Maybe this time Harmon would rocket another moon-shot high and deep over the left-field fence.

Fans watched with glee as, after a monumental swing, he would stand at the plate and admire the flight of the ball as if he were an artist applying the final stroke to a painting.

He was Harmon Killebrew. In baseball parlance, he was pure power; 573 times he circled the bases with home runs. He played fourteen years with the Minnesota Twins. For most of those years, his name was synonymous with baseball in Minnesota.

Born June 29, 1936, in Payette, Idaho, Harmon loved baseball from childhood.

In the days before televised games of the week, he followed baseball through radio's "Game of the Day." Harmon didn't have a particular hero. He just admired major-league players.

One of his favorite memories of youth concerns baseball. With his brothers and neighborhood friends, Harmon loved to play baseball in the Killebrew yard. The grass suffered, and his mother complained to his father about the worn spots. The elder Killebrew responded, "We're not raising grass, we're raising boys." Harmon related that story at his Baseball Hall of Fame induction ceremony in Cooperstown, New York. He strongly believes that baseball shapes character.

Harmon wanted to play baseball from the moment he started in second grade.

Many young boys can only dream to follow Killebrew's progression. He started playing when he was seven years old and kept on right through high school ball. Then, while playing semi-pro ball, Washington Senators' Farm Director Ossie Bluege scouted him; Idaho Senator Herman Welker had recommended that Bluege take a look at Killebrew.

Harmon's power came naturally. His father, Clay, was a great college football fullback. His grandfather, Culver Killebrew, was reputed to be the heavyweight champion of the Illinois detachment of the Union Army in the Civil War.

Harmon was fortunate to have strength in his family, for in those days weights and strength training were frowned upon. It was feared that baseball players would get too muscle-bound.

Killebrew signed with the Senators at age seventeen as a third baseman. He was their first "bonus baby." For two years under bonus rules, he stuck with the Senators but was used very little.

During the next three seasons, he played parts of each year for the Senators but spent the bulk of his days in the minor leagues. For the first time in Harmon's pro career, he played regularly during stints in Charlotte (North Carolina), Chattanooga (Tennessee) and Indianapolis. His 1957 season in Chattanooga foreshadowed the future; he drilled twenty-nine home runs with 101 RBIs.

In 1959, Senators owner Calvin Griffith called aside manager Cookie Lavagetto and told him that it was time to play the young Idahoan full time.

Harmon immediately rewarded Griffith's confidence in him. It proved to be his breakthrough year, for Killebrew hit .242 with forty-two home runs (tying a club record) and 105 RBIs.

It was the beginning of a remarkable run. After one more year in Washington, D.C., the team moved westward and became the Minnesota Twins. There Harmon would go on to win five home run titles, lead the league three times in RBIs, and top it twice with his slugging percentage.

In the field, he moved from third to first base. Then Harmon played left field for three years and moved back and forth between first and third again. But the many defensive shifts did not distract him at the plate, where he continued his powerful display.

Some of Harmon's blasts were especially memorable. In 1960, he became the first player in twenty-five years to hit a homer onto the left-field roof at Tiger Stadium in Detroit. Two years later, Harmon topped that by rocketing one completely over the Detroit left-field roof. He came just short of putting one out of Memorial Stadium in Baltimore.

At the Twins' own Metropolitan Stadium in suburban Bloomington, the "Killer" clobbered one 462 feet in distance and fifteen feet up the green batter's eye in center field. On July 4, 1961, Harmon hit the first inside the park home run in Met Stadium history after Chicago outfielder Jim Landis collided with the center-field fence in a futile attempt to catch the blast.

Killebrew played a key role when the Twins became the first American League team to have players hit two grand-slam home runs in the same inning. Harmon and his roommate, Bob Allison, each wiped the bases clean in the first inning against Cleveland on July 18, 1962. The club record eleven-run inning helped the Twins coast to a 14-3 win. Killebrew's shot came off future Twins teammate Jim Perry.

Harmon was part of another awesome display of power when he became the fourth consecutive Twin to hit a home run in the same inning. The outburst came in the eleventh stanza of a game played May 2, 1964, against the Los Angeles Angels; it tied a major-league record.

Killebrew and four teammates surpassed that with an even more impressive feat when they slammed five home runs in one inning, carving a record against Kansas City in the seventh frame on June 9, 1966. Rich Rollins, Zoilo Versalles, Tony Oliva, Don Mincher, and Killebrew were the first in American League history to achieve this. The Twins won 9-4.

Harmon's most monumental home run came at Metropolitan Stadium on June 3, 1967, against the Angels. He rifled a shot six rows into the upper deck in left field, shattering two seats, 530 feet from home plate. The spot is now commemorated with a red chair mounted high on a wall in the Mall of America, which was built at the former Met Stadium site. Home plate's location is commemorated as well by a metal plaque in a main-level floor at the mall.

Eight times Killebrew hit over forty home runs in a season. During ten seasons, he cracked over thirty homers, and nine times he drove in over 100 runs. Harmon was named the American League's MVP in 1969 when he hit forty-nine home runs, drove in 140 runs and walked 145 times to lead the league in all three categories.

Ever the team player, Harmon credited Cesar Tovar, Rod Carew, and Tony Oliva with helping his RBI total.

"Tovar was great. The year I drove in 140 runs, he was leading off most of the year. He scored ninety-nine runs," Killebrew said.

As teammates from 1965 to 1971, Harmon witnessed the day when Tovar (now deceased) became the only Twin to play every position in one game. Cesar accomplished that feat on September 22, 1968.

Harmon was an All-Star thirteen times. He homered in three of the contests. One homer was a two-run shot that propelled the American League to a 6-5 win in Detroit.

Killebrew's glove work didn't get the credit it deserved, according to Sam Mele, his manager from 1961 to 1967. "Harmon was a better fielder than people think," Mele related. "He wasn't fast, but he was quick. His initial moves were good. His hands were quick. I had him for some games in the outfield, but he was better in the infield."

In a career of monumental home runs, many are memorable for Harmon, among them his first, his last (against the Twins' Eddie Bane), and one he slammed just before the All-Star Game in 1965.

That last one came with the Twins playing the long-dominant Yankees. A win would mean a four-game lead for Minnesota going into the break; a loss would result in a margin of just two games. Killebrew's rocket in the ninth off Pete Mikkelsen beat the Yanks, and the Twins never looked back. They stayed in first place the rest of the season as they won their first American League title.

Minnesota advanced to face the Dodgers in Harmon's only World Series. The classic went seven games before the Dodgers prevailed. Killebrew hit .286 in the Series and launched a home run off ace Don Drysdale. The World Series was the highlight of Harmon's career.

"It's what every player plays for," he commented.

The Twins won the A.L. West championship in 1969 and 1970. Both times they went on to lose the pennant to the Baltimore Orioles.

In a career of records and honors, "Being the number-one right-handed homerun hitter in American League history stands out," Killebrew said. "Being second to Babe Ruth in the American League is quite an honor."

What makes a great hitter? "Concentration," Killebrew answered. "After good fundamentals, having the ability to concentrate on the baseball is most important."

Harmon terrorized some of the greatest pitchers in baseball history. But who gave him fits? "The guy who gave me more trouble than anybody else was a little relief pitcher, Stu Miller. The first time I saw him was in the All-Star Game in '61 in Candlestick Park.

"Then he was with Baltimore. I think I got two hits off him in five years. Miller was slow, but his motion was so deceptive. He was the first pitcher I ever saw who took a stretch with nobody on base.

"Nowadays pitchers do it for control. He was doing it for deception. He'd throw his hip and his shoulder, his back and everything he had at you. His arm would stay back and never seem to get up there."

Sadly, Killebrew played his last year in Kansas City. The Twins released him after the 1974 season. Calvin Griffith offered Harmon an opportunity to coach at the major-league level or manage AAA ball. But Killebrew felt like he had a couple of playing years left in him. The artificial turf in Kansas City was hard on the slugger's knees, and after one season there he stopped playing. However, his legendary career is forever part of Twins history. He hit 573 home runs, which is fifth all-time in major-league baseball and second only to Babe Ruth in the American League.

As of spring 2001, Killebrew still held team records for home runs, runs-batted-in, and walks. Harmon's jersey number 3 was retired by the Twins in a ceremony on August 11, 1974. He became the first Twin elected to the Baseball Hall of Fame on January 10, 1984.

Baseball was and still is Harmon's life. "Everything that I've ever had I owe to baseball. I've loved the game since I was a kid and it's been everything to me," he said in a phone interview for this book.

After his playing career ended, Killebrew returned to Idaho, where he joined a former United States congressman in an insurance business, Killebrew & Harding, Inc. From 1976 to 1984, Harmon worked with his partner selling business insurance and estate planning.

The business expanded in 1979, when E.F. Hutton Financial Services joined forces with Killebrew & Harding. They opened an office in Boise, Idaho, and made Harmon the vice president of operations. Adding a third partner in 1984, the company became Killebrew, Harding and Harper.

Harmon left the insurance business in 1987 to devote time to his automobile dealership, Harmon Killebrew Motors, begun in 1984 in Ontario, Oregon. He sold the dealership in 1990 and moved to Scottsdale, Arizona, where he established his current business, Professional Endorsements.

In addition to his business pursuits, Killebrew coached in spring training one year for the Twins under Gene Mauch and worked as a Twins television broadcaster.

Harmon also broadcast games for the Oakland A's for four years, doubling as a hitting instructor with them. For one year, he worked as a TV broadcaster for the California Angels.

Harmon lives in Scottsdale, Arizona, with his wife, Nita. Together they have nine children.

In retirement, Harmon smashes golf balls near his home instead of baseballs out of American League parks. Killebrew still does special events for the Twins several times a year. He is a sentimental favorite on the Twins Caravan, a regional tour that takes past and present Twins figures on the road to meet fans each winter.

He also does extensive work for a hospice group in Arizona called Vista Care. Harmon is Vista Care's national spokesman. He holds a golf tournament each year to raise money for the Harmon Killebrew Foundation, which distributes funds to charity.

Killebrew is also on the board of directors of an organization called the World Children's Baseball Fair, founded by Japanese star Sadaharu Oh. Killebrew explained, "We bring kids aged nine to eleven from all over the world and teach them how to play baseball. We've been in Japan eight times, the United States twice, and in Canada once."

His love and respect for the game at which he excelled are still evident. When asked for his favorite memory of baseball, Harmon responded, "The game itself. Every day when I walked on the field is my favorite memory."

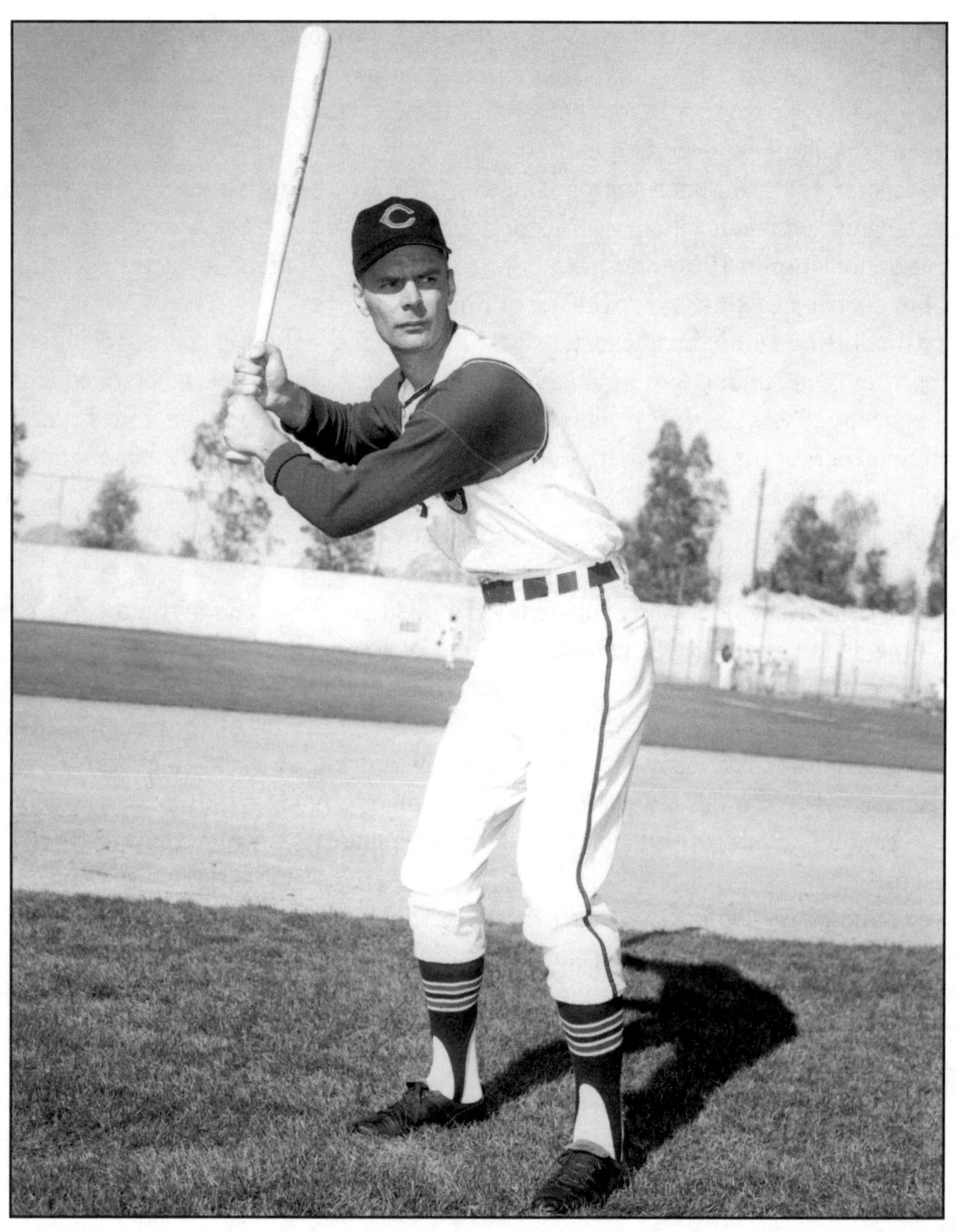

Jerry Kindall

Bats: Right
Throws: Right
Height: 6' 2"
Weight: 175 lbs.
Born: May 27, 1935, in Minnesota

YEAR	TEAM	LG	AVG	G	AB	R	H	2B	3B	HR	RBI	BB	K	OBP	SLG
1956	*ChN*	*NL*	*.164*	*32*	*55*	*7*	*9*	*1*	*1*	*0*	*0*	*6*	*17*	*.246*	*.218*
1957	*ChN*	*NL*	*.160*	*72*	*181*	*18*	*29*	*3*	*0*	*6*	*12*	*8*	*48*	*.196*	*.276*
1958	*ChN*	*NL*	*.167*	*3*	*6*	*0*	*1*	*1*	*0*	*0*	*0*	*0*	*3*	*.167*	*.333*
1960	*ChN*	*NL*	*.240*	*89*	*246*	*17*	*59*	*16*	*2*	*2*	*23*	*5*	*52*	*.253*	*.346*
1961	*ChN*	*NL*	*.242*	*96*	*310*	*37*	*75*	*22*	*3*	*9*	*44*	*18*	*89*	*.288*	*.419*
1962	*Cle*	*AL*	*.232*	*154*	*530*	*51*	*123*	*21*	*1*	*13*	*55*	*45*	*107*	*.290*	*.349*
1963	*Cle*	*AL*	*.205*	*86*	*234*	*27*	*48*	*4*	*1*	*5*	*20*	*18*	*71*	*.266*	*.295*
1964	*Cle*	*AL*	*.360*	*23*	*25*	*5*	*9*	*1*	*0*	*2*	*2*	*2*	*7*	*.407*	*.640*
1964	*Min*	*AL*	*.148*	*62*	*128*	*8*	*19*	*2*	*0*	*1*	*6*	*7*	*44*	*.199*	*.188*
1965	*Min*	*AL*	*.196*	*125*	*342*	*41*	*67*	*12*	*1*	*6*	*36*	*36*	*97*	*.274*	*.289*
			AVG	*G*	*AB*	*R*	*H*	*2B*	*3B*	*HR*	*RBI*	*BB*	*K*	*OBP*	*SLG*
			.213	*742*	*2,057*	*211*	*439*	*83*	*9*	*44*	*198*	*145*	*535*	*.266*	*.327*

The skinny eighth grader sneaked into Norton Fieldhouse on the Hamline University campus to shoot baskets. He loved sports and had a strong work ethic instilled by his father. Little did he know the success that dedication to work and sports would bring.

Jerry Kindall attended Washington High School in St. Paul. He entered the University of Minnesota in 1953, ironically with a basketball scholarship.

Jerry had offers to sign with four or five major-league baseball teams out of high school. But he wanted to play for the great Dick Siebert, coach of the Gophers' baseball squad. Dick and the basketball coach worked out an arrangement whereby Jerry would receive a basketball scholarship and play both sports.

But it was baseball in which Kindall excelled. In 1956 he was named an All-American shortstop. The Gophers won the College World Series that same year. After the tournament, the Chicago Cubs made a good offer. Kindall accepted.

He fell under the bonus player, two years in the majors rule. Kindall made his major-league debut on July 1, 1956. In limited action, Jerry hit below .200 in each of his first two seasons. He knew that he wasn't ready; besides, the Cubs already had a pretty good shortstop, Ernie Banks.

Thus, Kindall wasn't really disappointed to play with Fort Worth in 1958 and 1959, first in the Texas League and then in the American Association. His team won its division in 1959 and played the Minneapolis Millers in brand-new Metropolitan Stadium. At stake was the right to play in the Little World Series against the International League Champion. Fort Worth lost out to the Millers.

Kindall was called up to play for the Cubs in 1960. He played second base and had a solid year, appearing in 154 games and batting .240. With the backing of his manager, Lou Boudreau, he decided to experiment with switch hitting to take more advantage of his speed to first base.

In the last series of the season against the Los Angeles Dodgers, Kindall brought his experiment onto the field. He faced Don Drysdale and other Dodger pitchers batting left-handed. While Jerry didn't get any hits from the port side, he made solid contact with the ball and was encouraged enough to keep up the effort.

Kindall worked hard training to hit from the left side during the off-season. Maury Wills, the speedy switch-hitting Dodger infielder, motivated him. He continued to hit left-handed in 1961 spring training.

Then Boudreau resigned and Charlie Grim took over. The new regime wanted Jerry to end his switch-hitting attempts, citing his good power and the friendly confines that Wrigley Field presented to righties.

Stubbornly, Jerry insisted, "No, I'm going to switch hit. It's going to enhance my career."

After a prolonged debate, the Cubs management agreed, "Okay, you can switch hit, but you're going to do it in Des Moines."

That ended the argument. Kindall never again batted left-handed in a big-league game. It wasn't worth heading to the minors for an experiment.

Jerry stuck with the Cubs throughout 1961 and had another good year with nine homers and forty-four RBIs. But the Cubs wanted to go in another direction. In their minor-league system, Chicago had a terrific young player named Ken Hubbs; his readiness, coupled with the need for right-handed pitching, made Kindall expendable.

Jerry was traded to the Cleveland Indians for pitcher Bobby Locke prior to the 1962 season. In the long run, it didn't work out for the Cubs. Locke developed arm trouble and didn't finish out the year.

Hubbs played second base and was named National League Rookie of the Year. Then, tragically, he was killed in a plane crash after the season ended.

"It was a good trade for me," Jerry commented. "Although I loved being a Cub, I had a good year in Cleveland and established myself." In 1962 Kindall reached career highs in at-bats (530), home runs (thirteen) and RBIs (fifty-five).

The high-water mark of his year was a series against the Yankees in June. In the four-game set, Jerry rapped three hits in the first contest, four in the second, and hit two home runs in the Sunday doubleheader before more than 70,000 fans. His performance in that series helped propel the Indians into first place as they swept the Yankees.

A back injury the next year limited Jerry's playing time to eighty-six games.

After appearing in twenty-three games in the 1964 campaign, Jerry was traded to the Twins. He was joyful.

"It was the best thing that could happen to me, because I got to come home."

Bernie Allen and Kindall traded off at second base for most of 1964. In the championship season of 1965, Jerry was the regular second baseman for much of the year, appearing in 125 games. However, he was injured in Chicago when he was wiped out at second while turning a double play.

For three weeks, Jerry was on the shelf, and Frank Quilici came up from the Twins' minor-league Denver team to replace him. Quilici did a great job and, when Jerry's leg healed, there was no need for Manager Sam Mele to replace Frank. Kindall was in a utility role the remainder of the season.

But Jerry fondly remembers the Twins' first championship season, especially a game against the Washington Senators.

"We were struggling to stay in first place near the end of the season, and I pinch hit a home run to tie the game in the bottom of the ninth. Then Jimmie Hall came up to hit a home run to win it," Kindall said.

"I also won a game against knuckleball reliever Hoyt Wilhelm in Baltimore. Hitting a knuckleball was an act of divine intervention, and I did hit one in the late innings to help win the game.

"But just being on the championship team was my biggest thrill in baseball."

At the end of 1966 spring training, Calvin Griffith called Jerry into his office. Kindall was hoping that maybe Calvin had agreed to the raise he sought.

Instead Griffith said, "Look, here's your release. I just made a trade for Chuck Schilling. You two players are very much alike, good fielders, but don't hit much. I don't need both of you, so here's your release."

That proved to be it for Jerry's major-league career. He tried unsuccessfully to catch on with several other teams and then returned to the Twin Cities.

While he was playing baseball, Jerry had returned in the off-season to the University of Minnesota to work toward his master's degree. Basketball coach John Kundla recruited him to be a volunteer freshman basketball coach. After leaving the Twins in Florida, Kindall was contacted by his alma mater.

"When I was released, Athletic Director Marsh Ryman invited me to come on full time as assistant basketball coach and chairman of the Williams Scholarship Fund.

"It was a crossroads for me," Jerry recalled. "It was a wonderful blessing. I mourned the end of my baseball career because I was only thirty-one. I felt I could play some more. But when the opportunity came to coach at Minnesota, I was really happy for that.

"So I began my coaching career. I coached basketball three years, two under Kundla and one under Bill Fitch."

After two years of coaching basketball, Kindall expanded his scope when an opening occurred on Dick Siebert's baseball staff. Jerry became an assistant under his former mentor. For one year he assisted full time in both sports.

But Bill Fitch needed another full-time basketball coach under him. Kindall, when asked to choose one sport or the other, chose baseball. From 1968 to 1972 he was Siebert's assistant.

"My best baseball education came under Dick Siebert," Jerry said. "He was a terrific coach."

Kindall's brother in Phoenix phoned Jerry in the summer of 1971 to alert him that the head baseball coaching position at the University of Arizona was opening up. With Siebert's recommendation, Arizona hired Kindall in February of 1972. Essentially, he was coach-in-waiting because Wildcat head coach Frank Sancet was going to retire after the 1972 season.

Jerry's first year at the helm in Arizona was 1973. In Kindall's impressive twenty-four-year tenure in Tucson, he took five teams to the College World Series, winning the national championship three times, 1976, 1980, and 1986.

Each of those seasons Jerry was also named College Baseball Coach of the Year. Eleven times his teams were NCAA Regional finalists or champions.

The *Sporting News* added to Kindall's honors by naming him College Coach of the Year in 1980.

Jerry retired from the University of Arizona after the 1996 season with 861 wins and a .620 winning percentage. He became the senior advisor for U.S.A.

Baseball, overseeing three of America's national teams. They send out three teams for international competition. The Senior National Team is the college all-stars; the Junior National Team is made up of seventeen- and eighteen-year olds; and the Junior Olympians are fifteen and sixteen.

Jerry has coached a few years for U.S.A. Baseball, which is the national governing body in the Olympic movement for baseball, and also does clinics.

Education remains a big part of Kindall's life. He has authored an instructional book, *Sports Illustrated Baseball,* as well as numerous magazine articles on coaching, and four instructional videos for coaches and players. Jerry has also served as editor of *The Science of Baseball,* as well as co-editor of *The Baseball Coaching Bible.*

In January of 1991 Kindall was inducted into the College Baseball Coaches Hall of Fame. The University of Minnesota and the University of Arizona enshrined him in their respective Halls in 1995 and 1996.

Kindall continues to live in Tucson, Arizona. His first wife, Georgia, to whom he was married for thirty-one years, died in 1987 of Lou Gehrig's Disease. Ironically, Gehrig was Jerry's boyhood baseball idol, along with a St. Louis Cardinals shortstop named Marty Marion.

A year later he married Diane, whose first husband also died in 1987. Jerry had four children with Georgia, and Diane had two with her husband. Together they have twelve grandchildren.

Baseball has been Jerry Kindall's life. "I always wanted to play in the major leagues. It was a dream shared by most every boy who ever played Little League. I had some very good coaches who encouraged me at Washington High and North End American Legion Post 474.

"My dad was my biggest booster; he was a railroad man and a blue-collar guy. My mother was ill with multiple sclerosis. Dad had to do so much around the house. But he was always encouraging his three boys to play sports. He was a very stern guy but a very tender, loving, godly man.

"He always encouraged me and found money enough to buy me a glove. He worked two jobs, because we had a lot of medical expenses. We were a poor family, although I didn't know it at the time. So my dad is my hero.

"I had all these adults in my life who were encouraging me. Then I went to the University of Minnesota, and Dick Siebert was my best teacher. He knew the game. He was the best college baseball coach I ever knew. A terrific man.

"So what did baseball mean to me? It meant that I had all that support and encouragement and good teaching. When I got the chance to play ball professionally, the Cubs signed me. I was well along the way, because I had been given such good coaching.

"I had confidence, some skills, and a lot of support. When I got to the major leagues, it wasn't easy, but I thought I could make it."

Both as a player and a coach, Jerry Kindall made it. He is a true example of what good teaching, support, and hard work in developing skills can do.

Andy Kosco

Bats: Right
Throws: Right
Height: 6' 3"
Weight: 205 lbs.
Born: October 5, 1941, in Ohio

YEAR	TEAM	LG	AVG	G	AB	R	H	2B	3B	HR	RBI	BB	K	OBP	SLG
1965	Min	AL	.236	23	55	3	13	4	0	1	6	1	15	.241	.364
1966	Min	AL	.222	57	158	11	35	5	0	2	13	7	31	.251	.291
1967	Min	AL	.143	9	28	4	4	1	0	0	4	2	4	.200	.179
1968	NYA	AL	.240	131	466	47	112	19	1	15	59	16	71	.268	.382
1969	LA	NL	.248	120	424	51	105	13	2	19	74	21	66	.282	.422
1970	LA	NL	.228	74	224	21	51	12	0	8	27	1	40	.230	.388
1971	Mil	AL	.227	98	264	27	60	6	2	10	39	24	57	.291	.379
1972	Cal	AL	.239	49	142	15	34	4	2	6	13	5	23	.267	.423
1972	Bos	AL	.213	17	47	5	10	2	1	3	6	2	9	.260	.489
1973	Cin	NL	.280	47	118	17	33	7	0	9	21	13	26	.346	.568
1974	Cin	NL	.189	33	37	3	7	2	0	0	5	7	8	.311	.243
			AVG	G	AB	R	H	2B	3B	HR	RBI	BB	K	OBP	SLG
			.236	658	1,963	204	464	75	8	73	267	99	350	.273	.394

"Sudden" Sam McDowell threw hard in 1965. The Cleveland lefty looked to make short work of the strapping right-handed rookie outfielder who was batting in his first major-league game. But Andy Kosco caught up with McDowell's fastball and drove it out of Cleveland's Municipal Stadium.

That first taste of power in the "bigs" was thrilling for Kosco. However, he was quickly brought down to earth by the Indians' ace, who struck him out his next three times up.

The Detroit Tigers signed the Youngstown, Ohio, native out of Struthers High School in 1959. The Tigers moved Kosco around plenty in their minor-league system over the next five years: Durham, North Carolina; Knoxville, Tennessee; Birmingham, Alabama; and back to Knoxville. Then Andy was sent to the Tigers' Northern League affiliate in Duluth, Minnesota.

He was traded to the Twins about one month into the season. They assigned him to their club in the Northern League, Bismarck (North Dakota). Kosco wound up winning the Triple Crown in the league that year despite playing on a last-place team. Andy also was voted Minor League Player of the Year.

Andy went to 1965 spring training with the Twins and made the club. But he had another option year available, so he could be sent to a minor-league team without being lost to another club. Minnesota sent him to Denver for about half of the 1965 season. He was leading the league in batting, home runs, and RBIs when the Twins called him up.

"Being on a pennant winner right away was a highlight of my Twins career," Andy related. "That and hitting a home run my first game off Sam McDowell. That was special. It was in Cleveland, and my family was there."

Although Kosco was on the Twins World Series roster, he didn't play. He got only fifty-five at-bats his first season. Regardless, he has a treasured memento for his role with the 1965 Twins.

"It was nice to get a World Series ring your first year." Andy looked down and read from his ring as he talked. "It says 'American League Champions.' The winners' ring says 'World Series Champions.'"

Andy got more playing time in 1966, appearing in fifty-seven games.

"The Twins had such a good team; being an outfielder, it was tough to get into games. They had Harmon Killebrew, Bob Allison, Jimmie Hall, Tony Oliva. It was hard to move ahead of those guys."

That led to Andy's being sent back to AAA ball in Denver after half of the 1967 season. "Since I wasn't playing, and they didn't want me just sitting around, they sent me to the minor leagues."

Kosco was traded to the Yankees in 1968. He played one year in the "Big Apple."

"I played quite a bit. I didn't at first, but then worked my way into the line-up. It was another highlight of my career to be able to play with Mickey Mantle. I idolized him when I was growing up. I was the player who replaced Mantle in his last game. To be on the same team with him was one of my big moments.

"There was a tremendous magnetism Mantle generated with the fans. People just wanted to touch him; it was unbelievable. I had played with Killebrew, Rose, Bench, and Mike Schmidt. I played with a lot of these players, but none had the magnetism that Mickey did.

"People just wanted to be around him. And when I say touch him, that's really all they wanted to do. He was like a god."

From New York, Andy was traded to the Dodgers. Yankees' Skipper Ralph Houk called Kosco in and told him he was going to L.A. for his own good, saying, "Maybe you can hit some home runs there."

Andy hit fifteen home runs for the Yankees, but by broadcaster Phil Rizzuto's count he had hit twenty-four to the warning track in the left field power alley for fly ball outs.

"If I'm not mistaken," Andy said, "there were only about twenty home runs hit out to left in the history of Yankee Stadium before they remodeled. I was the last player out of fourteen total players to do that."

The fence was only 301 feet down the line at Yankee Stadium but quickly dropped off toward center, where it was 461 feet. The Yankees thought they'd do Kosco a service by sending him to a friendlier park. Dodger Stadium wasn't much better, although Andy did crack nineteen homers his first year there.

Kosco's at-bats with the Dodgers dropped from 424 in 1969 to 224 in 1970. "We had a bunch of outfielders, and they were rotating everybody." Then they got into a youth movement, and Andy started to move around.

With Milwaukee in 1971, he played some outfield and first base. Then Kosco went to the Angels until Boston purchased him. He pinch hit, played against left-handed pitchers and saw spot duty.

"When I was traded to the Reds in '73, I played considerably more again," Kosco said. "I got in sometimes in right field, a little bit of center and a little bit at third base. I had a real good year."

"I hurt my back during the 1974 season in a fight in Pittsburgh and had to have surgery. It was kind of hard to come back and play. I hurt it during the season and tried to come back after three weeks, but it was premature, and it didn't heal properly," Kosco continued.

"I rushed it because they had a chance to get into the World Series, and I wanted to be ready for that. But they released me during the winter.

"I ended up going to the Phillies. So I went to spring training with the Phillies and did well. Then my back started getting sore again. So I ended up going down and playing in the minor leagues. I was kind of a player-coach for a while. But my back kept bothering me, and I just quit playing."

Andy had been attending Youngstown State University in the off-season, working on his degree. He had done some substitute teaching during the winter months.

"I went into the insurance business with a friend who had played for the Phillies and was considerably older than I was. I gave it a try and took a liking to it. I've been able to do very well in the business."

With his wife, Cathy, Andy has five grown children. The couple resides in his native Youngstown.

Baseball was something that Andy always wanted to do. "I had the ability and the size to make that a reality," he said. "Being from this area and having played and then coming back here, there was not only self-satisfaction, but being treated well by my home-area people was very nice.

"I've made a lot of wonderful friendships in this area, and a lot of it's been because of baseball. It's given me exposure and allowed me to be successful in this business.

"I liked the excitement of being able to play in front of large crowds and also the friends that you establish when you're playing ball."

Frank Kostro

Bats: Right
Throws: Right
Height: 6' 2"
Weight: 190 lbs.
Born: August 4, 1937, in Pennsylvania

YEAR	TEAM	LG	AVG	G	AB	R	H	2B	3B	HR	RBI	BB	K	OBP	SLG
1962	*Det*	*AL*	*.268*	*16*	*41*	*5*	*11*	*3*	*0*	*0*	*3*	*1*	*6*	*.279*	*.341*
1963	*Det*	*AL*	*.231*	*31*	*52*	*4*	*12*	*1*	*0*	*0*	*0*	*9*	*13*	*.344*	*.250*
1963	*LAA*	*AL*	*.222*	*43*	*99*	*6*	*22*	*2*	*1*	*2*	*10*	*6*	*17*	*.264*	*.323*
1964	*Min*	*AL*	*.272*	*59*	*103*	*10*	*28*	*5*	*0*	*3*	*12*	*4*	*21*	*.303*	*.408*
1965	*Min*	*AL*	*.161*	*20*	*31*	*2*	*5*	*2*	*0*	*0*	*1*	*4*	*5*	*.250*	*.226*
1967	*Min*	*AL*	*.323*	*32*	*31*	*4*	*10*	*0*	*0*	*0*	*2*	*3*	*2*	*.382*	*.323*
1968	*Min*	*AL*	*.241*	*63*	*108*	*9*	*26*	*4*	*1*	*0*	*9*	*6*	*20*	*.274*	*.296*
1969	*Min*	*AL*	*.000*	*2*	*2*	*0*	*0*	*0*	*0*	*0*	*0*	*0*	*1*	*.000*	*.000*
			AVG	*G*	*AB*	*R*	*H*	*2B*	*3B*	*HR*	*RBI*	*BB*	*K*	*OBP*	*SLG*
			.244	*266*	*467*	*40*	*114*	*17*	*2*	*5*	*37*	*33*	*85*	*.291*	*.321*

Frank Kostro came from a tiny coal-mining town in Pennsylvania called Blough, population seventy-five. He grew up playing baseball and following the exploits of Pittsburgh Pirates' great Ralph Kiner. Kostro went to Forbes High School and graduated in 1956 dreaming of a future in baseball.

Kostro was signed by the Detroit Tigers and sent to their rookie farm team at Janestown, New York. Frank made stops in Durham, North Carolina; Birmingham, Alabama; Charleston, West Virginia; and Denver, Colorado, in the Tigers' minor-league system. He was called up to the Tigers in 1962.

Kostro's first major-league hit was a double off Twins great left-hander Jim Kaat. Frank hit .268 in forty-one at-bats his first year in the bigs. He was also thrilled to be interviewed by his boyhood hero, then a baseball broadcaster, Ralph Kiner.

Frank was traded to the Los Angeles Angels early in the 1963 season. One of Kostro's career highlights came during his short stay with the Angels, when he hit his first major-league home run off his former Tigers' teammate, Jim Bunning.

Kostro was traded to the Minnesota Twins before the 1964 season in a three-way deal involving Boston and Los Angeles. Essentially, the Twins received Kostro, and Lenny Green went to Boston.

His first season with the Twins was Frank's most productive. Kostro was a role player who saw limited action. But he was valuable because he could play a variety of positions, both infield and outfield, a true utility man.

Frank batted 103 times, hit three home runs and drove in twelve while hitting .272 in 1964. He led the Twins with ten pinch hits, including four in a row, a feat Frank accomplished twice in his career.

"To be a good pinch hitter, get good and loose," Frank advised. "Now it's a little different. They have batting cages right there. These guys are takin' batting practice. Someone calls back and says, 'Come on up, you're gonna hit in five minutes.'

"I always thought the key for me, and Don Mincher was the same way, was to have a little bit of lead time. This is where Sam Mele was so good. He was the manager when I had four hits in a row."

Kostro was injured for part of the Twins American League championship season in 1965 and saw very limited action. While on the team, Frank was not on the World Series roster. But he did receive a seventy-five percent share of the postseason paycheck and wears a World Series ring.

Frank was back in the minors in 1966 and much of 1967. He got into thirty-two games with the Twins that year.

In 1968, Frank saw the most major-league action of his career, appearing in sixty-three games and getting 108 at-bats. It was at the end of spring training, prior to the start of the 1968 season, that he earned his enduring nickname.

While waiting for the start of an exhibition game in the Houston Astrodome, Frank was discussing his varied fielding assignments with a fellow Pole, Twins reliever Ron Perranoski.

"Since I'm Polish, does that make me a utility Pole?" Frank recalls asking Ron. "We chuckled a bit, but there wasn't much said about it. But a newspaper guy overheard it, and that's how it got out that I was 'The Utility Pole.'"

For twenty-five years, the sobriquet was little remembered. But, Frank reported, it has suddenly sprung into the public eye again. In the last few years, he has received news clippings from various cities about the "Utility Pole," and a friend has printed up shirts with the words.

People liked Kostro, who was known for an active sense of humor. He had a conversation with a local sportswriter in which he talked about a fishing trip he and Ted Uhlaender had taken to Lake Minnetonka.

"Ted and I went fishing," Frank told the writer. "I caught one, but I handed Ted the pole and said, 'Here, Ted, you-land-er.'"

After another minor-league campaign and getting into just two games with the 1969 Twins, Frank headed east to Japan. He played with the Hyunku Braves in 1970 and then retired from professional baseball.

"My favorite memory is just getting to the major leagues," Frank related, "then some of the games and people I played with, like Harmon Killebrew and Tony Oliva. Harmon was a first-class guy.

"Baseball meant a lot to my life business-wise after I retired. I got into the credit life insurance business with car dealers. [Baseball] opened a lot of doors, and I got to know a lot of people when I was playing who knew car dealers.

"But while baseball meant much to my business, I think the best thing that happened is all the great people that you get to meet in the game, whether they're ballplayers or not ballplayers."

Frank is still active with Kostro Insurance Agency in Denver. He is married and has two grown sons.

Jim Lemon

Bats: Right
Throws: Right
Height: 6' 4"
Weight: 200 lbs.
Born: March 23, 1928, in Virginia

YEAR	TEAM	LG	AVG	G	AB	R	H	2B	3B	HR	RBI	BB	K	OBP	SLG
1950	Cle	AL	.176	12	34	4	6	1	0	1	1	3	12	.243	.294
1953	Cle	AL	.174	16	46	5	8	1	0	1	5	3	15	.224	.261
1954	Was	AL	.234	37	128	12	30	2	3	2	13	9	34	.283	.344
1955	Was	AL	.200	10	25	3	5	2	0	1	3	3	4	.286	.400
1956	Was	AL	.271	146	538	77	146	21	11	27	96	65	138	.349	.502
1957	Was	AL	.284	137	518	58	147	23	6	17	64	49	94	.345	.450
1958	Was	AL	.246	142	501	65	123	15	9	26	75	50	120	.314	.467
1959	Was	AL	.279	147	531	73	148	18	3	33	100	46	99	.334	.510
1960	Was	AL	.269	148	528	81	142	10	1	38	100	67	114	.354	.508
1961	Min	AL	.258	129	423	57	109	26	1	14	52	44	98	.329	.423
1962	Min	AL	.176	12	17	1	3	0	0	1	5	3	4	.286	.353
1963	Min	AL	.118	7	17	0	2	0	0	0	1	1	5	.167	.118
1963	Phi	NL	.271	31	59	6	16	2	0	2	6	8	18	.353	.407
1963	ChA	AL	.200	36	80	4	16	0	1	1	8	12	32	.304	.263
			AVG	G	AB	R	H	2B	3B	HR	RBI	BB	K	OBP	SLG
			.262	1,010	3,445	446	901	121	35	164	529	363	787	.332	.460

Dubbed the "Covington Clouter," Jim Lemon was among the American League's most-feared power hitters from 1956 to 1960. If not for a stint in the Korean War and an injury, his impact would have been even greater.

A native of Covington, Virginia, Lemon signed with the Cleveland Indians after his high-school years. He spent three years in Cleveland's minor-league system, rapping thirty-nine home runs for their Oklahoma City affiliate in 1950.

That earned Jim a call up to the big club in August 1950. Just as he thought he was on his way in the major leagues, Uncle Sam called. Lemon spent the next two years in the service during the Korean War.

Jim returned to baseball in 1953. He appeared in sixteen games for the Indians but spent the bulk of the year in Indianapolis. After the season the Indians sold Lemon to the Senators.

"When I came back from the service, I was rusty," Jim explained. "I had to relearn. It took me three years to put it back together."

But put it together he did. In 1956 Lemon hit .271 with twenty-seven homers and ninety-six RBIs. He rapped three home runs in one game off the Yankees' Whitey Ford with President Eisenhower in attendance.

Strikeouts, a byproduct of power hitting, were also common for Lemon. For three seasons, from 1956 to 1958, he led the league in whiffs. Jim's biggest years came in 1959 and 1960, when he hit thirty-three and thirty-eight dingers, respectively, and drove in 100 runs each year.

In 1959 Jim tied two major-league records by hitting two home runs (one a grand slam) and driving in six runs in one inning. In the 1960 campaign, Lemon battled for the American League home run championship with Mickey Mantle and Roger Maris. He lost out to Mantle, 40-38. Jim was named to the 1960 All-Star squad.

Lemon excelled while the Senators kept losing. "We had a good offensive group," Jim related, "with Roy Sievers, Harmon, Bob Allison, Pete Runnels. But we didn't catch the ball too good. We had some pitching; Pedro Ramos was a great athlete who had a real rubber arm."

The 1961 season, the first the team played as the Twins, opened at Yankee Stadium. Jim Lemon batted cleanup and played left field in the first Twins lineup.

In his prime, the "Covington Clouter" was fast, powerful and had an exceptional arm. But years lost to the military cut into his potential. Lemon was thirty-two when he arrived in Minnesota. As a Twin, he was unable to duplicate his prowess of previous years.

"I had a tough time," Jim remembered. "We were about a third into the season, and I tore a muscle in my left shoulder. It never healed. I had surgery in 1962 and spent most of the year on the disabled list, but I never got my strength back."

Lemon hit .258 in 1961. He slipped from his peak thirty-eight homers from the year before to just fourteen. It was a tough adjustment for the slugger. "When you have lived your whole life being able to swing a bat, it's hard to not do what you did before," Lemon said. "When you used to see a pitch and say, 'Look out!' when you hit it, it was disgusting to see the same pitch and not be able to get to it."

There were moments of glory. Jim hit one homer for the Twins in 1962. It came during one of the contests that skipper Sam Mele recalled as special. Mele sent Lemon in to pinch hit late in a game against Baltimore's Chuck Estrada.

Jim recalled, "He gave me a high fastball. I hit it out and we won the game." It was his last Twins homer.

In 1963 Lemon played for three teams: the Twins, the Phillies, and the White Sox. He even tried some first base, but it was apparent that time and injury had caught up with Jim. He retired after the season.

The Washington Senators hired Lemon to manage their York, Pennsylvania, minor-league club in 1964. The following season the Twins brought big Jim back to Minnesota to be a first-base coach and hitting instructor. He was with the Twins as they won the 1965 American League title.

Lemon returned to manage the Senators in 1968, but when Bob Short purchased the team, he cleaned house and fired Jim.

"New brooms sweep clean," Jim said philosophically.

For the next twelve years, Lemon was out of baseball. He and a partner ran a grocery business in Maryland. Then, in 1981, the Twins called again. Jim returned as a base coach and hitting instructor through the 1984 season. When Carl Pohlad purchased the Twins, he replaced Jim with Tony Oliva. Essentially, the two switched jobs; Lemon became the Twins' minor-league hitting instructor. He stayed with the Twins in that position until 1995.

When Jim looks back on his pro baseball career, he sees beyond playing the game. "The most satisfaction I got from the game was that someone, meaning the Twins and Senators, had enough confidence in me as a person and a player to let me teach.

"I became a hitting coach and a minor-league manager. In the minors, you do a multitude of things. You instruct, manage, scout, you do all of the things.

"Then I became a manager in the big leagues. Looking back over my career, I think I'm most proud of that. People had enough confidence in me to let me teach their players. I still enjoy that.

"Baseball meant everything to me. It was my livelihood. It gave travel opportunities. I enjoyed every bit of it."

Jim and his wife, Ella, are retired and live in central Florida. They have a daughter, who works in the investment business, and two sons. One son is a nursing-home administrator, and the other is a prosecuting attorney.

Twins

Sam Mele
Manager

Managerial Record—all with the Twins
1961 45-49
1962 71-91
1963 91-70
1964 79-83
1965 102-60
1966 89-73
1967 25-25
.548 winning percentage

The New York kid in the Boston Red Sox uniform was playing in Yankee Stadium. He was competing against the team for which he had grown up rooting. His family and friends were seated in the Yankees' familiar confines.

Sam Mele ripped his first major-league home run that summer day in 1947. One of Sam's greatest memories in baseball was circling the bases and spying his parents, two Italian immigrants, cheering in the stands with looks of jubilation on their faces.

Mele was signed by the Boston Red Sox after his third year at New York University, where he also played basketball.

Sam was privileged to play with some of the finest players of his era. Dom DiMaggio and Ted Williams were his outfield mates.

Asked what made Williams such a great hitter, Mele responded, "He was a fantastic student on hitting. He wanted to know everything about a pitcher: What he threw; what did he like to throw in a tough situation? What does his ball do? Does it move in, down, out or whatever?

"If there was a new guy on the mound he'd go up and down the bench. He wanted to know if anybody had seen this guy before and who'd he remind you of.

"Ted always did exercises with his wrists and forearms, which he said was so important for the velocity of the bat. He had an excellent eye at the plate. He was a student who asked questions and questions and questions.

"Williams would have me sit beside him on bus trips in spring training, and when you got off that bus you felt like you were the greatest hitter in the world. All he talked about was hitting and hitting.

"I went to Williams one day in the outfield to ask him about fielding. He said, 'Don't ask me about fielding. You go to that little guy in center field, Dom DiMaggio, he can help you more than I can. I'll tell you about hitting.'"

Mele played for seven teams in eight years. He moved from Boston to the Senators in 1949 and then to the Chicago White Sox, Baltimore, Boston again, and then Cincinnati before wrapping up his big-league playing career in Cleveland in 1956.

Mele had a career batting average of .267. His best overall season was his rookie year, when he batted .302 with twelve home runs and seventy-three RBIs.

In 1951, as Washington's right fielder, he tied for the American League lead in doubles with thirty-six. In his biggest single game, Sam, then a White Sox, hit a three-run homer and a three-run triple in one inning in a game at Philadelphia.

In 1953, for Chicago, he set a record for most consecutive errorless games by an outfielder in a season, 131, as he handled 212 chances.

Sam related this account of a game in St. Louis. "I was playing for Joe McCarthy, manager of the Red Sox. McCarthy had a bad drinking problem. He really didn't play me much at all. One game, we were playing St. Louis, they locked him in his hotel room, and third-base coach Del Baker was the acting manager.

"I was on second, and Birdie Tebbits was on first. Baker gave us the hit-and-run sign. When I slid into third, I threw out my ankle and knee. McCarthy had gotten out of his hotel room. He walked across the diamond.

"Mickey Harris said, 'Somebody get a stretcher!'

"McCarthy said, 'Since when do they have to take a guy off on a stretcher?'

"I replied, 'I'll walk.' But they wouldn't let me.

"McCarthy got after Del Baker for giving that sign. Baker said, 'Hell, you gave it to me to give to them.'"

After Sam's playing career ended in 1958, he became a scout for the Senators. On July 3, 1959, Calvin Griffith called and asked Mele to become a first-base coach for Washington.

Mele went to Minnesota with the Twins and became manager Cookie Lavagetto's third-base coach. On June 23, 1961, Calvin Griffith fired Cookie and Sam Mele became the second Twins' skipper.

Sam was asked what it takes to make a good manager.

"Being fair and still being firm. But what helped me a great, great deal," Mele said, "I had Harmon Killebrew, Camilo Pascual, Bob Allison, and Earl Battey. All the players respected them so much that the problems got taken care of before they came to me.

"I had a bunch of good guys that made it easy to manage."

Mele also cited the coaches with whom he worked. Jim Lemon became his first-base coach and also worked frequently as a hitting instructor with Harmon Killebrew.

Killebrew had many managers. In commenting on their styles, he said, "There were two ways to manage: through fear, like Billy Martin, or be like Sam Mele and just let the players play.

"Sam was the best at keeping players who weren't playing regularly happy."

Mele's highest praise was reserved for Billy Martin, who had played second base for Sam in 1961 and became his third-base coach.

"He made Carew into a second baseman, and he made the '65 Twins run. In spring training of '65, Zoilo Versalles let a ball get by to his right. It pissed me off! I took him out right away and put someone else at short.

"Zoilo mouthed off in the dugout. I said, 'That's a $100.' He said some more and I said, '$200, $300.' Then Billy came over and took Zoilo away. Billy took care of him that year, treated him like a father. He taught Zoilo what it means to win. Versalles was the League MVP that year.

"Some people thought Billy was after my job. That wasn't true. Whenever he helped us to win, it helped me keep my job that much longer."

They did joke about it, however. Sam and Billy occasionally fished together. On one Minnesota lake, Sam put a little extra effort into a cast and fell out of the boat. Standing neck deep in water, his feet mired in muck, Sam cried to Martin for help.

Billy stood in the boat and said, "Ya know, I really do want your job." Then he picked up the anchor and pretended to heft it at his manager, before laughingly helping Sam into the boat.

The 1965 Twins led the American League for most of the season. They cemented their lead at four games at the All-Star break and never looked back, winning the title by seven games.

"One of the keys," Mele said, "was that we beat the Red Sox seventeen out of eighteen games that year."

Solid hitting, good power and sterling pitching by Jim Grant, Jim Kaat, and others led the way to Minnesota's first championship.

The Twins won the first two games of the 1965 World Series in Minnesota, then dropped three in Los Angeles. After Jim Grant beat the Dodgers in the sixth game in Bloomington, the stage was set for Game 7 at Metropolitan Stadium.

Sandy Koufax, the great Dodgers lefthander and Game 2 loser, was on the hill for L.A., facing Jim Kaat.

"Koufax couldn't get his curve over," Sam remembered. "They had Don Drysdale warming up in the bullpen more than once."

"But Koufax beat us anyway, a three-hitter, 2-0. He was one of the greatest pitchers I ever saw."

The Twins' best chance to mount a serious threat went by the boards when Dodger third baseman Junior Gilliam made a great stab at a shot by Versalles with Rich Rollins on base.

Dodger pitcher (and later Twins pitching coach) Johnny Podres told Mele, "Those were the kind of plays that Gilliam would make, but if you hit one hard right at him he might have booted it."

"It was a great series," Mele continued. "I watch that Game 7 on Classic Sports. I must have seen it ten times, and we lose every time. But it was a thrill."

Sam Mele was named the *Sporting News* Manager of the Year for 1965. He ranks second to Billy Martin in winning percentage for a Twins manager.

By virtue of the Twins' first-place finish in 1965, Mele had the honor of managing the 1966 All-Star Game. He had no reason to suspect that the excitement surrounding the event would be heightened by threats to his personal safety.

Mele's duties included naming players. Yankee star Mickey Mantle was picked for center field. Featuring Mantle at his home, Yankee Stadium, for the All-Star Game created a match beyond compare for the Mick's devoted following.

Mele recounted how the drama began unfolding in Baltimore, where the Twins were playing prior to the All-Star Game.

"I was having breakfast," Mele recalled. "Billy Martin joined me. He wanted steak and eggs, and he knew that the manager paid.

"Then he got a phone call. It was Mickey Mantle, and he wanted to talk to me. Mantle wanted the three days off. His legs hurt. He wrapped them from ankle to thigh every game. I said okay and replaced him with Tommy Agee.

"When I got to New York for the All-Star Game, I got a call in my hotel. Someone was outraged that I had replaced Mantle. He didn't know that Mickey wanted off the team.

"The guy said he'd shoot me and Tony Oliva at the game. Well, if he shot Oliva, he might as well have shot me. Oliva should be in the Hall of Fame today.

"I called Calvin and told him about the threat. We had cops on the bus, cops around the dugout and ballpark guarding us.

"When the time came to bring out the lineup cards to home plate, I called Martin over. 'You always wanted to be a manager,' I said. 'You take the card to the plate. I'll even let you wear my uniform top.'

"Martin said, 'B— S—!' And left me to go to home plate. I went out where the umpires were standing in a circle by the plate and stood in the middle of them."

The game proceeded without violence.

The Twins had another good year in 1966 but dipped to second place, six games out. In 1967, the team got off to a slow start. They were 25-25, still just six games out of first place, when team owner Calvin Griffith decided to replace Mele as manager.

"I have no idea why Calvin fired me," Mele stated. "I went to the ballpark very early. My family had flown out that morning from the East. I put them at the hotel and went to the park.

"I had a message to go up and see Calvin. Calvin and his son Clark were in his office. Calvin said, 'I'm gonna make a change, but I want you in the organization.'

"That's all Calvin said to me. I really don't know why I was fired. We were at .500. When I left the park, I ran into Bob Allison. He said, 'Where're ya goin'?' When I told him, he said, 'You're kidding!' Then I ran into Billy Martin, we grabbed each other; he cried, I cried.

"I still liked Calvin an awful lot," Mele concluded, "he gave me my first chance." Sam's managerial record was 522 wins and 431 losses, a winning percentage of .548.

Tom Yawkey, Boston owner, had once told Sam that a job awaited him with the Red Sox if he ever needed it.

Sam said, "Calvin offered me a job, but Boston was my first choice. As soon as I called Mr.Yawkey, he said, 'You're working for me.'"

From 1965 through the early 1990s, Sam Mele worked for the Red Sox as a hitting instructor, outfield instructor and ran the minor-league camp. He scouted all over the country for the Sox.

Now retired, Sam still takes part in fantasy camps.

Sam and Connie Mele have been married fifty-two years. They have lived all that time in Quincy, Massachusetts. The Meles have five grown children: three daughters and two sons.

Twins

Don Mincher

Bats: Left
Throws: Right
Height: 6' 3"
Weight: 205 lbs.
Born: June 24, 1938, in Alabama

YEAR	TEAM	LG	AVG	G	AB	R	H	2B	3B	HR	RBI	BB	K	OBP	SLG
1960	*Was*	*AL*	*.241*	*27*	*79*	*10*	*19*	*4*	*1*	*2*	*5*	*11*	*11*	*.330*	*.392*
1961	*Min*	*AL*	*.188*	*35*	*101*	*18*	*19*	*5*	*1*	*5*	*11*	*22*	*11*	*.333*	*.406*
1962	*Min*	*AL*	*.240*	*86*	*121*	*20*	*29*	*1*	*1*	*9*	*29*	*34*	*24*	*.406*	*.488*
1963	*Min*	*AL*	*.258*	*82*	*225*	*41*	*58*	*8*	*0*	*17*	*42*	*30*	*51*	*.351*	*.520*
1964	*Min*	*AL*	*.237*	*120*	*287*	*45*	*68*	*12*	*4*	*23*	*56*	*27*	*51*	*.300*	*.547*
1965	*Min*	*AL*	*.251*	*128*	*346*	*43*	*87*	*17*	*3*	*22*	*65*	*49*	*73*	*.344*	*.509*
1966	*Min*	*AL*	*.251*	*139*	*431*	*53*	*108*	*30*	*0*	*14*	*62*	*58*	*68*	*.340*	*.418*
1967	*Cal*	*AL*	*.273*	*147*	*487*	*81*	*133*	*23*	*3*	*25*	*76*	*69*	*69*	*.367*	*.487*
1968	*Cal*	*AL*	*.236*	*120*	*399*	*35*	*94*	*12*	*1*	*13*	*48*	*43*	*65*	*.312*	*.368*
1969	*Sea*	*AL*	*.246*	*140*	*427*	*53*	*105*	*14*	*0*	*25*	*78*	*78*	*69*	*.366*	*.454*
1970	*Oak*	*AL*	*.246*	*140*	*463*	*62*	*114*	*18*	*0*	*27*	*74*	*56*	*71*	*.327*	*.460*
1971	*Oak*	*AL*	*.239*	*28*	*92*	*9*	*22*	*6*	*1*	*2*	*8*	*20*	*14*	*.375*	*.391*
1971	*Was*	*AL*	*.291*	*100*	*323*	*35*	*94*	*15*	*1*	*10*	*45*	*53*	*52*	*.389*	*.437*
1972	*Tex*	*AL*	*.236*	*61*	*191*	*23*	*45*	*10*	*0*	*6*	*39*	*46*	*23*	*.384*	*.382*
1972	*Oak*	*AL*	*.148*	*47*	*54*	*2*	*8*	*1*	*0*	*0*	*5*	*10*	*16*	*.281*	*.167*
			AVG	*G*	*AB*	*R*	*H*	*2B*	*3B*	*HR*	*RBI*	*BB*	*K*	*OBP*	*SLG*
			.249	*1,400*	*4,026*	*530*	*1,003*	*176*	*16*	*200*	*643*	*606*	*668*	*.348*	*.450*

"We've got Minch in the pinch!" was a cry that echoed throughout Metropolitan Stadium in the early and mid-1960s as Don Mincher strode to the plate in critical situations.

The big left-handed slugger from Alabama often came through as a pinch hitter. In 1962 he had twenty-nine hits and twenty-nine RBIs. He pinch hit two homers and drew sixteen walks, two short of Elmer Valo's record for pinch hitters.

Mincher was born in Huntsville, Alabama, where he attended high school, graduating in 1956. Don was signed to a contract by the Chicago White Sox and sent to their Duluth-Superior farm club.

He spent four years in the White Sox minor-league system, also at Davenport, Iowa, and Charleston, West Virginia, before being traded, along with Earl Battey, to the Washington Senators for Roy Sievers.

Don started 1960 with the Senators, making his major-league debut on April 18, 1960. But he spent most of the year in the minors at Charleston.

Mincher made the move with the Senators to Minnesota in 1961 to become a Twin. He hit just .181 his rookie year, but five of his nineteen hits were home runs. Don had a knack for making his hits count.

Mincher doesn't think anyone really wants to be a pinch hitter. They'd rather be playing regularly.

"But," Don said, "that role is there, and it's important to be able to follow the actions of the game and realize from the fifth inning under what conditions you might be used as a pinch hitter and against whom.

"You know who the other team's pitchers are and who might be used against you if you pinch hit. Stay alive and stay into the game. Always know that your time at bat is going to be just as valuable as anyone else's because normally pinch hitters are reserved for big situations.

"Be mentally alert and ready to stay in the game."

Mincher's playing time grew during 1962, 1963, and 1964. He pinch hit and backed up Vic Power, Bob Allison, and Harmon Killebrew at first base.

Don made the most of his opportunities. When Vic Power was injured in the middle of a game in Cleveland, Mincher replaced him and rapped two home runs, one a grand slam. In a six-game span begun that day, he drove in fourteen runs and hit five home runs, including another grand slam.

Mincher's play earned him more game time. In 1964 he batted just 287 times but he hit twenty-three home runs. It earned him the lead position in a first-base platoon for the American League champs in 1965.

Don rewarded manager Sam Mele's faith in him with twenty-two home runs, sixty-six RBIs and a .251 average in 346 at-bats. That year—1965—and the World Series were the biggest moments in his years with the Twins.

"Without a doubt the 1965 World Series and being able to hit a home run off Don Drysdale in my first at-bat at Metropolitan Stadium was a personal highlight," Mincher said.

"But the whole year, 1965, winning the pennant and all that was absolutely unbelievable."

Mincher helped make baseball history on June 9, 1966, when he hit one of five Twins home runs in one inning; the five homers set an American League record.

But Don's power numbers fell off in 1966 to fourteen homers, and he was traded to the Angels for Dean Chance. He bounced up to a .273 average and twenty-three home runs with the Angels in 1966, but in April of 1968, he was beaned on the head by fastballer Sam McDowell. He suffered from dizziness for much of the rest of the season and didn't get back on track offensively.

Some players have great difficulty coming back from a serious beaning. Twin Jimmie Hall was never again the same hitter after being hit on the head. Don talked about coming back after getting beaned.

"It's hard. You can't get it out of your mind until you get back in there, and it doesn't occur until you face that same pitcher again.

"McDowell was just as shaken as I was about the whole situation. Most of my at-bats after that he walked me, kinda afraid to come inside. Once I got past facing him again, it was all forgotten.

"You clear it out of your mind. Except when that one pitcher faces you, it brings back memories."

The Angels left him unprotected in the expansion draft, and the Seattle Pilots picked up Mincher. The move was a good one: The big guy was back. He slammed twenty-five home runs and drove in seventy-eight runs for Seattle.

"Every hitter, no matter what they tell you, plays the game off the fastball," Don explained. "You look for that up to two strikes and then you might start anticipating the breaking ball.

"But I think ninety percent of the game is played off the fastball and that's what I looked for, especially 2-0 and 3-1."

The Oakland A's, looking for left-handed power, traded four players for him in 1970. Mincher rewarded them with the best power show of his career, twenty-seven homers.

However, Don dropped off considerably and was traded to the Senators. He was with them when they moved to Texas, becoming the only person to play for both Senators teams that transferred from Washington, D.C.: the Twins and the Rangers.

In 1972 the A's called him back for one more pennant drive. He played in just forty-seven games and hit only .148 but had one more moment in the sun. In Game 4 of the 1972 World Series against Cincinnati, the A's trailed 2-1 in the ninth inning. With one out and two runners on base, Don came up to pinch hit. His single tied the game. The A's went on to win the game and the series.

Mincher retired from major-league baseball after the 1972 season and returned to Alabama.

Don was grateful for the education that baseball provided him. A southerner from a middle-lower-income family, Mincher gained from baseball the opportunity to travel and see America and other parts of the world.

"I learned a lot through baseball," Mincher said.

Baseball was too important for Don to stay away. "Baseball is my life," Mincher explained. "It's all I've ever done, everything I have, everything I own, everything I hope to own is baseball. I signed out of high school, played a career, got out, was in the sports retail business for a couple of years, and when minor-league baseball came to Huntsville in 1985, I became general manager, and I've been in minor-league baseball there ever since that time.

"So there's nothing else in my life that even comes close to baseball. It is my life."

Don and his wife, Pat, live in the Huntsville area. Don was the general manager and part-owner of the Huntsville Stars in the Southern League. He has recently become president of the Southern League. The Minchers have three grown children: Mark, Donna, and Lori.

Tony Oliva

Bats: Left
Throws: Right
Height: 6' 1"
Weight: 175 lbs.
Born: July 20, 1940, in Cuba

YEAR	TEAM	LG	AVG	G	AB	R	H	2B	3B	HR	RBI	BB	K	OBP	SLG
1962	Min	AL	.444	9	9	3	4	1	0	0	3	3	2	.583	.556
1963	Min	AL	.429	7	7	0	3	0	0	0	1	0	2	.429	.429
1964	Min	AL	.323	161	672	109	217	43	9	32	94	34	68	.359	.557
1965	Min	AL	.321	149	576	107	185	40	5	16	98	55	64	.378	.491
1966	Min	AL	.307	159	622	99	191	32	7	25	87	42	72	.353	.502
1967	Min	AL	.289	146	557	76	161	34	6	17	83	44	61	.347	.463
1968	Min	AL	.289	128	470	54	136	24	5	18	68	45	61	.357	.477
1969	Min	AL	.309	153	637	97	197	39	4	24	101	45	66	.355	.496
1970	Min	AL	.325	157	628	96	204	36	7	23	107	38	67	.364	.514
1971	Min	AL	.337	126	487	73	164	30	3	22	81	25	44	.369	.546
1972	Min	AL	.321	10	28	1	9	1	0	0	1	2	5	.367	.357
1973	Min	AL	.291	146	571	63	166	20	0	16	92	45	44	.345	.410
1974	Min	AL	.285	127	459	43	131	16	2	13	57	27	31	.325	.414
1975	Min	AL	.270	131	455	46	123	10	0	13	58	41	45	.344	.378
1976	Min	AL	.211	67	123	3	26	3	0	1	16	2	13	.234	.260
			AVG	G	AB	R	H	2B	3B	HR	RBI	BB	K	OBP	SLG
			.304	1,676	6,301	870	1,917	329	48	220	947	448	645	.353	.476

Sunday afternoons under a bright tropical sun meant baseball in rural Cuba. The country boys played only once a week, trying to emulate heroes like Pedro Ramos and Minnie Minoso. But once a week was enough for a certain twenty-year-old, left-handed outfielder to impress Roberto Fernandez, a former Washington Senators outfielder.

Fernandez recommended young Pedro Oliva to Senators' scout Joe Cambria, who signed him to a contract in 1960. Because of hostile political relations between Cuba and the United States, Pedro traveled to America by way of Mexico using his brother Tony's passport. From that time on, Pedro became Tony Oliva, changing the identity he'd carried since birth on July 20, 1940, in Pinar del Rio, Cuba.

The Senators became the Twins. Tony was sent to Wytheville, Virginia, in the Appalachian League. Fernandez' faith in Oliva was soon justified. Tony won the Silver Louisville Slugger as the top hitter in professional baseball after hitting .410 in 1961.

The Appalachian League fans were treated to watching a player who would become one of the most graceful, natural hitters of all time. Line drives ripped from his bat as his smooth stroke drove balls to all fields or deep into the gaps.

His outfield play left room for improvement, but his bat more than made up for any fielding deficiency. Tony spent most of 1962 and 1963 in the minor leagues; but in brief stints with the Twins, he hit over .400 in each season.

Tony Oliva earned a starting spot in Minnesota's outfield in 1964. He played right field on a powerful team.

Tony related, "They wanted somebody on base for [Harmon] Killebrew and [Bob] Allison. When I started to play, I hit home runs, too. I think the long ball was contagious on the Twins."

In his first big-league season, Oliva surprised everyone with his power. He cracked thirty-two home runs. But that was merely a small part of a tremendous rookie campaign that garnered him Rookie of the Year honors.

Tony batted .323 to lead the American League. He also led with 217 hits (an A.L. rookie record), forty-three doubles, and 109 runs. Tony led the majors with 374 total bases, eighty-four extra-base hits, and seventy-one multi-hit games.

The next year, 1965, marked a milestone in Minnesota baseball history. The Twins won their first pennant and played in their first World Series. It was also another big year for Tony. For the second time he led the league in hitting with a .321 average and 185 hits.

In Game 2 of the series, Tony ripped a big double off Dodger ace Sandy Koufax to help beat him 5-1.

The series and the 1965 team were certainly highlights in Tony's career. The team had excellent pitching and a power-laden lineup. Ironically, two of the team's stars had off-seasons due to injuries. Camilo Pascual won just nine games, and Harmon Killebrew hit only twenty-five home runs, which were still respectable seasons but definite drop-offs from their previous years.

But Tony led the league with a .321 average and was named the *Sporting News* Player of the Year. Shortstop Zoilo Versalles was named the American League's MVP. Jim "Mudcat" Grant won twenty-one games to pace the A.L., while Jim Kaat added eighteen victories.

The Twins dropped to 150 homeruns, down from 1964's tally of 221, but they were well distributed. Don Mincher jacked twenty-two and Versalles had nineteen. Oliva's outfield mates, Jimmie Hall and Bob Allison, smacked twenty and twenty-three, respectively. Tony played right, with Hall in center and Allison in left.

The hits kept coming throughout Tony's career. He won his third batting championship with a .337 mark in 1971. He was again named the *Sporting News* American League Player of the Year. In six of his twelve full seasons, Tony hit over .300, rapping out 1,917 safeties. He slugged 220 home runs and drove in 947 runs.

But when asked what honor he most valued, Tony didn't mention the three batting titles or being named to the All-Star Game his first six seasons. Instead, Oliva cited the Gold Glove he won for his fielding in 1966. By his own admission, he started as a poor outfielder and worked hard to improve. It paid off.

Baseball fans were cheated in 1971. In the midst of his .337 season, Tony dived for a bloop hit to right field off the bat of the Oakland A's Joe Rudi. His right knee slammed into the ground. Tony would never again be the same.

The next year, with the exception of ten games in June, Tony was unable to play. Fortuitously, the advent of the Designated Hitter (DH) rule in the American League allowed Tony to prolong his career, which otherwise would have ended.

Oliva became the first great DH. Although forced to limp around the bases, he hit .291 with sixteen homers and ninety-two RBIs. Tony slugged the first home run ever recorded by a DH on April 6, 1973, in Oakland.

For the next two seasons Tony put up respectable numbers as a DH, but he dropped off drastically in 1976, hitting just .211 in 123 at-bats. Tony's knee, operated on seven times, just wouldn't let him play anymore. He retired after that summer with a lifetime batting average of .304.

Tony had played in an era of great pitchers. He cited two as particularly tough: Sam McDowell and Nolan Ryan.

"Both threw very hard and were a little wild," Oliva remembered. "You didn't want to get hit by them."

It was a very impressive career, but many wondered what might have been had Tony not injured his knee. At the very least, it cost him sure entry into the Baseball Hall of Fame, an honor that still awaits Tony.

Those in baseball speak with admiration and respect about Oliva. He is the only player to win the league batting championship his first two years in the big leagues. Five times he led the American League in hits. His 220 home runs are third all-time for the Twins. On July 14, 1991, his jersey number 6 was retired by the team with which he spent his entire career.

Tony loves to talk about the game. Of all his hits, he highlighted one, a homer that he smashed 517 feet, lofting it completely out of the ballpark in Kansas City in 1967.

"Just to be able to play," Tony responded when asked the highlight of his Twins career. "Also, the 1965 pennant when I played and 1987 World Series champions when I was the hitting coach."

It almost didn't happen. Bernie Allen attended a rookie camp with Tony and got a first look at him in 1962. "Tony got in the batting cage and took ten swings," Bernie commented. "He didn't hit one ball out of the infield. Then the coach said, 'On the last swing, no matter where you hit the ball run to second. Tony took off and fell over when he tripped on first base.

"When he got into the outfield, Tony dropped the first two balls hit to him. The coach yelled, 'Who is this guy? Send him back to Cuba!'"

The Twins and baseball fans everywhere were lucky they didn't.

Baseball was the key to the future for Tony Oliva. "God, family, and baseball are the most important," he said. "Without baseball, I would have stayed in Cuba and been a farmer, maybe played amateur ball and coached. I wouldn't have met my wife or had my family. It opened doors to meet great people."

Since he retired as an active player in 1976, Tony has worked for the Twins as a base coach and hitting coach. He has worked at spring training, as a minor-league hitting instructor, and has scouted in the Dominican Republic, where the Twins also have a baseball school. Tony continues to make public relations appearances for the Twins as well.

With his wife, Gordette, Tony lives in the Twin Cities. He has three grown children. One son was given his father's original name, Pedro. He played a year for the Twins in their rookie league before, ironically, he hurt his knee.

Camilo Pascual

Bats: Right
Throws: Right
Height: 5' 11"
Weight: 170 lbs.
Born: January 20, 1934, in Cuba

YEAR	TEAM	LG	ERA	W	L	Sv	G	IP	H	R	ER	BB	K	AVG. A
1954	Was	AL	4.22	4	7	3	48	119.1	126	65	56	61	60	.276
1955	Was	AL	6.14	2	12	3	43	129.0	158	94	88	70	82	.311
1956	Was	AL	5.87	6	18	2	39	188.2	194	131	123	89	162	.261
1957	Was	AL	4.10	8	17	0	29	175.2	168	85	80	76	113	.258
1958	Was	AL	3.15	8	12	0	31	177.1	166	66	62	60	146	.248
1959	Was	AL	2.64	17	10	0	32	238.2	202	80	70	69	185	.226
1960	Was	AL	3.03	12	8	2	26	151.2	139	65	51	53	143	.240
1961	Min	AL	3.46	15	16	0	35	252.1	205	114	97	100	221	.217
1962	Min	AL	3.32	20	11	0	34	257.2	236	100	95	59	206	.241
1963	Min	AL	2.46	21	9	0	31	248.1	205	76	68	81	202	.224
1964	Min	AL	3.30	15	12	0	36	267.1	245	121	98	98	213	.241
1965	Min	AL	3.35	9	3	0	27	156.0	126	67	58	63	96	.217
1966	Min	AL	4.89	8	6	0	21	103.0	113	63	56	30	56	.278
1967	Was	AL	3.28	12	10	0	28	164.2	147	73	60	43	106	.237
1968	Was	AL	2.69	13	12	0	31	201.0	181	72	60	59	111	.239
1969	Was	AL	6.83	2	5	0	14	55.1	49	42	42	38	34	.239
1969	Cin	NL	8.59	0	0	0	5	7.1	14	7	7	4	3	.424
1970	LA	NL	2.57	0	0	0	10	14.0	12	4	4	5	8	.231
1971	Cle	AL	3.09	2	2	0	9	23.1	17	9	8	11	20	.205
			ERA	W	L	Sv	G	IP	H	R	ER	BB	K	AVG. A
			3.63	174	170	10	529	2,930.2	2,703	1,334	1,183	1,069	2,167	.244

Scout Joe Cambria was impressed as he watched a youth from Havana play baseball in the Cuban amateur league. He threw the ball hard when he pitched, had a decent curve and hit well, too.

The boy's brother Carlos was nicknamed "Potato," meaning "small." Cambria dubbed young Camilo Pascual "Little Potato" and signed him to a contract with the Washington Senators in 1950 when he was only seventeen years old.

Camilo never dreamed he'd be a pro baseball player, let alone a pitcher. "I always played other positions," he said. "I liked to hit, and I played shortstop and third base. When I was about twelve to fourteen years old, I started working on my curveball, but I don't know how I became a pitcher. I mostly played other positions."

The young man divided his time in 1951 between Senator farm clubs in Big Springs, Texas; Chickasha, Oklahoma; and Geneva, New York. He totaled 8-3 with the three clubs. In 1952 and 1953, Pascual returned home to play for Havana in the Florida International League.

Camilo made his first major-league appearance with the Senators on April 15, 1954. The young man from Havana was now facing men he had idolized, players including Ted Williams, Joe DiMaggio, and Bob Feller.

Pascual pitched in several memorable opening days for the Senators. In 1956, which featured an opening-day matchup between the Senators and Yankees, each team hit three home runs. Mickey Mantle rapped two homers: a couple of tape-measure shots off Camilo. In 1960, with President Dwight Eisenhower in attendance, he struck out fifteen batters.

Despite playing for a bad team, Pascual became one of the dominant pitchers in the American League in the 1950s. His fastball clocked in the mid- to low-nineties. His control was excellent, and the curveball he started working on as a boy developed into one of the wickedest breaks baseball has ever seen.

He moved with the Senators to Minnesota in 1961 and became a Twin. Camilo was 15-16 in the Twins' first season in Minnesota. He pitched back-to-back shutouts three times that year. He led the league with 221 strikeouts, the first of three consecutive strikeout-leading seasons.

Camilo's ERA was a respectable 3.46, but he lost six one-run games. Through the mid-1960s, he was the ace of the Twins pitching staff. In addition to his strikeout leadership, Pascual topped the league in complete games in 1962 and 1963, and in shutouts in 1961 and 1962. Despite recurring arm injuries, he pitched 200-plus innings his first four years in Minnesota.

Camilo also led the Twins in victories from 1961 to 1964, including twenty-victory seasons in 1962 and 1963. His twenty-win seasons were even more remarkable considering that he missed three or four weeks each year with injuries to his arm.

The key to Pascual's success was his curveball, which he could throw with a hard, fast break or a slow, big drop. It was the best curveball of his time.

Earl Battey, his catcher, said that Camilo was easy to catch. "His pitches didn't do much damage to a catcher's hands. Some throw a heavy sinking ball that tears up your hands. Camilo didn't throw that kind of ball. I could have caught him with a pair of pliers."

Pascual used his bat as well as his arm. He led American League pitchers with a .302 average in 1959. He repeated the feat with a .267 mark in 1962. That year he led pitchers of both leagues with twenty-six hits, thirty-six total bases and nineteen RBIs.

Pascual was named to the American League All-Star Team from 1959 to 1962 and again in 1964. In a 1961 All-Star Game, he pitched three hitless innings and fanned four.

After going 21-9 in 1962, Camilo hoped to be amply rewarded by his team owner, Calvin Griffith. He was dismayed when Calvin, a master negotiator, sent him a contract considerably lower than Camilo expected.

Pascual recalled, "I was really upset. I ripped the contract into three pieces and sent it to Calvin. He taped it together and sent it back to me. I held out into spring training that year, but we finally agreed on a contract."

The Twins' first magical season, 1965, as they won their first American League pennant. Unfortunately, it was not a banner year for Pascual. His arm miseries—brought on, Camilo believed, by years of pitching winter ball—led to an operation in July. He had gone 9-3, mainly spot starting when he was healthy.

It looked like he might be out for the season, but Camilo was determined to pitch in the World Series. He sped up his rehabilitation program and managed to get in three or four games at the end of the season. By his own admission, Camilo wasn't at his best as he lost Game 3 to the Los Angeles Dodgers by a score of 4-0.

Another sub-par year for "Little Potato" was 1968. He was 8-6. Camilo was traded after that season to the new Washington Senators, where he won twenty-five games over the next two years.

The next three seasons were divided between Cincinnati, Los Angeles, and Cleveland. But his arm was worn out, and Camilo appeared in only twenty-four games over those years and won just twice.

Pascual retired from playing after the 1971 season. He found new roles in baseball, first as a pitching coach with the Twins from 1977 until 1980, and then as a scout for twenty-three years. The last twelve he has scouted for the Los Angeles Dodgers.

As he reflected upon his career, Camilo was satisfied with his eighteen years in the major leagues.

"Baseball was my life," he said. "I never dreamed I would be playing at the premier level of baseball for so long. Baseball players are great today, but I believe that it doesn't matter what era you're in. If you were a good pitcher, you could pitch now and then."

What gave Camilo the most satisfaction?

"My twenty-win seasons," he replied. "I managed to do it even when I was hurt part of each year."

In addition to scouting for the Dodgers, Camilo runs a baseball academy in Venezuela. He lives in Miami, Florida.

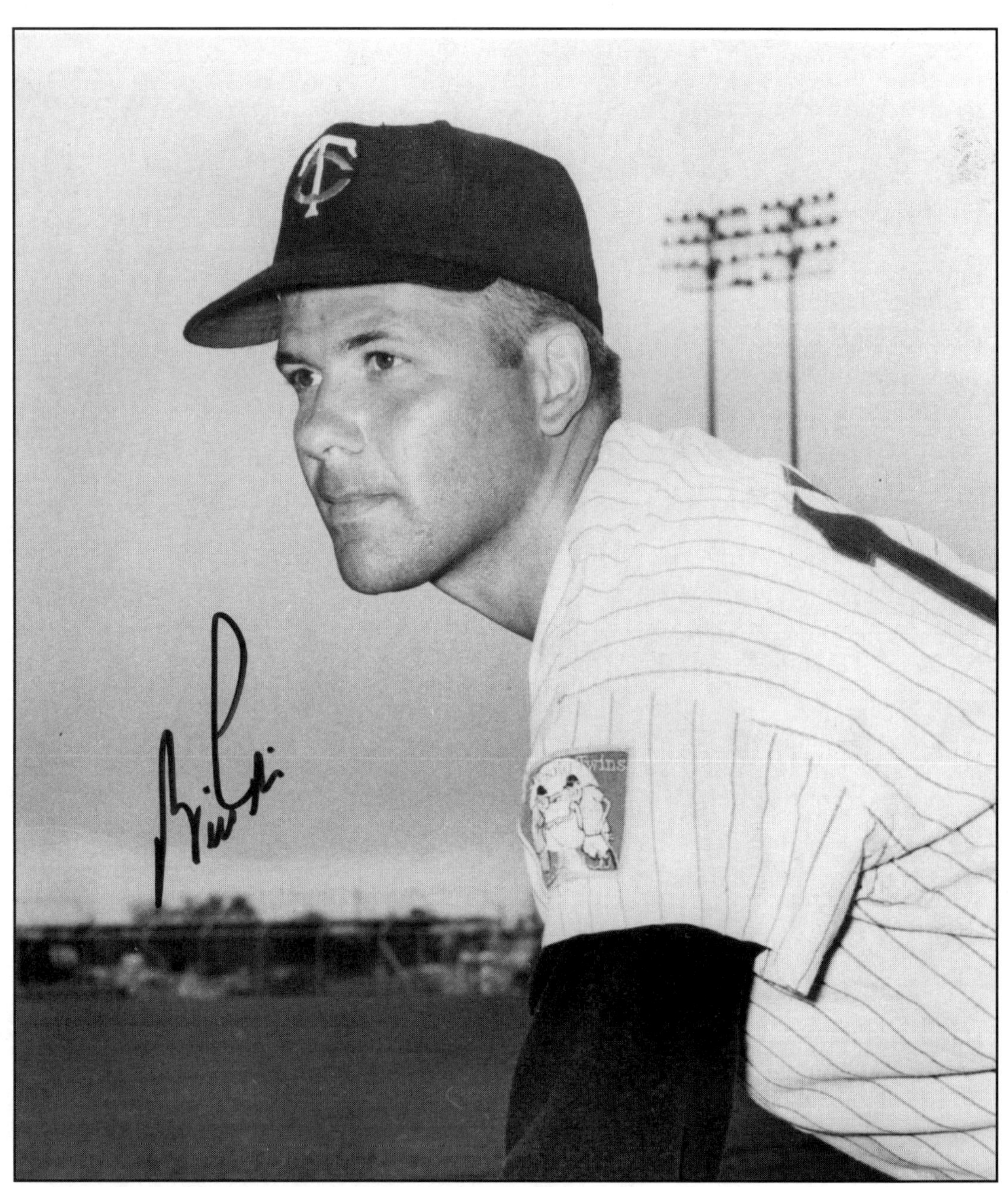

Bill Pleis

Bats: Left
Throws: Left
Height: 5' 10"
Weight: 170 lbs.
Born: August 5, 1937, in Missouri

YEAR	TEAM	LG	ERA	W	L	Sv	G	IP	H	R	ER	BB	K	AVG. A
1961	*Min*	*AL*	*4.95*	*4*	*2*	*2*	*37*	*56.1*	*59*	*35*	*31*	*34*	*32*	*.266*
1962	*Min*	*AL*	*4.40*	*2*	*5*	*3*	*21*	*45.0*	*46*	*27*	*22*	*14*	*31*	*.264*
1963	*Min*	*AL*	*4.37*	*6*	*2*	*0*	*36*	*68.0*	*67*	*37*	*33*	*16*	*37*	*.258*
1964	*Min*	*AL*	*3.91*	*4*	*1*	*4*	*47*	*50.2*	*43*	*23*	*22*	*31*	*42*	*.232*
1965	*Min*	*AL*	*2.98*	*4*	*4*	*4*	*41*	*51.1*	*49*	*20*	*17*	*27*	*33*	*.250*
1966	*Min*	*AL*	*1.93*	*1*	*2*	*0*	*8*	*9.1*	*5*	*6*	*2*	*4*	*9*	*.152*
			ERA	*W*	*L*	*Sv*	*G*	*IP*	*H*	*R*	*ER*	*BB*	*K*	*AVG. A*
			4.07	*21*	*16*	*13*	*190*	*280.2*	*269*	*148*	*127*	*126*	*184*	*.251*

Bill Pleis was a relief pitcher for the Twins from 1961 to 1966. A left-handed "stuff" pitcher with good control, he was a tough challenge for left-handed hitters.

"Shorty," or "Bulldog," as he was also called, was born August 5, 1937, in St. Louis, Missouri.

He grew up admiring the power and grace of Cardinal outfielder Stan Musial. Pleis attended Kirkwood High School and led his team to two state baseball championships.

Signed from a tryout camp by a scout, Bill eventually became the property of the Boston Red Sox. From 1956 to 1959, he pitched in the minors for Orlando, Louisville, Lafayette (Louisiana), Magic Valley (Idaho), Allentown (Pennsylvania), and Memphis. After the 1959 season, he entered the United States Army.

He was discharged six months later only to discover that the Red Sox no longer had a place for him in their organization. Upon the recommendation of Washington Senators assistant farm director George Brophy, scout Bill Messman signed the young lefty in 1960. Bill was assigned to Charlotte, North Carolina, where he went 10-4 with a 2.73 ERA.

After a short stint in Syracuse in 1961, Pleis joined the Twins, the new name given the Senators after their move to Minnesota. Ironically, his first big-league game was in Boston, the home of the team that had let him go.

Pleis went three innings to earn a save for his roommate, Jim Kaat. He retired the dangerous Sox outfielder Jackie Jensen in nailing down the win.

Shorty had been a starter his entire career. But left-handed relief pitchers were a valued commodity, and that became his role in the major leagues.

In 1961, Bill Pleis was the Twins' best reliever from the middle of August until the end of the season. In his final eleven games, spanning twenty innings, no one scored against him.

He split 1962 between Vancouver and the Twins, going 2-5 for the big club. Shorty even started a game against the mighty New York Yankees that season. His left-handed slants were effective against the Bronx Bombers. In three appearances in 1962, he gave up only one earned run while striking out ten in nine innings.

Part of his success against the Yankees was owed to the fact that Shorty had good luck pitching to the great Mickey Mantle.

"Watching Mantle hit, I knew that he sat on the fastball whenever he got ahead in the count," Pleis explained. "If you threw a fastball then, he ripped it. I intentionally got behind in the count and threw him off-speed pitches. It worked pretty well for me against him.

"Mantle was great. People loved him. No one today compares with the feeling people had about Mantle."

Pleis said that another baseball legend posed a greater challenge to him. "The hitter I couldn't get out much was the Tigers' Al Kaline. He hit line drives everywhere. Even his outs were line drives."

Pleis recalled that Calvin Griffith, Twins owner and president, once made a deal with him that if he were still on the team on June 15, Griffith would give him a $5,000 bonus.

Pleis pitched well, and June 15 came and went, but no bonus check appeared. He waited into July and then dropped by Griffith's office before a game. As they exchanged pleasantries, Calvin complimented Pleis on his season. Shorty took that opportunity to remind Griffith of his $5,000 promise.

Looking perplexed, Calvin asked, "Do you really think you've pitched well enough to deserve that?"

Shorty lost his cool, made a couple of heated remarks to his boss and slammed the office door behind him as he left. When he arrived home, he suggested to his wife, Sue, that they start packing.

Bill expected to receive reassignment to the minor leagues when he got to the ballpark the next day. Instead he found a $5,000 check awaiting him.

The Twins in the early 1960s were a power-laden team just reaching its potential. But Bill Pleis remembers them as a fine group of people as well. Just playing with that ball club was the highlight of his playing career.

They didn't just play baseball. Golf and other forms of entertainment added to the comaraderie. Greg Matthews, a Litchfield (Minnesota) high school teacher, recalled a golf outing in which he caddied for Pleis and Billy Martin, who was a Twins' scout at the time. Two Twins' front office employees rounded out the foursome.

"The Twins office guys played quite a bit with Billy, and they teased him mercilessly," Matthews related. "If he missed a putt or something, they'd really tear into him. Billy was the fiercest competitor I ever saw when I caddied. He really wanted to win, and he really wanted to beat these two guys because of how they got on him.

"We were at Southview Golf Course," Matthews continued. "Billy needed a good shot on a hole. We were in a position where no one could see us. Martin had seen me hitting a golf ball with other caddies and said, 'Hit this shot for me.'

"I replied, 'Aren't you playing for money?' He said, 'Sure, that's why I want you to hit the shot.'"

"'But I'm left-handed,' I told him.

"'That's okay. So's Shorty,' Billy replied as he pulled out a club from Pleis' bag. Caddies carried two bags. I had both Shorty's and Martin's.

"Since caddies didn't really care much for those particular Twins front office guys, I hit the ball. It landed on the green.

"I liked caddying for both Pleis and Martin," Matthews continued. "They treated us well. Billy even played with the caddies on Caddy Day once."

Shorty went 4-4 with a 2.98 ERA for the American League pennant-winning Twins in 1965. He pitched against the Dodgers in the World Series even though he had injured his arm previously.

Late in the year, after pitching several games in a row, he felt something was wrong with his arm in a contest against the White Sox in Comiskey Park.

When the team returned home, Shorty pitched again on a cold night. His arm hurt more. Pleis had torn the rotator cuff on his left arm. He didn't know it then, but his career was about over.

Surgery to repair injuries such as Shorty suffered was not nearly as successful in the sixties as it is today. After appearing in only eight games in 1966, the pitcher was released.

To make matters worse, Shorty was about a month short of the five years' minimum requirement for a major-league pension. When word of this reached

Calvin Griffith, he sent out word to find Bill and bring him back to the Twins for the final month of the 1967 season. Unfortunately, finding Shorty wasn't easy.

"I owe a lot to my former roommate, Jim Kaat," Pleis explained. "Not only was he a great roommate, he tracked me down when I needed that time on my pension.

"Calvin could not find me, but Jim did. We were on vacation at the Lake of the Ozarks. I still don't know how he found us."

Pleis' entire career was spent with Minnesota. He won twenty-one games, lost sixteen, had a 4.07 ERA and recorded thirteen saves.

For the last twenty-three years, Bill Pleis has stayed in baseball as a scout for the Los Angeles Dodgers. He likes to golf, but he still misses the competition of pro baseball. It's something he says he'll never forget.

In comparing today's players with those of his era, Pleis says that although there are more good players today, the elite of yesteryear compares well with the elite of today.

The money is, of course, much different today. Current athletes are paid in the millions. Pleis and his contemporaries had to have winter jobs to supplement their baseball incomes.

Bill lives with Sue, his wife of forty-one years, in Parrish, Florida. They have three children: a daughter, Stacey, and two sons, Scott and Steven.

Stacey operates a gymnastics school.

Scott, who was drafted by the Toronto Blue Jays as an infielder, hit over .300 in rookie league but hurt his arm, ending his baseball career. He turned to golf and was doing well, playing some Nike tournaments, when he hurt his back in an automobile accident. He got back into baseball as a scout and is based in Florida, scouting for the New York Yankees.

Steven is currently trying to make his mark as a professional golfer. He has been playing in golf tournaments including Nike events, as he tries to qualify for the PGA tour.

FORT LAUDERDALE STADIUM

Pedro Ramos

Bats: Both
Throws: Right
Height: 6′ 0″
Weight: 175 lbs.
Born: April 28, 1935, in Cuba

YEAR	TEAM	LG	ERA	W	L	Sv	G	IP	H	R	ER	BB	K	AVG. A
1955	Was	AL	3.88	5	11	5	45	130.0	121	62	56	39	34	.253
1956	Was	AL	5.27	12	10	0	37	152.0	178	95	89	76	54	.299
1957	Was	AL	4.79	12	16	0	43	231.0	251	131	123	69	91	.271
1958	Was	AL	4.23	14	18	3	43	259.1	277	133	122	77	132	.273
1959	Was	AL	4.16	13	19	0	37	233.2	233	127	108	52	95	.257
1960	Was	AL	3.45	11	18	2	43	274.0	254	126	105	99	160	.245
1961	Min	AL	3.95	11	20	2	42	264.1	265	134	116	79	174	.258
1962	Cle	AL	3.71	10	12	1	37	201.1	189	104	83	85	96	.246
1963	Cle	AL	3.12	9	8	0	36	184.2	156	74	64	41	169	.226
1964	Cle	AL	5.14	7	10	0	36	133.0	144	84	76	26	98	.273
1964	NYA	AL	1.25	1	0	8	13	21.2	13	3	3	0	21	.183
1965	NYA	AL	2.92	5	5	19	65	92.1	80	34	30	27	68	.237
1966	NYA	AL	3.61	3	9	13	52	89.2	98	43	36	18	58	.283
1967	Phi	NL	9.00	0	0	0	6	8.0	14	8	8	8	1	.412
1969	Pit	NL	6.00	0	1	0	5	6.0	8	4	4	0	4	.320
1969	Cin	NL	5.16	4	3	2	38	66.1	73	41	38	24	40	.284
1970	Was	AL	7.56	0	0	0	4	8.1	10	7	7	4	10	.294
			ERA	W	L	Sv	G	IP	H	R	ER	BB	K	AVG. A
			4.08	117	160	55	582	2,355.2	2,364	1,210	1,068	724	1,305	.261

A black Pontiac convertible pulled up to the Twins' Orlando, Florida, training camp in 1961. A man dressed in black Western clothing climbed out of the car. One pearl-handled pistol was holstered on each hip. "Pistol Pete" Ramos, who would become Minnesota's first opening-day pitcher, had arrived.

Pedro Ramos was yet another baseball talent discovered by Washington Senator scout Joe Cambria. Pedro (Pete) came from the rural area near Pinar del Rio, Cuba.

His family worked in the tobacco fields, and by the age of six, young Pete was helping out. He was expected to work from 6:00 A.M. to 11:00 A.M. and then attend school in the afternoon. On more than one occasion, the lad managed to elude his father or a teacher to pursue his real love, baseball.

Pete Ramos loved the game from early childhood and began playing when he was six. A gifted athlete, he was lightning fast afoot, hit for power and played excellent defense. Young Ramos played shortstop, outfield, first base, and even caught long before he began playing at the position where he would be featured in the major leagues. He finally started pitching when he was fifteen. He blossomed quickly.

Pete grew up hoping that someday he could play in Havana, 150 miles away, where they had a pro league. But he also yearned for the American major leagues as he sat before an old four-foot-high radio and listened to broadcasts of the World Series. Names like Berra, McDougald, DiMaggio, and Garagiola excited the youth and heightened his dreams for the future.

The first step of Ramos' dream was realized in 1953, when Cambria signed the seventeen-year-old country youth to a contract with the Washington Senators as a pitcher.

Pete toiled in the minors in Morristown (Tennessee), Hagerstown (Maryland), and Kingsport (Tennessee) before making the Senators out of spring training in 1955. He was 5-11 his first year, as he began a career of pitching good baseball for bad clubs. He had a blazing fastball in the mid-nineties, but wasn't an overpowering strikeout pitcher early in his career.

As Pete developed a more effective curveball in the late 1950s, his strikeout total mounted. But the Washington teams, with whom he played, while blessed with some good hitters—Jim Lemon, Roy Sievers, and later Harmon Killebrew—were woeful defensively.

"My infielders didn't have much range, and if I got a win for every ball my outfielders dropped, I'd have been one of the best pitchers in the league," Pete said.

It was tough to get wins for the Senators, but Ramos managed a 14-18 year in 1958. Following the season he talked contract with owner Calvin Griffith and asked for a $1,000 raise.

"Well, Pete, I'm gonna give you $500," Griffith responded. "If you like it, you sign. If you don't, go back to Cuba and cut sugar cane."

"With my fielders, I'm lucky I didn't lose my head," Ramos answered Griffith. But he signed for the $500 raise.

Pete's pitching philosophy was simple. "If you throw strikes, you can win. If you throw ball one, ball two and walk 'em, those hitters are gonna kill you, so you better get ahead and throw strikes.

"If you throw strikes and are around the plate, you gonna get hit a little more than some other pitchers, but you're gonna be in less trouble than by walking guys. A walk is as good as a base hit, so you gotta own it.

"I'd rather give up a base hit than a base on balls. I wasn't afraid to challenge. Sometimes I win, sometimes I lose. One time I told Mickey Mantle I would only throw him fastballs, my best against him. The first two times up I struck him out, the third time he hit one 600 feet."

Home runs were not a rare occurrence when Ramos pitched. He set a since-broken American League mark of surrendering forty-three home runs in a season. It came from challenging hitters and not backing down.

When asked what his best pitch was, Pete laughingly said, "The home run."

Ramos had other memorable encounters against some of baseball's best during his career. In a phone interview for this book, Ramos told of the day in Boston when his catcher, Clint Courtney, came to the mound and gestured to the waiting batter. Ramos recalled the conversation:

"Hit 'em, Pete."

"I don't want to hit him," Ramos objected.

"Look, you yellow Cuban, I said hit 'em!" Courtney rejoined.

"But he's Ted Williams!" the pitcher pleaded to no avail.

Pete plunked Boston's "Splendid Splinter" on the back of the leg. The next time up, Williams lofted the ball over the scoreboard.

"I never hit him again," Pete said.

Ramos had his most success against the Red Sox, winning twenty-two times. In one memorable series he won three out of four games, one starting and two in relief.

In another game Ramos faced Jimmy Piersall, an outfielder subject to sometimes-bizarre behavior. Ramos recalled that Piersall began to sing, "I got the whole world in my hand," as he batted.

After strike three, catcher Courtney held the ball out to Jimmy and said, "I got your whole world right here."

Ramos was named to the American League All-Star Team in 1959, in the midst of a 13-19 season. He didn't get to play but was warming up in the bullpen as pitcher Cal McLeish struggled to finish the game.

"It was the only time I ever hoped a teammate would get bombed," Pete remembered. "I wanted to play."

The Senators played an exhibition game in Cuba in 1960. That nation's new leader, Fidel Castro, was scheduled to throw out the first ball for the 9:00 A.M. game. He didn't show up until ten o'clock and then kept throwing warm-up pitches from the mound.

"I asked him if he wasn't just supposed to throw out the first pitch," Ramos said in a phone interview. "Castro replied he wouldn't stop until he was throwing strikes.

"I heard that he was supposed to be a major-league prospect once," Pete continued. "If he was a prospect, I was President of the United States."

Cuba has a rich baseball tradition and has turned out many great players. "Baseball is number one in Cuba," Ramos explained. "They play all year 'round. With the flood plains, there are good flat places to play, and the weather is good."

Pete Ramos moved with the Senators to Minnesota in 1961. On April 11, he was the opening-day pitcher in the Twins' inaugural home game. Ramos beat the Yankees and Whitey Ford by a 6-0 score. He pitched a three-hitter and drove in two runs himself.

Later that night he got a phone call from the Castro-controlled newspaper in Cuba. The Cuban leader had put his Communist government into action. Word was out that Ramos had spoken out against Castro during spring training.

Pete had told a West Palm Beach newspaper, "The least a man can do is give up his life for his country." The newspaper suggested that Ramos might join the rebels against Castro and "throw grenades instead of baseballs."

The caller from Cuba asked, "Is it true you would go to fight against your brothers in Cuba?"

"You can't always believe what you read," the pragmatic pitcher responded. His family was still in Cuba. Pete couldn't risk any retaliation against them.

The 1961 Twins went 71-91. They showed promise and had some good hitting, but their fielding was still erratic. Pete went 11-20 with a respectable 3.95 ERA. It was Ramos' only year in Minnesota, for he was traded to Cleveland the next spring for Vic Power and Dick Stigman.

While pitching with the Indians, Ramos continued his quest to prove that he was the fastest player in baseball. He routinely challenged known speedsters to race. He had beaten Richie Ashburn, Don Houk, Zoilo Versalles, and Willie Davis and, in Pete's words, "I beat everybody that I raced."

But one player eluded him, Yankee great Mickey Mantle. When challenged, Mickey offered to race for a $1,000 bet. Ramos wasn't in the big money and didn't want to risk the cash. When he got to Cleveland, he told General Manager Gabe Paul about it.

Paul said he'd put up $2,000, "$1,000 for each leg."

"So I went to Mickey," Pete explained. "I said, 'I have $2,000 to race.'

"'No, Pedro, I don't wanna race you,' Mantle said.

"When I went to the Yankees," Ramos continued, "I asked Mickey, 'Why didn't you race me?'

"'Well, I don't need $2,000,' Mantle answered. 'You could have beat me, or I could have hurt myself. And if you would have beat me, it would have hurt my reputation.'

"If I would have beat him, it would have been nose to nose," Ramos concluded.

After a few years in Cleveland, once again playing for a bad team, Pete finally got a break when he was traded to the Yankees on September 5, 1964. Even that good fortune turned sour because the World Series roster was set September 1. Pete helped the Yankees get there. He was 1-0 with a 1.25 ERA and eight saves down the stretch. But he was ineligible for the series.

Skipper Ralph Houk turned Pete into a relief pitcher, a closer who earned nineteen saves in 1965 and thirteen in 1966. But much to Ramos' disappointment, the mighty Yanks fell on hard times, finishing last in 1966.

"Every team I went to started dying when I got there," Pete lamented. "Only the Twins got better."

Pete missed the opportunity to run and hit when he pitched relief. With the Twins and Senators, he pinch ran about ten times a year. He also smacked fifteen home runs, including a grand slam off Baltimore's Chuck Estrada.

"I would have been a good center fielder. I could hit and run and throw. But Washington needed pitching. I think I could have hit a couple of hundred home runs if I played in the field."

Pete wound down his career from 1965 to 1970 with a variety of teams, playing for Philadelphia, Pittsburgh, Cincinnati, and finally back to the new expansion Senators.

"Being in the big leagues was great," Ramos said. "I didn't care where I played. But I wish I could have played for a team like the Yankees earlier in my career. It would have meant five or six more wins a season to me. Instead of twelve wins a year, I could have had eighteen."

Baseball was in Pete's blood forever. After leaving the major leagues, he played in the Mexican League from 1970 to 1975. He made a return to American ball in 1972 by playing for the Tidewater Mets.

Even today, at the age of sixty-five, he plays in a men's league in Miami. In the fall of 2000, he pitched three innings, with a fastball in the mid-sixties. Pete gave up one run and got a hit in his only at-bat.

"Baseball has been my whole life," Ramos commented. "I started playing when I was six, and I'm still playing."

He started a cigar company in the mid-1970s. From a factory in Nicaragua he produces Don Pedro Ramos Cigars. Ramos has two children; one works with metro police, and the other is a paramedic. He lives in Miami, Florida.

Baseball has been good to the Cuban tobacco farm boy. It changed his life. Without it, he probably would have stayed in Cuba and fought Castro and maybe, as Pete pondered, "would have been executed for fighting for freedom."

Rich Rollins

Bats: Right
Throws: Right
Height: 5' 10"
Weight: 185 lbs.
Born: April 16, 1938, in Pennsylvania

YEAR	TEAM	LG	AVG	G	AB	R	H	2B	3B	HR	RBI	BB	K	OBP	SLG
1961	Min	AL	.294	13	17	3	5	1	0	0	3	2	2	.400	.353
1962	Min	AL	.298	159	624	96	186	23	5	16	96	75	61	.374	.428
1963	Min	AL	.307	136	531	75	163	23	1	16	61	36	59	.359	.444
1964	Min	AL	.270	148	596	87	161	25	10	12	68	53	80	.334	.406
1965	Min	AL	.249	140	469	59	117	22	1	5	32	37	54	.309	.333
1966	Min	AL	.245	90	269	30	66	7	1	10	40	13	34	.286	.390
1967	Min	AL	.245	109	339	31	83	11	2	6	39	27	58	.305	.342
1968	Min	AL	.241	93	203	14	49	5	0	6	30	10	34	.287	.355
1969	Sea	AL	.225	58	187	15	42	7	0	4	21	7	19	.270	.326
1970	Mil	AL	.200	14	25	3	5	1	0	0	5	3	4	.276	.240
1970	Cle	AL	.233	42	43	6	10	0	0	2	4	3	5	.283	.372
			AVG .269	G 1,002	AB 3,303	R 419	H 887	2B 125	3B 20	HR 77	RBI 399	BB 266	K 410	OBP .328	SLG .388

A few years ago Rich Rollins received a phone call from a sportswriter from Fargo, North Dakota. "Do you remember signing a baseball for an elderly man in Fargo when you did the Twins speaking tour?" he was asked.

Rollins recalled the incident well. "I remember because the man had an antiquated box," Rich told the writer. "I asked, 'Whose signature is that?' He said, 'Babe Ruth.' Then he asked me to sign it. I told him it would devalue the ball, but he really wanted me to sign it. I'd had a good year, so I autographed the ball."

"Roger Maris signed the ball next," the writer informed Rollins. "It was quite a ball, three autographs, Babe Ruth, Roger Maris, and Rich Rollins. They just put it up for auction for charity."

"Didn't my signature devalue it?" Rich wondered.

"No," the writer chuckled, "they had yours professionally erased."

Was Rich insulted? No, Rollins understood the game of baseball and his place in it. He played ten years of major-league baseball, at times brilliantly, but always with respect for the game.

Rich was born in western Pennsylvania and raised near Cleveland, Ohio. He was a big fan of the Cleveland Indians, especially the 1948 pennant winners.

Rollins attended Parma Senior High School and then went to college at Kent State. After earning his degree in 1960, Rich had already lined up a teaching job when a baseball scout, Floyd Baker, invited him to a Senators tryout camp in Washington, D.C. Baker had been following the young redhead since high school.

There was no draft in those days, and about fifty hopefuls showed up for the camp at Griffith Stadium. Rich played well and was offered a contract by Joe Haynes.

But Rollins didn't grab a pen right away. He had done some consulting with his father and had prepared for this possibility ahead of time. He had a degree and a teaching job, he was twenty-two, and he was not desperate to play pro ball.

"I want to start in Class B in Wilson, North Carolina, and $15,000," Rollins told Haynes.

Haynes replied that he had to go to Fort Walton Beach for rookie ball. Rollins said he'd just go home to Parma, then. When he got home, his mother said Haynes had phoned and left a message for Rich to call.

Rich had returned home at 3:00 P.M. By 5:30 P.M. he was on his way to Wilson. Haynes had reconsidered.

It was discouraging at first. "It was the beginning of an education," Rich recalled. "After two weeks I hardly played at all. Then my manager, Jack McKeon, played me at second base. I had a good night and played regularly after that.

"Then early one morning, after an all-night bus trip, when we got back to Wilson another player said, 'Rich, McKeon wants to see ya.'"

The manager told Rollins, "They want me to send you to Fort Walton Beach, but I'm not gonna let you go."

His skipper's faith and insight was a big break in Rollins' career. He wound up hitting third in the Carolina League that year and was in good position to move up the next year.

A six-month tour of military duty interrupted Rich's start to the 1961 season. After his release from his commitment to Uncle Sam, the Twins designated Rich for their Class AAA team in Syracuse, New York.

Rich never really got to play for them. The team traveled to play in San Juan, Puerto Rico, about two weeks into the season. Rollins was sent in to pinch run at second. He got picked off and did not play for them again.

He was sent to Charlotte, North Carolina, to play third base in May of 1961. After only a month, Rollins got the call from the Twins. He met the team in Chicago and spent the next seven years with a "TC" on his hat.

Cookie Lavagetto was the Twins' manager when Rich reported. He had a team of veterans; Rollins sat. Late in June, when Sam Mele replaced Cookie at the Twins' helm, Rich's status didn't change. He watched.

"I had the jitters," Rich admitted. "I gained experience just by being there. The pressure was tough, and there's a big mental adjustment. I was lucky to make it."

Rollins got into only thirteen games his first season and batted just seventeen times. One of his five hits was a bases-loaded triple off the Angels' Ryne Duren.

The 1962 season was the type of year young kids dream of having. Rollins was ticketed for assignment to minor-league Vancouver. But he played so well in spring training that the starting hot-corner job was his on Opening Day.

Rich hit safely the first twelve games of the season and battled for the league batting title over half the year. In the early 1960s two All-Star games were played each summer. Rollins was named the starting third baseman in both. He received more votes than any other American League player did in a year when the team was selected by a vote of the players.

Rich commented, "The All-Star games were my fondest memories. I don't know how it happened, it just did.

"I went to Washington, D.C., on cloud nine. Stan Musial was the oldest player. I was the youngest. We were both on the *Today Show*. Ted Williams was in town as a representative for Sears. I spent the evening with him.

"After the third inning, I got taken out, along with Mickey Mantle. In the locker room Mantle said, 'I'm going to the airport, wanna come with me?' It was me and Mick in a cab. Later he got criticized for leaving the game early. They didn't notice me."

At first, playing in the big leagues was a star-struck experience for Rollins. In his Cleveland suburb, Rich had attended a church also frequented by Roger Maris and Rocky Colavito, then with the Indians.

Now Rocky was sliding into third and asking Rollins, "How's the family doin'?" Rich soon proved he belonged. He won Sophomore of the Year honors for his great second season. He had hit .298 with sixteen homers and ninety-six RBIs.

Rollins followed that up with .307 the next year. The following seven years saw his batting average drop a little each season.

Certain home runs or hits don't weigh heavily in Rollins' mind when he recalls his career. The biggest highlight was a whole season, 1965.

"We lost twenty-two games in spring training," Rich said. "It was great to see it all come together. We were positive we could win each game. The chemistry of that team became a life lesson to me. I don't remember the hits. I remember the ultimate team game.

"The World Series was unbelievable. I was on first base in Game 7 when Junior Gilliam dived and made the great play at third that ended our best chance to win."

Rollins hurt his right knee during the 1968 campaign and only got 203 at-bats. After the season ended, he was scheduled for an operation. One Saturday morning he was in a Richfield car wash when he heard over the radio that the expansion Seattle Pilots had selected him.

"I learned a big lesson. When I asked the Twins about my operation, scheduled for Monday morning, they told me, 'You're a Pilot now. It's up to them.'" Rich got his operation two months later, courtesy of Seattle.

The next three seasons, Rollins played for the Pilots, Milwaukee, and Cleveland. He was now mainly a utility role player and never again approached his heady early years as a Twin.

"I had hurt my right knee and couldn't push off. I'd make solid contact and the ball would get caught on the warning track," Rollins said.

After his retirement as a player from professional baseball, Rollins went to work for the Cleveland Indians, first as a scout and later in the front office.

When he reflected on his playing days, Rich commented, "Baseball is an endurance contest. Who can master the fundamentals? Games are lost, not won, by mental errors. My whole personality was in front of the public for ten years. I looked at baseball as a job. But it was my whole life, from when I was a kid.

"I miss the camaraderie of the people I was with. The game was natural. I made lifelong friends and influence. I still miss the players."

The best hitter Rich saw? Tony Oliva. "He should be in the Hall of Fame. Ask any pitcher in the sixties who the toughest hitter was. They'll tell you it was Tony."

He noted that the life of a baseball player can be hard as well. "Many of the players and their wives are divorced."

With his wife of thirty-eight years, Lynn, Rich lives in suburban Cleveland. He has been retired from the Indians since 1993. Now he does baseball clinics and goes to fantasy camps.

Lynn and Rich have three grown sons and three daughters. Now, instead of the thrill of packed stadiums, they enjoy their grandchildren.

Frank Quilici

Bats: Right
Throws: Right
Height: 6' 1"
Weight: 170 lbs.
Born: May 11, 1939, in Illinois

YEAR	TEAM	LG	AVG	G	AB	R	H	2B	3B	HR	RBI	BB	K	OBP	SLG
1965	Min	AL	.208	56	149	16	31	5	1	0	7	15	33	.280	.255
1967	Min	AL	.105	23	19	2	2	1	0	0	0	3	4	.227	.158
1968	Min	AL	.245	97	229	22	56	11	4	1	22	21	45	.305	.341
1969	Min	AL	.174	118	144	19	25	3	1	2	12	12	22	.236	.250
1970	Min	AL	.227	111	141	19	32	3	0	2	12	15	16	.297	.291
			AVG	G	AB	R	H	2B	3B	HR	RBI	BB	.K	OBP	SLG
			.214	405	682	78	146	23	6	5	53	66	120	.281	.287

Frank Quilici played for three championship teams for the Twins: the 1965 American League pennant winners, and the 1969 and 1970 Western Division champs.

He grew up in Chicago, eventually honing his baseball skills in the park leagues. But he didn't start playing baseball until he was thirteen. Prior to that he played softball and hung around with the men's team on which his dad, Guido, played.

Then young Frank turned to baseball. Chicago's park system boasted 432 parks. Quilici's team won the park league championship five years out of the seven that he played.

Following high school, Frank went to Western Michigan University in Kalamazoo, Michigan, and played baseball. His talent gained a wider audience when Western played in the 1961 College World Series. Dick Wiencek, the head scout for the Twins, signed Quilici after the CWS.

For the next several years, Quilici labored in the minor leagues with stops at Erie, Pennsylvania, in the Penn State League; Wytheville, Virginia; Wilson and Charlotte, North Carolina; and finally Class AAA Denver.

The Twins were in the middle of a pennant run on July 18, 1965, when Quilici was called up to the big leagues for a doubleheader against the Los Angeles Angels. The twenty-six-year-old infielder faced Bob Lee late in the first game and popped up in his first major-league at-bat.

In the second game, Frank started at second base. He drilled a double down the left-field line off Angels' ace pitcher Dean Chance for his first big-league hit. It remains one of the biggest thrills of Frank's playing career. After five years of toiling in the minor leagues, he had finally made it to the "bigs."

In the World Series that fall, Frank experienced another high point in his professional life. In Game 1 of the 1965 Series, Quilici smacked two hits in the same inning off Dodger star Don Drysdale. Frank's mother, father, and sister were there to watch it happen.

Quilici still chuckles as he recalls that Dodger Manager Walter Alston must have greatly regretted two decisions he made in that series. Twice he had pitchers intentionally walk the relatively light-hitting Quilici to face Twins pitchers,

Kaat and Grant. The results: Jim Kaat singled in two runs, and Jim "Mudcat" Grant hit a three-run homer after Frank was put on first base.

Manager Sam Mele appreciated how Quilici bolstered the infield in 1965, but the 1966 season found Frank back in the minors. The skipper told his second baseman that although he'd like to keep him with the Twins, Mele wasn't the only one making decisions. Frank also had five options left; those options made it easy for the teams to send down and bring back players.

Quilici stuck with the team in 1967, even though Cal Ermer replaced Mele as manager in midseason. But he appeared in only twenty-three games the whole campaign.

1968 was Quilici's best year with the Twins. He hit .245, played in ninety-seven games and drove in twenty-two runs while playing solid defense. At the end of the season, Ermer was fired. The new skipper was Billy Martin, a former Twins player and coach who was taking on his first job as a major-league manager.

Martin used Frank as a defensive replacement. He told Quilici, "I don't care what you hit. I just want you to quell riots on the bench and be ready to play when I put you in on defense."

Since regular second baseman Rod Carew had weekend military duty in 1969, Quilici became his replacement in that capacity as well. Billy got Frank into 118 ball games, the most of his career.

But it wasn't always easy playing for the fiery Martin. In a game at Oakland, Quilici, who was in the game for his defense, made an error at third base. His manager was livid. An argument ensued in which Martin accused Frank of not being ready.

Quilici recalled telling Martin, "I know what my job is. You just do your job. I just missed the ball."

Jim Kaat went on to pitch ten shutout innings, and the Twins won the game. When Martin suggested that he and Quilici go out for drinks afterward, Frank told him, "Go crap in your hat."

"You see," Frank explained, "you had to know how to play for Billy. Billy Martin knew the strengths and weaknesses of all of his players, and he wasn't afraid to do Little-League things at a big-league level to win a ball game.

"And he'd keep you in a game, too. He'd walk over to you on the bench and say, 'What's the count? What're ya gonna do here? You gonna bunt? You gonna hit and run? You gonna take?' He'd keep you in the game."

The Twins won the Western Division title in 1969 but lost the playoff series for the A.L. pennant in three games to the Orioles. Calvin Griffith had questioned some of Billy Martin's methods and behavior during the season. When Martin started a pitcher of whom Griffith disapproved in the final game, it was the last straw. The Twins owner fired his popular winning manager.

The next season Frank played for new skipper Bill Rigney. He was used similarly to the previous season, appearing in 111 games and hitting .227. The 1970 campaign proved to be his last playing major-league ball.

The next year Frank was named a player-coach. He did not get into a game as a player during 1971.

Quilici's career average was just .214. However, his value as a player and student of the game went far beyond his hitting.

Perhaps more than some modern players, Quilici simply appreciated where he was. He loved putting on a big-league uniform and stepping onto the field each day. Baseball meant a lot to his life.

Frank commented, "Baseball is a lesson in human beings, people's dispositions and how they handled themselves. You got a good read on people, how they perform under pressure and everything else. It helped me in twenty-five years in business to know how people respond. Baseball was really, truly a life lesson."

Quilici carries memories of contributions by Bob Allison, his famed teammate of the mid-sixties.

"No one worked harder to make himself into a baseball player than Bob Allison. He was a good-looking, rugged guy who set the tone for our ball club. He slid hard, starting about three feet from the base, and would sometimes tear them out of the ground.

"When teams played the Twins, they knew they were in for a good, clean, tough ballgame, and Bob had a lot to do with that. He was a classy guy on the field and in the community.

"Bob was an All-Star in 1963 and '64, Rookie of the Year in 1959, and Harmon Killebrew's roommate. He was a leader of the 1965 team."

From World Series Game 2 an image of Bob Allison is frozen in time as he slid, diving across the left-field foul line to make a tremendous back handed catch. But the Dodgers won the Series, four games to three.

Frank Quilici became manager of the Twins in midseason of 1972, at the age of thirty-three. He served in that position through the 1975 campaign and gained a 280-287 record. Frank asserts that he would have done better, but Calvin was cutting back on expenses. One fact not often mentioned is that after the Twins' pennant victory in 1965, they had one of the highest payrolls in baseball.

Griffith's cuts in the mid-1970s left Quilici short of players, both in quality and numbers. He did have some great ones like Carew and Blyleven, and his teams were respectable. However, playing was much more to Quilici's liking than managing.

"Managing sucked," Frank said, "In managing, you're not in control of your own destiny. Calvin and I disagreed on players. We were always fighting on that stuff. I think Calvin thought I was too young to get involved in the player selection and, as a result, we often had a difference of opinion."

Quilici recalled a memorable conversation that took place after the 1975 season. He walked into Griffith's office and greeted him. "How ya doin', Calvin?"

Griffith answered, "I'm doing okay, but you're not going to be."

"Why not?" Quilici wondered.

"Because I'm not gonna rehire you for next year."

Quilici replied, "Well, you haven't talked to me since July. I knew this was coming. But what about the radio job?"

"I'll get you that," the owner responded. "But I wanna talk to you about your managing."

"What do you wanna talk to me about that for?" his now ex-skipper asked. "It's evident you didn't like what I was doing."

Griffith got Frank a job as a Twins broadcaster. The two men remained friends until Calvin's death in 1999.

"We didn't mix business and friendship," Quilici remembered. "Two weeks before his death, my mother and I were at a Twins preseason game. Calvin left the press box and came down, with difficulty, to the handicapped area and said to my mother, 'I miss your sausage sandwiches, Mrs. Quilici.'"

Frank spent five years as a Twins broadcaster: 1976, 1977, and 1980 to 1982. In the late 1970s, he developed the Accubat, a racquet to aid in hitting fungo tosses.

One of Quilici's favorite memories of his time with the Twins concerns an award called the "Nummy," given for actions of the bonehead variety.

Jim Merritt, a left-handed hurler who pitched for the Twins from 1965 to 1968, was one "Nummy" recipient. Quilici and Dave Boswell both recalled the prize, dubbed the "Crash at Lake Eola."

It seems that Merritt had borrowed a car during spring training. The car—memories get a little fuzzy here—belonged to one of the Griffiths, either Calvin or Clark, Jr.

Merritt was cruising the Griffith car around Lake Eola, near Orlando, one night when he unexpectedly came upon a crowded lovers' lane. Jim crashed into the end car in a string of cars containing romantic couples and started a chain reaction that resulted in numerous vehicles smacking into one another.

Both Frank and Dave agreed that it was a well-deserved "Nummy."

Quilici lives with his third wife in Burnsville. He has been in business there for twenty years and has been vice president of Webster Diversified Insurance. He has four grown children and five grandchildren.

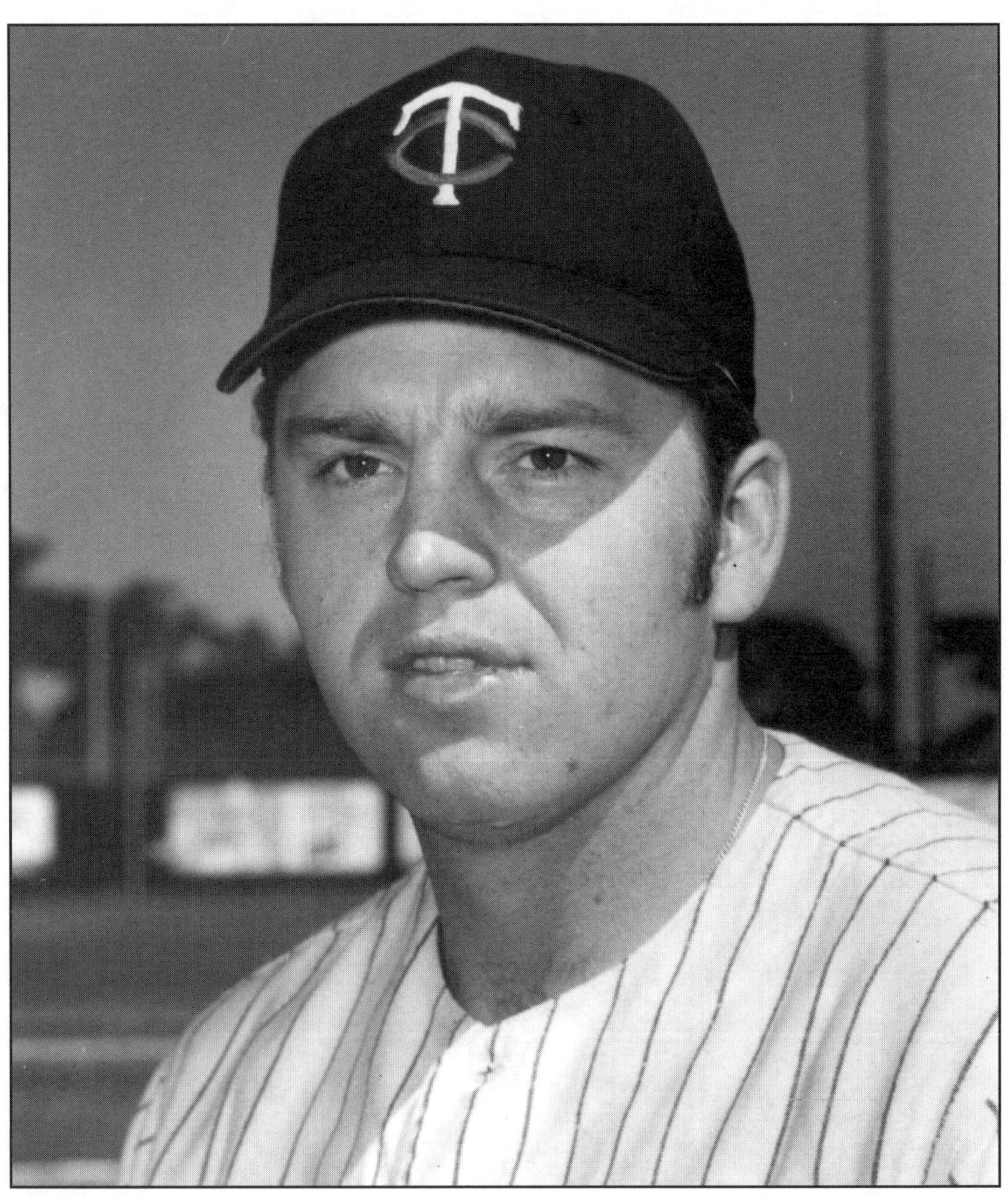

John Sevcik

Bats: Right
Throws: Right
Height: 6' 2"
Weight: 205 lbs.
Born: July 11, 1942, in Illinois

YEAR	TEAM	LG	AVG	G	AB	R	H	2B	3B	HR	RBI	BB	K	OBP	SLG
1965	*Min*	*AL*	*.063*	*12*	*16*	*1*	*1*	*1*	*0*	*0*	*0*	*1*	*5*	*.118*	*.125*
			AVG	*G*	*AB*	*R*	*H*	*2B*	*3B*	*HR*	*RBI*	*BB*	*K*	*OBP*	*SLG*
			.063	*12*	*16*	*1*	*1*	*1*	*0*	*0*	*0*	*1*	*5*	*.118*	*.125*

Some players hang around the major leagues for ten to twenty years. Others appear in only one inning. More commonly they get in a few years. John Sevcik was with the Twins for one full season and got into only twelve games. But while his playing time was short, his memories of one glorious year in Twins history are rich.

John and his twin brother, Jim, were from the Chicago suburb of Berwyn, Illinois. They attended Morton High School and then went to the University of Missouri on football scholarships.

But while football became the means to an end, namely a college education, the boys had always considered baseball their favorite sport. They had been Cubs and Sox fans and had even had a youthful experience with Ted Williams.

As the young Sevciks and their father awaited a cab at Comiskey Park after a Sox game, the legendary player asked if he could share their cab. It was quite a thrill for John and Jim to share a ride with one of baseball's all-time greats.

In the Sevcik's senior year at Missouri, their team played in the College World Series in Omaha. Coming through the losers' bracket, they wound up playing the University of Minnesota for the championship. The Gophers won the game, but scouts had taken an interest in several players.

The Twins signed four players from the Missouri squad, scouted by Billy Martin. They included John and Jim Sevcik.

John reported to rookie league in Cocoa Beach, Florida. His stay there was short. The catcher for the Wisconsin Rapids team had broken his finger; a replacement was needed. Also, team officials decided, they could use another outfielder.

The Sevcik brothers—catcher John and outfielder Jim—were selected to fill those spots. They headed north to spend the summer playing ball for Wisconsin Rapids.

1965 found John at the Twins' spring training camp in Orlando. The way rosters were constructed at that time, three bonus players were designated on the forty-man major-league roster. Eventually, the roster was to be cut to twenty-five for the trip to Minnesota, but two of the three bonus players had to be kept. The Twins decided to keep pitcher Dave Boswell and John Sevcik. The third bonus player was Rod Carew; he was sent to the minors.

John was a backup catcher in 1965, behind two Twins stalwarts, Earl Battey and Jerry Zimmerman. Sevcik was a good receiver who liked working with the pitchers. He spent a lot of time in the bullpen warming up Twins' hurlers, but rarely got into games.

It wasn't for lack of trying. Along with Frank Kostro, Andy Kosco, and other part-timers, John was a member of the "Scrubeenies." Led by Kostro, they occasionally lobbied for playing time.

Sevcik said that sometimes he and Frank Kostro would stand by the batting cage watching hitters along with Manager Sam Mele.

Sevcik recalled, "Frank would walk around the cage and say to Mele, 'Sevey and I are in there tonight, aren't we?'

"Mele would just look at him with his hands in his back pockets and shake his head from side to side like, 'You gotta be kiddin' me.'

Sevcik continued, "Kostro would ask Mele, 'Are ya hittin' us four and five, or three and four? You're playing us tonight, aren't ya. Goin' with percentages, they don't know us.' It would always be against some ace, like Gary Peters or Sam McDowell.

"Mele would give him a stone-cold look, and Kostro would say to me, 'I don't know. I'll probably get in. You'll be backin' up.'"

Occasionally, in the late innings, he'd catch an inning or two and maybe get an at-bat. He hit against the likes of Whitey Ford and Sam McDowell. But he was along for the pennant-winning ride.

John recalled, "When we clinched the pennant, we did it in Washington. We partied all night and then bussed over to Baltimore.

"The first game in the series against Baltimore, Mele put out a makeshift lineup. I was catching. There were some guys playing who'd been called up. It wasn't the regulars.

"So we played Baltimore, and Wally Bunker was pitching for 'em, and I hit his first pitch off the left-field fence. It was a curveball that looked like a beach ball.

"Ted Uhlaender retrieved the ball and inscribed it. 'Sept. 28 in the 158th ballgame of the year, 1965, John Sevcik hit the first pitch off Wally Bunker off the left field wall for a stand-up double. His first major league hit.'"

It would be his only major-league hit. Today it's the highlight of his career. "It was about a foot from the top of the wall. I thought it was a home run," Sevcik said.

The year itself created many snapshots in John's memory, including one of Harmon Killebrew lining a shot over the left-field fence off the Yankees' Pete Mikkelsen, and others of being on the field with the greats of the game.

"There was a Cleveland pitcher named Gary Bell, one of the few at-bats I got was against him in Cleveland. I was mopping up, and he was a closer. Bell was a side-arming right-hander who threw real hard.

"I batted right-handed and was in the bullpen when the phone rang. Mele said, 'Send Sevcik in to pinch hit.'

"I was leading off, Jimmie Hall was on deck. He said, 'Just look for heat. He don't throw nothin' but heat.' Bell wound up and threw. I started swinging as soon as this guy let go and I hit a bolt down the left-field line that curved foul and rattled around the corner.

"I was heading for second. The umpire put up his arms and said, 'Foul ball!' I ran across the infield back to the plate. Bell was rubbing up a new ball. When I ran by the mound, he took a couple steps toward me and said, 'You take another rip like that and I'll stick the next pitch in your ear.'

"I was nervous when I got in the box. The next pitch came at my head, not a real brushback, but kind of high and tight. It didn't knock me down, but I had to spin back.

"The next ball I hit off the end of the bat. A weak ground ball to the infield. Bell just glared at me.

"It was fun, even though I didn't get a chance to stick around. I got a taste of it. Glenda, my wife, mentioned what a thrill it was. One year we were in college, and the next we were flying chartered jets to World Series games."

John didn't see any action in the World Series, but he did warm up Jim Kaat prior to Game 7. Both teams' bullpens were on the first-base side. The Twins' catchers and the opponent's pitchers were back to back with a screen between them.

After Kaat completed his warm-up tosses, Sevcik turned to watch the Dodger starter, Sandy Koufax.

"He was poppin' his fastball, hitting corners and breaking off his curve. He looked great. Then he turned to me, stretched out his left arm and said, 'I just can't get loose.'

"I went to Jerry Zimmerman and I said, 'I think it's gonna be a long day.'" It was. The Dodgers prevailed 2-0 to win Game 7 and the Series on Koufax's three-hitter.

John was sent to Charlotte, North Carolina, in 1966. He spent the next several years in the Twins farm system at Wilson (North Carolina), Evansville (Indiana), and then played AAA at Denver and Portland, Oregon. But he never made it back to the "bigs."

"I could catch, but I wasn't a real good hitter. I was big and not real flexible. Good fastballs ate me up," Sevcik said.

In Sevcik's last year at Portland, AAA skipper Ralph Rowe told him that Calvin would be calling and that they wanted John to become a minor-league manager.

Rowe said, "You'd be perfect for it. You've got the right disposition. You're a catcher, they like catchers as managers, you had to bat so you know something about hitting. You've worked with pitchers, you've had the whole field in front of you. It makes good sense. You'd be good at it."

Calvin called and offered Sevcik a contract to manage in the rookie league. Griffith also offered Frank Quilici a minor-league managerial job, and they sat side by side considering their futures.

Calvin offered John $11,500, which was more than the going rate for first-year skippers. But Sevcik ultimately turned him down. "I just didn't want to baby-sit kids in a rookie league," he said.

John was twenty-nine years old. He went back to Minneapolis, where he went into the construction equipment business. From 1971 to 1997, he lived in the

Twin Cities. In 1993, he took a job with Jim Beam Brands that eventually necessitated a move to San Antonio.

Stories of other players remain a big part of John's memories. One was particularily unforgettable. "We were on a road trip," John related. "I got a phone call from another player to come into his room.

"When I knocked on his door I heard, 'What's the password?' I answered, "What do you mean? You called me. Let me in.

"The door opened," John continued, "and my friend was standing in the doorway, stripped to the waist with a shoulder holster draped down one side. He started doing kung fu moves and waved a pistol while singing 'Secret Agent Man.'

"Then the guy went to a window and shot up the side of the hotel. When he looked down and said, 'Ya know, John, a fella could pick people off easy from up here,' I decided it was time to leave."

"I was always active in sports," John remembered, "but baseball was my favorite. It was something I wanted to do since I was a young kid. My brother and I were baseball addicts. We followed the Cubs and Sox. Ernie Banks was my favorite, along with Ted Williams.

"When you play sports at a professional level, a certain bond is formed that time doesn't change. I don't miss playing, just the friendships. It is nice to see the guys at alumni golf outings. I have contact and competition with them there."

John lives with his wife, Glenda, near San Antonio.

Twins

Ted Uhlaender

Bats: Left
Throws: Right
Height: 6' 2"
Weight: 190 lbs.
Born: October 21, 1940, in Illinois

YEAR	TEAM	LG	AVG	G	AB	R	H	2B	3B	HR	RBI	BB	K	OBP	SLG
1965	Min	AL	.182	13	22	1	4	0	0	0	1	0	2	.182	.182
1966	Min	AL	.226	105	367	39	83	12	2	2	22	27	33	.280	.286
1967	Min	AL	.258	133	415	41	107	19	7	6	49	13	45	.285	.381
1968	Min	AL	.283	140	488	52	138	21	5	7	52	28	46	.324	.389
1969	Min	AL	.273	152	554	93	151	18	2	8	62	44	52	.328	.356
1970	Cle	AL	.268	141	473	56	127	21	2	11	46	39	44	.321	.391
1971	Cle	AL	.288	141	500	52	144	20	3	2	47	38	44	.336	.352
1972	Cin	NL	.159	73	113	9	18	3	0	0	6	13	11	.246	.186
			AVG	G	AB	R	H	2B	3B	HR	RBI	BB	K	OBP	SLG
			.263	898	2,932	343	772	114	21	36	285	202	277	.311	.353

Ted Uhlaender grew up in McAllen, Texas, where he graduated from high school in 1957. He played baseball at Baylor University and earned a degree. He aspired to play the sport professionally after graduating from Baylor. However, no major-league team had contacted him, no scouts seemed interested, and there was no draft at the time.

So Uhlaender went to Victoria, Texas, to work out with an AA club in hopes of signing an independent contract. While he was there, a scout from Minnesota noticed the speedy, left-handed-batting outfielder. The Twins were looking for players for their Wytheville, Virginia, team in the Rookie League.

The scout offered the young Texan $350 a month if he made the team. Accepting the opportunity, Ted made the long drive from Texas to Virginia in hopes of being selected. The tryout attracted eighty other players. Ted landed a spot on the team.

He spent the next several years working his way through the Twins' minor-league system with stops in Erie, Pennsylvania; Wilson and Charlotte, North Carolina; and Denver.

Ted was on the Charlotte roster for the third straight year in the spring of 1965. Then, Denver Manager Cal Ermer gave him a shot at making the Twins' Denver ball club, just one level from the big show.

"He kept me as the last roster spot," Ted recalled. "The rest is history. Cal is a fine person, good manager, and loves the game of baseball."

Uhlaender led the Pacific Coast League in hitting with a .340 average while playing with Denver for the 1965 season. He was called up to the Twins in September and played in his first big-league game on September 4, 1965. Ted got into thirteen games with the American League champs.

Uhlaender regularly patrolled center field between Bob Allison and Tony Oliva from 1966 to 1969. Despite the fact that Ted led all major-league outfielders with a .996 fielding percentage in 1967, Paul Blair won the Gold Glove. It was just one of five seasons in which Uhlaender had fewer than three errors.

He developed into a solid hitter but was overshadowed by great hitters like Harmon Killebrew and Tony Oliva.

When asked about hitting and fielding, Ted remarked, "As long as we won a game, it gave me great satisfaction. I just enjoyed playing the game. I liked to make good defensive plays, but I think the key was that when you weren't hittin', you can't just take your hitting with you to the field. You have to play defense.

"The ability to make a good play and help the team when you weren't hittin' is what kept you on the field."

Uhlaender recalled several highlights of his Twins career. "I got to score Harmon Killebrew's 1,000th RBI; I had games where I got five hits; getting to play on two championship teams. I don't believe I've ever been around a finer gentleman in my playing or coaching career than Harmon Killebrew. That was a privilege as a player for me.

"The attitude toward the game is different today. Too many guys are complacent. Who cares about going to the World Series and winning $300,000 when you've got twenty million in the bank? You just waste another month of your time, you're gonna get paid anyway. If you're a superstar, you can pick up half a million in one appearance."

Uhlaender was among the league leaders in hitting for much of the 1968 season. Around midseason, he hurt his hand, and his average suffered, but he still hit .283, fifth in the American League.

As a youth, Ted admired Chicago White Sox second baseman Nellie Fox. Like Fox, Ted used a thick-handled bottleneck bat. For part of his pro career, he used a Nellie Fox model bat.

New skipper Billy Martin relied heavily upon Ted in 1969. He played in more games, 152, and had more at-bats than in any other year in his career. The Twins won the Western Division title that year.

The season ended when the Baltimore Orioles swept the Twins in three games. Uhlaender, Martin, and Rich Reese went hunting afterward near Denver. Then a call reached them with the news that Calvin Griffith was firing Billy Martin as manager.

"I don't think he expected it," Uhlaender said of Billy. "He went back and stayed in his room about two days and didn't come out. He made phone calls, and after he finally settled down he came out and was still pretty upset. Billy told me that since he was gone, I was gone. About two weeks later they called me and told me I was traded."

Uhlaender liked his years in Minnesota and appreciated his owner, Calvin Griffith. "I liked Calvin, he didn't pay so well, but he treated you well. When you got to Minnesota, they helped you find a place to live.

"I lived in a person's home up there for about $220 a month. It was a real nice home. They gave us the keys to a new Ford to drive for the summer.

"We traveled first class. They gave us the finest food. It's just that when it came time for contracts he didn't want to pay a lot."

Uhlaender, Dean Chance, Graig Nettles, and Bob Miller were traded to the Cleveland Indians for Stan Williams and Luis Tiant. Ted played regularly for the next two seasons. He had his highest average in 1971, hitting .288 to lead the Indians.

Uhlaender left the Indians for a short time that season. It was announced that he was considering retirement. Ted related that the real story was something different.

"My daughter had stepped next to a heater when she was five or six years old. Her housecoat caught on fire and burned her leg real bad. She had a scar around her knee. The doctors said they needed to remove it, otherwise, the scar was going to tighten up and not let her leg extend, and she'd be crippled. So, she went into the children's hospital in Cleveland, and I just wanted to attend the operation.

"Alvin Dark and I were a little at odds because he decided not to play me against left-handed pitching. They went to New York and were facing three left-handers, so instead of getting on a plane in Detroit to go to New York, I went to Cleveland and went to the hospital.

"The last day in New York someone asked Alvin Dark where I was, and he didn't know I was gone. When he got back, we had a discussion about it. In order for them to make things look good, they said I quit. I never did; I just went to the hospital."

Another result of Ted's discussion with his manager was that Dark decided to let Uhlaender hit left-handers again. That night the Indians faced Vida Blue, who was having a tremendous year. Ted got the game-winning hit to beat Blue. He played against righties and lefties the rest of the season.

Uhlaender was traded to the Cincinnati Reds after the 1971 season. It was with his new team that he got pulled into the struggle between the players' union and baseball owners. After attending a strike meeting on behalf of the Reds players, Ted had the duty of reporting to management that the players had voted to strike. That year his at-bats fell to 113 and Ted hit only .159. The next season he couldn't catch on anywhere.

Uhlaender returned to Texas to work with his father in the family's electronic business. He stayed until his father retired and then began to make calls to get back into baseball.

"The guy who actually helped me get back in was Lou Pinella. He was GM for a little while for New York. He put my name down, and when he took the job to manage again, my name was sitting there when the new Yankees' GM took over. He called me, and I got a job that fall in 1989."

Ted worked for the Yankees until 1993 as a minor-league coach. From 1994 to 1995, he was their major-league advance scout. He then followed former Yankee skipper Buck Showalter to Arizona. There Ted did scouting work on the major- and minor-league levels for the expansion draft.

After the draft, Uhlaender worked for the San Francisco Giants' organization on special assignment and did scouting work in 1998 and 1999.

Ted joined a former Twin teammate, Charlie Manuel, in Cleveland in the 2000 season. Manuel was the new manager of the Indians, and Ted became his first base coach.

Throughout his career, Uhlaender played for some of baseball's finest managers, with Billy Martin, Alvin Dark, and Sparky Anderson among them.

"I respected Billy a lot as far as knowledge of the game was concerned. His decisions about the game were very good. I liked Billy, but my favorite manager and the nicest person was Sam Mele. He's about as fine a person as you'd wanna meet. He gave me my chance to play." Mele managed the Twins from 1961 to 1966.

Baseball has always meant much to Uhlaender. "Since I've been old enough to talk, I've wanted to be a major-league baseball player. I never made a lot of money. But there's not many people that can stand up before a bunch of kids and look 'em in the eye and say, 'Look, this is what I wanted to do in life, and I accomplished it by the time I was thirty years old.' Some people never accomplish what they want to do in their whole lifetime. I've been very lucky.

"Everything I have came from the game. I've got a home in Texas, a farm, a house in Colorado, a twin engine aircraft. The chance to participate, and the reputation you get and the things that come with baseball, the pension, it's been very good to me.

"I'm very thankful that God gave me the tools to play the game."

Ted lives in McGregor, Texas, with his wife, Karen, and two children. He has three grown children with his previous wife. The Uhlaenders also spend time at their place in Colorado, where Karen works as a ski instructor.

Twins

AL WORTHINGTON

Bats: Right
Throws: Right
Height: 6' 2"
Weight: 195 lbs.
Born: February 5, 1929, in Alabama

YEAR	TEAM	LG	ERA	W	L	Sv	G	IP	H	R	ER	BB	K	AVG. A
1953	NYG	NL	3.44	4	8	0	20	102.0	103	55	39	54	52	.258
1954	NYG	NL	3.50	0	2	0	10	18.0	21	7	7	15	8	.333
1956	NYG	NL	3.97	7	14	0	28	165.2	158	82	73	74	95	.254
1957	NYG	NL	4.22	8	11	4	55	157.2	140	75	74	56	90	.237
1958	SF	NL	3.63	11	7	6	54	151.1	152	72	61	57	76	.255
1959	SF	NL	3.68	2	3	2	42	73.1	68	34	30	37	45	.253
1960	Bos	AL	7.71	0	1	0	6	11.2	17	12	10	11	7	.340
1960	ChA	AL	3.38	1	1	0	4	5.1	3	2	2	4	1	.176
1963	Cin	NL	2.99	4	4	10	50	81.1	75	34	27	31	55	.248
1964	Cin	NL	10.29	1	0	0	6	7.0	14	11	8	2	6	.400
1964	Min	AL	1.37	5	6	14	41	72.1	47	18	11	28	59	.183
1965	Min	AL	2.13	10	7	21	62	80.1	57	25	19	41	59	.207
1966	Min	AL	2.46	6	3	16	65	91.1	66	26	25	27	93	.199
1967	Min	AL	2.84	8	9	16	59	92.0	77	36	29	38	80	.229
1968	Min	AL	2.71	4	5	18	54	76.1	67	26	23	32	57	.238
1969	Min	AL	4.57	4	1	3	46	61.0	65	31	31	20	51	.278
			ERA	W	L	Sv	G	IP	H	R	ER	BB	K	AVG. A
			3.39	75	82	110	602	1,246.2	1,130	546	469	527	834	.243

Baseball has had great impact on players, families, and even society. Sometimes the changes wrought by playing a game dramatically alter the everyday approach a player takes in living his life.

Jerry Kindall once described Al Worthington as "mean, rough-looking, and often appearing unshaven. He was intimidating. They called him Red."

Then one day in 1958, while serving as a pitcher for the San Francisco Giants, Worthington attended a Billy Graham Crusade at the Cow Palace. That day changed his outlook on life and baseball forever. As he committed his life to Jesus Christ, he was "saved and born again."

Al Worthington was from Birmingham, Alabama. He attended high school there, graduating in January of 1948. For three and one-half years, he attended the University of Alabama.

Al's Alabama baseball team qualified for the 1950 College World Series in Omaha. But a greater prize awaited the pitcher from Birmingham. The manager of a semi-pro team from Fulda, Minnesota, was in attendance in Omaha. He offered Al a job pitching for his club that summer. Al went north to Minnesota, where he met the skipper's niece, Shirley. They were married that December.

Al had planned to return to Minnesota to pitch in Waseca the next summer. However, he was offered a minor-league contract to play for Nashville, Tennessee, and he signed. Al pitched for Nashville in 1951 and 1952. His first professional start was against his hometown Birmingham team.

Al won and admitted, "It was kind of exciting, since they didn't try to sign me, either."

The New York Giants bought Al's contract from Nashville in 1953. Out of spring training that year Worthington was sent to the Giants' minor-league team, the Minneapolis Millers. Midway through that season, the Giants called him up.

Al made an auspicious major-league debut. His first two starts were 6-0 whitewashes of the Pirates and Dodgers on July 7 and 11. Worthington's shutout of Brooklyn also halted the Dodgers' consecutive-game home-run streak. They had cracked thirty-nine homers during the streak.

But Al knew it wouldn't be that easy all the time.

"I was lucky," he recalled.

He was right. The rest of 1953 and the first half of 1954 he totaled 2-10 in a mixture of starting and relieving. Worthington's ERA, however, was very respectable, in the mid-threes.

Al was back in Minnesota pitching for the Millers again the second half of 1954 and in 1955.

Starting in 1956, Worthington was a member of the Giants pitching staff until Boston picked him up in 1960 for a short stint. Then it was on to the Chicago White Sox, but only for four games. For a couple of seasons Al was back in the minors.

The Cincinnati Reds signed Al in 1963 and made him a relief pitcher. He saved ten games for the Redlegs that year.

Worthington preferred to start, but "I wasn't good enough," he admitted.

He certainly was good enough to blossom into one of baseball's top relief pitchers when the Twins purchased his contract. They acquired him after the Reds sent him to the minors in San Diego early in the 1964 season.

His manager, Sam Mele, recalled Al's acquisition. "Al Worthington was a high-class guy. I tried to get him for years, but Calvin was concerned about his being so religious. I called Luke Appling, who had had Worthington in Atlanta. He said, 'Al's a great guy. There's no problem whatsoever.'

"When we got Al, I asked him, 'What about this religion thing?' He said, 'Maybe on a Sunday, I might be five minutes late.' He never was late."

Worthington fondly remembers the 1965 campaign. "We got in the lead early, and we never relinquished it. We just pulled together, and it was a great relationship with each player. You're more friends when you win, anyway, and we won the whole year. We had a great time."

It's also fun when you're pitching well. Al was 10-7 with a 2.13 ERA and twenty-one saves for the American League champions. His eighteen saves led the league in 1968.

"My fastball slid and sunk," Worthington related. "That was my main pitch. I threw inside a lot to left-handed hitters. I pitched right-handed hitters away because the ball slid away."

In his Twins career Al won thirty-seven games, lost thirty-one and had a 2.62 ERA with eighty-eight saves. His saves rank fourth all-time for the Twins.

Al continued to pitch for the Twins through the 1969 division championship season. Only once did his ERA top 3.00; he posted a 4.57 his final year.

Worthington became the Twins' pitching coach. He points with pride to his 1973 staff that set a Twins record for lowest ERA at 2.84.

Then Al left major-league baseball. He spent sixteen and one-half years at Liberty University in Lynchburg, Virginia. The first thirteen years he was head baseball coach; then he became athletic director.

Al has many fond memories about his career in baseball. "Playing so long, you get in habits. We'd get up early, usually five of us, and meet for breakfast. Travel was hard, but being with the other players was good."

But the memory of Billy Graham in San Francisco stands apart. "It changed everything about everything. It gave me a foundation, something to build on. It motivated me, all these things, every part of life it affects.

"I became a better man, a better pitcher, better husband, better daddy. Man is dead without God; he's just a creature. Without Christ he's just a walking-around dead man. That's what I was. [I had] no spiritual life, and I didn't until I was twenty-nine years old."

Al continues to make mission trips, taking one or two trips a year to places including Venezuela.

"My purpose in living is to tell people how to go to heaven. That's what I do since I stopped working to make a living. It's the greatest joy of my life."

Al and Shirley live in Sterrett, Alabama. They raised five children and have ten grandchildren.

"Baseball grows ya," Al concluded. "It's the greatest game in the world. If it hadn't been for baseball, I wouldn't have attended the crusade in San Francisco and been saved to witness for Christ.

"It was a nice life; without travel, perfect. There were many good times. The minors were actually more fun, but the big leagues is where you wanted to be."

Rod Carew

Bats: Left
Throws: Right
Height: 6' 0"
Weight: 170 lbs.
Born: October 1, 1945, in Canal Zone

YEAR	TEAM	LG	AVG	G	AB	R	H	2B	3B	HR	RBI	BB	[illegible]	[illegible]	[illegible]
1967	*Min*	*AL*	*.292*	*137*	*514*	*66*	*150*	*22*	*7*	*8*	*51*	*37*	*91*	*.341*	*.409*
1968	*Min*	*AL*	*.273*	*127*	*461*	*46*	*126*	*27*	*2*	*1*	*42*	*26*	*71*	*.312*	*.347*
1969	*Min*	*AL*	*.332*	*123*	*458*	*79*	*152*	*30*	*4*	*8*	*56*	*37*	*72*	*.386*	*.467*
1970	*Min*	*AL*	*.366*	*51*	*191*	*27*	*70*	*12*	*3*	*4*	*28*	*11*	*28*	*.407*	*.524*
1971	*Min*	*AL*	*.307*	*147*	*577*	*88*	*177*	*16*	*10*	*2*	*48*	*45*	*81*	*.356*	*.380*
1972	*Min*	*AL*	*.318*	*142*	*535*	*61*	*170*	*21*	*6*	*0*	*51*	*43*	*60*	*.369*	*.379*
1973	*Min*	*AL*	*.350*	*149*	*580*	*98*	*203*	*30*	*11*	*6*	*62*	*62*	*55*	*.411*	*.471*
1974	*Min*	*AL*	*.364*	*153*	*599*	*86*	*218*	*30*	*5*	*3*	*55*	*74*	*49*	*.433*	*.446*
1975	*Min*	*AL*	*.359*	*143*	*535*	*89*	*192*	*24*	*4*	*14*	*80*	*64*	*40*	*.421*	*.497*
1976	*Min*	*AL*	*.331*	*156*	*605*	*97*	*200*	*29*	*12*	*9*	*90*	*67*	*52*	*.395*	*.463*
1977	*Min*	*AL*	*.388*	*155*	*616*	*128*	*239*	*38*	*16*	*14*	*100*	*69*	*55*	*.449*	*.570*
1978	*Min*	*AL*	*.333*	*152*	*564*	*85*	*188*	*26*	*10*	*5*	*70*	*78*	*62*	*.411*	*.441*
1979	*Cal*	*AL*	*.318*	*110*	*409*	*78*	*130*	*15*	*3*	*3*	*44*	*73*	*46*	*.419*	*.391*
1980	*Cal*	*AL*	*.331*	*144*	*540*	*74*	*179*	*34*	*7*	*3*	*59*	*59*	*38*	*.396*	*.437*
1981	*Cal*	*AL*	*.305*	*93*	*364*	*57*	*111*	*17*	*1*	*2*	*21*	*45*	*45*	*.380*	*.374*
1982	*Cal*	*AL*	*.319*	*138*	*523*	*88*	*167*	*25*	*5*	*3*	*44*	*67*	*49*	*.396*	*.403*
1983	*Cal*	*AL*	*.339*	*129*	*472*	*66*	*160*	*24*	*2*	*2*	*44*	*57*	*48*	*.409*	*.411*
1984	*Cal*	*AL*	*.295*	*93*	*329*	*42*	*97*	*8*	*1*	*3*	*31*	*40*	*39*	*.367*	*.353*
1985	*Cal*	*AL*	*.280*	*127*	*443*	*69*	*124*	*17*	*3*	*2*	*39*	*64*	*47*	*.371*	*.345*
			AVG	*G*	*AB*	*R*	*H*	*2B*	*3B*	*HR*	*RBI*	*BB*	*K*	*OBP*	*SLG*
			.328	*2,469*	*9,315*	*1,424*	*3,053*	*445*	*112*	*92*	*1,015*	*1,018*	*1,028*	*.393*	*.429*

The bat was like a magic wand in Rod Carew's hands. He could slap a ball to left with a deft flick of his wrists or turn on a pitch and drive a ball down the line.

Both the left- and right-field gaps were his prey. While Rod hit home runs for double figures only twice in his nineteen-year career, he smacked the baseball inside the park like it was his personal pinball machine. And he was amazing on the bases as well.

His Twins teammate Frank Kostro said it simply. "The man could really, really hit, and he could really, really run."

Rod Carew was born on a train in the Panama Canal Zone. His parents, Olga and Eric, were heading for a hospital forty miles away, where medical facilities were better. But baby Rod couldn't wait.

Rod grew up in Gatun, a little town of 2,000 people near the Canal. He lived in the black section of town with his parents, a brother, and two sisters in a second-story, five-room apartment.

From the age of five, young Rod loved baseball. He and his friends, often using broom handles for bats and tennis balls instead of baseballs, played the game wherever and whenever they could. The joy of playing ball was countered by the realities of poverty, segregation and a sometimes-abusive father.

Seeking a better life for Rod and his siblings, Olga left her family for New York. In 1961, after his mother sent for him, Rod boarded a plane to join Olga in New York City. He was seventeen years old. Carew attended George Washington High School and played park league baseball his senior year. It was in that league that he attracted the attention of major-league scouts.

Rod signed with the Minnesota Twins one day after graduating from high school in 1964. The nineteen-year old reported to Elizabethton, Tennessee, to play in the rookie league.

Rod was a bonus player and, under baseball rules, was placed on the Twins' forty-man major-league roster. But after spring training back in 1965, one of the three bonus players on the roster could be sent to the minors.

The Twins kept a catcher, John Sevcik, and a pitcher, Dave Boswell. Rod went to the minors for two seasons. In 1967 he jumped from Class C to the big leagues.

Carew had a great first season with the Twins. He hit .292 and won American League Rookie of the Year honors. His second season was solid; he batted .273.

Rod's average would not dip below .300 for the next fifteen years. He would win seven American League batting championships, once flirting with .400, all with the Minnesota Twins. In 1972, he became the first player ever to win a batting championship without hitting a home run.

Rod was always a good hitter, but he worked at it. He would take extra batting practice, adjust to various pitches and vary his stance, especially if he was in a slump.

Carew was almost as dangerous on the bases. He stole second base, third base, and home in a game against Detroit on May 18, 1969. Twin Cesar Tovar also stole third and home that inning to tie a major-league record.

"Billy Martin motivated me to steal home," Rod offered. "He told me I was a great base-runner and should use the element of surprise."

Said Frank Quilici, another of his former managers, "There's nobody alive who could turn a single into a double, a double into a triple the way Rod could. He may have been the most complete player of his time."

"Rod ran effortlessly, and people miscalculated how fast he was. When you looked at the top half of his body, it didn't look like he was going that fast. But he was very powerful and would fool people. When Rod turned it on, he could fly."

Carew tied a major-league record when he stole home seven times in 1969. The Twins won the Western Division championship that year. They claimed the division title again in 1970, but Rod was injured. He played in only fifty-one games that season, although he did hit .366 in 191 at-bats.

The Twins teams of 1969 and 1970 were perhaps the finest blend of hitting, defense, and pitching in Minnesota history. They were a collection of talented players that featured two future Hall of Fame inductees, Harmon Killebrew and Rod, and other viable Hall candidates like Jim Kaat, Bert Blyleven, and Tony Oliva. They also had two Cy Young Award winners: Dean Chance from 1964, and Jim Perry from 1970.

In Perry's words, "There wouldn't be enough money for a franchise to pay that team today." Unfortunately, they ran into an excellent Baltimore team and were swept in postseason play twice.

Carew continued to play second base until 1975, when he was moved to first base in an attempt to avoid injury.

Rod was named to his first All-Star Game in 1967 and would have played continuously in the summer classic through 1984 had he not been sidelined three times because of injuries. In 1977 he set a mark with over four million All-Star votes. His two triples in the 1978 All-Star Game had never been achieved by a single player.

Carew's offensive exploits with the Twins were impressive. He amassed over 200 hits four times. Three times he led the league in hits, and once he led in runs scored. Rod's 239 hits in 1977 were the highest total in forty-seven years. The 128 runs he scored in 1977 were the most since 1961.

In a stellar career, 1977 was Carew's best year. He hit .388, drove home 100 runs and hit fourteen homers, feats that earned him American League MVP honors.

Forty-two times with the Twins Rod hit least four times per game. He holds the Twins' season records for runs, hits, batting average, singles, triples, and stolen bases.

Carew's highlights in Minnesota were the relationships he had with his teammates and fans treatment throughout his stay. He especially appreciated the fan support during 1977 when he flirted with a .400 batting average much of the year.

"I also fondly remember my relationship with Billy Martin, who turned me from a boy to a man, and my first major league hit, that proved to me that I belonged at the big-league level.

"I never would have gotten that hit if Calvin hadn't told Sam Mele at the beginning of spring training in 1967, 'This is your second baseman. End of discussion.'

"Billy Martin and Calvin Griffith were the only two people who believed I could do the job. Billy worked with me on playing second base, we talked baseball. When I was trying to hit homeruns, Billy advised me to use the whole field and not try to hit the ball out of the park."

Former manager Sam Mele talked about how Martin worked on fielding with Carew, "In spring training Billy would throw a ball against a wall and make Rod go to the left, right, straight at him, and bring the ball in nice and soft and not jab at it.

"When Rich Rollins got hurt I said, 'What'll we do?' Martin said, 'Send for Carew.' I said, he's not ready. Billy said, 'He's ready!' And boy was he ready!"

For all his success, Rod was faced with an issue that he believed made it impossible for him to continue to play for Calvin Griffith in Minnesota. The Twins' owner made a speech during the off-season in Waseca, Minnesota. In the talk, he cast aspersions on black baseball fans. Calvin said in effect that blacks were more interested in pro wrestling than baseball and that he had moved the team from Washington, D.C., because blacks didn't go to games. Griffith added, "We came to Minnesota because you've got good, hard-working white people here."

Rod felt that he could no longer play for an owner who had that kind of feelings about people and players of color. He couldn't play on Griffith's "plantation," he said. "I would have been happy playing in Minnesota for twenty years. I never wanted to leave, but I had no choice." Rod announced that he would play out his option and not re-sign with the Twins if they did not trade him.

On February 3, 1978, Rod got his wish. He was sent to the California Angels for Ken Landreaux, Dave Engle, Brad Havens, and Paul Hartzell.

For the next seven years, Carew played for the Angels. Twice he helped them into the League Championship Series, but they did not make the World Series.

Carew hit over .300 his first five years on the West Coast. Then his average dipped to .295 and .280 his last two seasons.

Rod became the sixteenth player ever to collect 3,000 hits when he blooped a single to left, fittingly off the Twins' Frank Viola, on August 4, 1985. But the Angels did not offer Carew a contract for the 1986 season, ending his playing career.

Carew finished with 3,053 hits. He was elected to the Baseball Hall of Fame on January 8, 1991. It was his very first year of eligibility for the Hall. Rod was pleased and excited when the Twins retired his jersey number 29 on July 19, 1987.

Rod commented, "Tony Oliva was critical in teaching me the art of hitting. He deserves to be in the Hall of Fame, and I want to go to Cooperstown for him."

Rod had respected and worked well with Calvin before the Waseca incident. He restored an amicable relationship with Calvin prior to Griffith's death on October 20, 1999, at age eighty-seven.

Carew has served as a hitting instructor with the California Angels and the Milwaukee Brewers. He lives in California with his wife, Marilynn.

John Castino

Bats: Right
Throws: Right
Height: 5' 11"
Weight: 175 lbs.
Born: October 23, 1954, in Illinois

YEAR	TEAM	LG	AVG	G	AB	R	H	2B	3B	HR	RBI	BB	K	OBP	SLG
1979	Min	AL	.285	148	393	49	112	13	8	5	52	27	72	.331	.397
1980	Min	AL	.302	150	546	67	165	17	7	13	64	29	67	.336	.430
1981	Min	AL	.268	101	381	41	102	13	9	6	36	18	52	.301	.396
1982	Min	AL	.241	117	410	48	99	12	6	6	37	36	51	.304	.344
1983	Min	AL	.277	142	563	83	156	30	4	11	57	62	54	.348	.403
1984	Min	AL	.444	8	27	5	12	1	0	0	3	5	2	.531	.481
			AVG	G	AB	R	H	2B	3B	HR	RBI	BB	K	OBP	SLG
			.278	666	2320	293	646	86	34	41	249	177	298	.329	.398

John Castino dived onto the Metropolitan Stadium dirt and speared a ball off the bat of Yankee star Dave Winfield. It was a fantastic defensive play. Twins fans immediately leapt to their feet with rousing cheers for the third baseman.

Castino didn't know what to do. No one had ever given him a standing ovation for a fielding play. Someone yelled, "You're supposed to tip your cap!" John did, and the crowd cheered louder. It was a moment that stood out in a career that was all too short for the player who grew up in suburban Chicago.

John Castino was a Cubs fan during his childhood. He admired players like Ernie Banks, Ron Santo, and Randy Hundley.

The Minnesota Twins drafted Castino in 1976, taking him in the third round out of Rollins College in Orlando. For three years he toiled in the minor leagues, first in Wisconsin Rapids (Wisconsin), then Orlando (Florida), and finally Visalia (California), before making the Twins squad out of 1979 spring training.

In his rookie season, after hitting .285 in 148 games, Castino was named Co-Rookie of the Year for the American League, sharing the honor with Alfredo Griffin.

John Castino loves baseball. His fondest memories concern the joy of playing in legendary parks like Yankee Stadium. But more than anything else, what John liked were the games themselves.

While he doesn't miss the travel or even the locker-room banter, Castino does miss the individual battles that major-league baseball afforded: getting the big hit to win a game; making a great defensive play to ice a victory. He was a slick-fielding third baseman who could hit for average and had some power.

The Twins teams of the late 1970s and early 1980s were not very successful on the field. Owner Calvin Griffith was battling with trying to put as good a team on the field as possible at the lowest possible price.

Castino recalled events that unfolded from a game in which Jerry Koosman was pitching for the Twins against Detroit. With a runner on first, Koosman forgot to go into his stretch and launched into a full windup. The runner easily stole second, and the Twins eventually lost the game.

Back in the Twin Cities, Griffith was livid. He called his team a bunch of scabs. By this time, Castino was a leader on the team, and he reacted to Calvin's comments by telling teammates that Calvin had built the team, and that if he didn't like what was happening, it was a reflection on his efforts.

Griffith responded by saying that if Castino were a man, he'd come and tell him what he thought face to face. Word got back to John, and when the team returned from the road trip, he went to Calvin's office.

Griffith said, "Castino, you're the most overrated, overpaid player in the league."

Castino answered, "Why don't you trade me, then. A lot of teams would want me."

"Because," Griffith countered, "you're the best third baseman in the league, and I'm not letting you go!"

Calvin's convoluted logic left John somewhat bewildered. While most stories about Griffith start and end with the owner's tight wallet, Castino made it plain that he admired and liked Griffith in spite of his frugality.

Castino's best season came in 1980. He batted .302 with thirteen homers and sixty-four RBIs while playing stellar defense. The next year he led the American League in triples with nine.

But 1981 ended on a sad note that foreshadowed the end of John's career. While diving for a ball near the end of the season, Castino suffered a hairline fracture of a vertebrate. After the season, spinal fusion was performed in his back.

Then, Gary Gaetti began his first full season with the Twins in 1982. The team tried Gaetti unsuccessfully as an outfielder. Searching for a place for Castino's potent bat in the order, Manager Billy Gardner asked whether he could play anywhere else. John offered to move to second, and Gaetti wound up on third.

After his fused-disc procedure, Castino played for two more full seasons and part of a third before chronic back pain forced him to give up the game he loved. He retired with a lifetime batting average of .278 with forty-one home runs and 249 RBIs.

Lessons learned in baseball stuck with him as he entered the business world after earning a master's degree from St. Thomas University in St. Paul, Minnesota.

"Baseball taught me commitment to goals and the importance of believing in yourself," John said. His only regrets are the injuries that shortened his career.

John lives in Edina, Minnesota, and works as an investment financial planner. His back still bothers him every day; he works from a special chair. He's married and has three children. One son followed John's footsteps to Rollins College, where he is captain of the 2001 baseball squad.

John still plays some amateur baseball, not as a fielder, but as a pitcher. It's not as stressful on his back, and it allows him to still enjoy the game he loves.

Dave Goltz

Bats: Right
Throws: Right
Height: 6' 4"
Weight: 200 lbs.
Born: June 29, 1949, in Minnesota

YEAR	TEAM	LG	ERA	W	L	Sv	G	IP	H	R	ER	BB	K	AVG. A
1972	*Min*	*AL*	*2.67*	*3*	*3*	*1*	*15*	*91.0*	*75*	*30*	*27*	*26*	*38*	*.224*
1973	*Min*	*AL*	*5.25*	*6*	*4*	*1*	*32*	*106.1*	*138*	*68*	*62*	*32*	*65*	*.318*
1974	*Min*	*AL*	*3.25*	*10*	*10*	*1*	*28*	*174.1*	*192*	*81*	*63*	*45*	*89*	*.282*
1975	*Min*	*AL*	*3.67*	*14*	*14*	*0*	*32*	*243.0*	*235*	*112*	*99*	*72*	*128*	*.255*
1976	*Min*	*AL*	*3.36*	*14*	*14*	*0*	*36*	*249.1*	*239*	*113*	*93*	*91*	*133*	*.254*
1977	*Min*	*AL*	*3.36*	*20*	*11*	*0*	*39*	*303.0*	*284*	*129*	*113*	*91*	*186*	*.247*
1978	*Min*	*AL*	*2.49*	*15*	*10*	*0*	*29*	*220.1*	*209*	*72*	*61*	*67*	*116*	*.253*
1979	*Min*	*AL*	*4.16*	*14*	*13*	*0*	*36*	*250.2*	*282*	*124*	*116*	*69*	*132*	*.288*
1980	*LA*	*NL*	*4.31*	*7*	*11*	*1*	*35*	*171.1*	*198*	*91*	*82*	*59*	*91*	*.299*
1981	*LA*	*NL*	*4.09*	*2*	*7*	*1*	*26*	*77.0*	*83*	*35*	*35*	*25*	*48*	*.288*
1982	*LA*	*NL*	*4.91*	*0*	*1*	*0*	*2*	*3.2*	*6*	*4*	*2*	*0*	*3*	*.353*
1982	*Cal*	*AL*	*4.08*	*8*	*5*	*3*	*28*	*86.0*	*82*	*43*	*39*	*32*	*49*	*.252*
1983	*Cal*	*AL*	*6.22*	*0*	*6*	*0*	*15*	*63.2*	*81*	*48*	*44*	*37*	*27*	*.315*
			ERA	*W*	*L*	*Sv*	*G*	*IP*	*H*	*R*	*ER*	*BB*	*K*	*AVG. A*
			3.69	*113*	*109*	*8*	*353*	*2,039.2*	*2,104*	*950*	*836*	*646*	*1,105*	*.269*

On a summer day in 1966 the sharp pop of a baseball smacking into a mitt echoed through the backyards of the small Minnesota town of Rothsay. It was not an unusual sound, especially in the Goltz backyard, where Dave threw occasionally.

But today was different. Angelo Guiliani, Billy Kane, and Johnny Mauer were watching the tall, lanky right-hander throw. The three were Twins scouts who operated the Twins baseball clinics.

Scouts had hoped to watch Goltz pitch in an American Legion tournament, but Dave's team had been upset and eliminated. This called for a visit to the Goltz home by the three Twins representatives.

The visit paid off. After graduating from Rothsay High School the following year, Dave was drafted by the Twins in the fourth round. He immediately was sent to Sarasota in the Gulf Coast Rookie League and began a tour of duty with various minor-league teams.

In 1968, he was in the Northern League in St. Cloud. Ironically, he stayed in the basement of a future teammate's parents. Goltz and that player, Greg Thayer, would eventually both pitch for the Twins.

Every fall Dave went back to school at Moorhead State College in Moorhead, Minnesota. In the spring of 1969, Goltz made the AA team in Charlotte, North Carolina. He was supposed to pitch opening night and was twice rained out.

Then he got a call from his army reserve unit. Dave had been called to active duty. He spent the next months in Ft. Benning, Georgia, and Ft. Rucker, Alabama.

That took care of the 1969 season as far as baseball was concerned. Late in the year, Dave was able to come back and take part in the Instructional League.

Goltz was assigned to AA Orlando after 1970 spring training. But in his first game, he pulled a muscle in his elbow and had to spend most of the summer in rehabilitation. By the time his arm came around, the season was pretty much over.

Goltz went back home and returned to school as he rested his arm. He was stronger in 1971. This time he was sent to Orlando again out of spring training, but to Class A.

About halfway through the season he moved up to Lynchberg, Virginia, a higher classification, where he went 14-3 with a seven-inning no-hitter. Then, it was to the Instructional League again in the fall.

Goltz reported to AAA at Tacoma in 1972. In July he finally got the call to the big league. He became the first native Minnesotan originally signed by the Twins to reach their major-league roster.

Dave would spend eight years with the Twins. As the fifth-winningest pitcher in Minnesota history, he would never have a record below .500. His teams in those years generally finished right around .500.

Goltz went 20-11 in 1977. One game from that year stands out in Dave's memory. "Against Boston I threw a one-hitter, and the only hit was a broken-bat single by Jim Rice, about six to eight inches out of the shortstop's reach."

When asked about his pitches, Dave replied, "I had a fastball that sank. It was a ground ball pitch. It was one of those pitches where they knew it was coming and would swing at it and still hit a ground ball.

"I threw a knuckle-curve in high school as a change up. The more I fooled around with it, the better I could control it. I could make it move various ways by the angle of my wrist. I could make it break away from a lefty like a screwball, or into him if I held it the other way, or straight down.

"That took a lot of pressure off the elbow, because you didn't twist it or cut it. You just pushed down. I could throw it at several different speeds and it moved a lot.

"It became a real important pitch to me, but the fastball was still prime. Later on I developed a fastball that ran, like a cut fastball. So, I had one that ran into a lefty and into a righty."

The arm speed and arm location at release were pretty much the same for the fastball and the knuckle-curve, making it even tougher to hit.

Dave went to for the Dodgers after the 1979 season.

"I didn't want to leave the Twins," Goltz said. "I was very comfortable there. I liked what the team had. Mauch was quite a motivator, he could get players to play a couple of levels above what they did for other teams. We had a good core of young players.

"But the Twins didn't even make me an offer. We talked with a lot of clubs and had it down to four. Three West Coast teams, San Diego, L.A. and California, and I really liked Milwaukee. That's basically where I wanted to go. Out of the clear blue my agent called and told me the Dodgers had made an offer, and he signed me with them."

The contract was for three million dollars over six years. But Dave was mystified why the Dodgers did it. They had five or six starting pitchers already. Manager Tommy LaSorda was in Japan with an All-Star team and apparently wasn't consulted about the trade.

Tommy wound up with three players that year with whom he'd had no role in obtaining: Goltz, Jay Johnstone, and Don Stanhouse. It translated into a bad situation for the pitcher from Rothsay.

"We got off on the wrong foot right away. I don't think he wanted us there, and I didn't want to be there," said Goltz.

Two sub-par years with the Dodgers resulted for Goltz before they released him in 1982. After several tryouts, his old skipper, Gene Mauch, now with the Angels, came to his rescue. The Angels needed pitching. Dave signed with California.

The Angels won the Western Division that year with Goltz pitching the clinching game against Texas. He relieved in one playoff against Milwaukee. California won the first two games at home and needed only one of three in County Stadium to go to the World Series. They lost all three.

After fifteen games in 1983, things didn't go well for Goltz.

"It was time, and I got released. I had two other teams call and want me to play. But I knew at that time that I was done. That extra little desire that you need just wasn't there anymore."

Dave's family was growing up, and he knew it was time to return to Minnesota. "I got into real estate in Fergus Falls for a while and then I got into insurance, and I've been doing that ever since.

"Baseball was a boyhood dream come true. I had the opportunity to make a success of it. It gave me the ability to travel and see a lot of the country. I met many interesting people."

Until his children became involved in sports, Dave did some umpiring for high school, VFW, and college games. In recent years, not wanting to miss his children's activities, he gave up officiating.

Dave and his wife, Sheri, live in Fergus Falls, Minnesota, and have three children. One son lives in Cambridge, Minnesota, a daughter is at St. Cloud State University, and a son is in high school.

Craig Kusick

Bats: Right
Throws: Right
Height: 6' 3"
Weight: 210 lbs.
Born: September 30, 1948, in Wisconsin

YEAR	TEAM	LG	AVG	G	AB	R	H	2B	3B	HR	RBI	BB	K	OBP	SLG
1973	*Min*	*AL*	*.250*	*15*	*48*	*4*	*12*	*2*	*0*	*0*	*4*	*7*	*9*	*.357*	*.292*
1974	*Min*	*AL*	*.239*	*76*	*201*	*36*	*48*	*7*	*1*	*8*	*26*	*35*	*36*	*.353*	*.403*
1975	*Min*	*AL*	*.237*	*57*	*156*	*14*	*37*	*8*	*0*	*6*	*27*	*21*	*23*	*.346*	*.404*
1976	*Min*	*AL*	*.259*	*109*	*266*	*33*	*69*	*13*	*0*	*11*	*36*	*35*	*44*	*.344*	*.432*
1977	*Min*	*AL*	*.254*	*115*	*268*	*34*	*68*	*12*	*0*	*12*	*45*	*49*	*60*	*.370*	*.433*
1978	*Min*	*AL*	*.173*	*77*	*191*	*23*	*33*	*3*	*2*	*4*	*20*	*37*	*38*	*.305*	*.272*
1979	*Min*	*AL*	*.241*	*24*	*54*	*8*	*13*	*4*	*0*	*3*	*6*	*3*	*11*	*.281*	*.481*
1979	*Tor*	*AL*	*.204*	*24*	*54*	*3*	*11*	*1*	*0*	*2*	*7*	*7*	*7*	*.302*	*.333*
			AVG	*G*	*AB*	*R*	*H*	*2B*	*3B*	*HR*	*RBI*	*BB*	*K*	*OBP*	*SLG*
			.235	*497*	*1,238*	*155*	*291*	*50*	*3*	*46*	*171*	*194*	*228*	*.342*	*.392*

As a youth, Craig Kusick would sit in the bleachers in County Stadium in his hometown of Milwaukee, Wisconsin, and watch his favorite team: the Milwaukee Braves. Hank Aaron, Joe Adcock, and other stars inspired his dreams of someday playing on that field.

Kusick graduated from a Milwaukee suburb, Greenfield High School, in 1966 and then attended the University of Wisconsin at LaCrosse. The Twins signed him out of LaCrosse in 1970. They assigned him to play rookie ball for the St. Cloud (Minnesota) Rox in the Northern League, a sixty-game schedule.

The next year Craig moved to Lynchberg, Virginia, for his first full season as a Class A ballplayer. He moved up to AA ball at Charlotte, North Carolina, in 1972. The following year he advanced to AAA Tacoma, Washington.

At 6' 3" and 210 pounds, the brawny Kusick exhibited a long ball stroke that the Twins hoped would be transferred to the major leagues. He was called up to the "bigs" in September of the 1973 season.

Craig stuck with the Twins in 1974 and played in seventy-six games, batting .239 with eight homers. He split his playing time between first base, pinch-hitting and designated-hitting.

Through the 1970s, Kusick played on teams that usually flirted on either side of .500. But the 1975 season generated considerable excitement as the Twins were in the race for their division title in September.

"It was us against the White Sox and Kansas City, all three of us were fighting for the pennant at that time. That was fun baseball," Craig recalled.

The Twins didn't gain the title that year. They faded to fourth under skipper Frank Quilici.

During the off-seasons of 1973, 1974, and 1976, he played winter ball in Venezuela, the first two years in Maricabo and then in Maracay.

He noted, "In Venezuela my family and I were afforded the opportunity of a cultural exchange as well as experiencing playing baseball in a foreign country."

In 1977 Kusick saw his most big-league action. He appeared in 115 games for the Twins that season. He also put up his best numbers with twelve homers and forty-five RBIs.

The Twins put Kusick on waivers in 1979, and Toronto purchased him. Craig agreed to report to the Blue Jays because the manager was Ray Hartsfield, who was the skipper in Hawaii when Kusick played for Tacoma in the Pacific Coast League. Hartsfield, a "fan" of Kusick's, wanted Craig to join him in Toronto.

Kusick's career in Toronto was a short one, but for him was marked by one memorable experience. He pitched three innings and did well in a blowout game.

"Unfortunately, we were new to the league and really bad. The Blue Jays cleaned house and got rid of all the managers and coaches. I was released and became a free agent. San Diego called up and asked if I'd be interested in being a kind of player-coach in Hawaii in 1980."

Kusick reported to the Islanders with an eye to lands farther east. At that time Hawaii was viewed as a kind of steppingstone to Japan. Former Twin Charley Manuel advised that it would be a good move for Craig.

It almost happened, but only two Americans could play at one time on a Japanese team, and there just wasn't room for Kusick. He did come close enough to be told to get a passport to Japan; however, they backed off and chose someone else.

Craig went back to the Hawaiian Islanders, a San Diego Padres' farm club, in 1981. But he was not the property of the Padres. The Islanders owned him directly.

Kusick was a player-coach again and enjoyed the fun, relaxed atmosphere in Hawaii. He did have one of the highlights of his professional career while playing for the Islanders.

"We were playing in Albuquerque. I was the leadoff hitter in the sixth inning. I had walked my first two times up. We were down about 6-2. I led off with a double. When I came up the second time in the inning with the bases loaded, I hit a grand-slam home run. That put us up 7-6," Kusick recalled.

"When I came up again in the seventh, I hit a three-run home run. In the eighth inning I came up with the bases loaded and hit a double to clear the bases. That was ten RBIs.

"In the ninth inning there were runners on first and second, and I hit a ball to deep center field. Mookie Wilson jumped over the fence and caught it to end the inning."

Craig recalled other personal highlights that came earlier during his years in the majors. "A few games, I hit a couple of home runs in them. I was never a full-time player, but there would be times when I'd play three or four games in a row.

"When Gene Mauch came in as manager in 1976, I was primarily a platoon player against left-handed pitchers, mostly at DH or first base, sometimes a little outfield." In 1977 he led the Twins with ten pinch-hits.

Craig fondly remembered hitting home runs against some of baseball's best. "I hit home runs against guys like Jim Palmer, Nolan Ryan, Mike Cuellar, Dave McNally, those were big highlights.

"I particularly enjoyed hitting a home run in Yankee Stadium before one of their packed houses there. It was off Ron Guidry the year he won the Cy Young.

"I remember Mark Latell, he was a reliever for Kansas City. I hit a home run off him late in a game there, I think we beat 'em. Until Chris Chambliss hit the home run in the playoffs off him, mine was the only home run he'd given up all year.

"Those were big, but coming back to Milwaukee and playing in front of a large number of relatives—including my parents, who lived in Florida and came up for a number of series there—coming back to Milwaukee and playing was a real thrill," said Kusick.

"I also tied a major-league record there by getting hit three times in one game. I wasn't crowding the plate; it was a left-handed pitcher. He threw a real hard-breaking slider that broke way inside.

"The first one hit me on my back foot on my toe. The next time up he hit me on my back leg on my shin. The next time on my back leg on my thigh. My only regret is that I didn't get hit a fourth time to set the record."

Craig retired after the 1981 season. He had opportunities to continue but had played twelve professional years and, with two young school-age children, Kusick had to decide whether to stay in baseball or go into teaching, which was what he was licensed to do.

Mexican teams and others called. But the road trips and conditions of minor-league baseball didn't appeal to Craig anymore. He chose to teach.

Craig accepted a contract to teach at Rosemount (Minnesota) High School in 1982, and has been there since. He's coached football, both boys and girls basketball, and began his eleventh year as head baseball coach in the spring of 2001.

"The playing part of baseball was very stressful," Kusick said. "It becomes a business real fast. You have only a short window of opportunity. Getting to the major leagues is very difficult, but staying there is even harder. There's always some young guy on your steps waiting to take your place if you slip just a little bit."

Baseball meant a lot to Kusick. "It was something a kid dreams of when he's little, to get to the major leagues and play there. To be able to do it, to have the gift and opportunity to be able to do that kind of thing and to be able to play for a period of time, was a huge thrill in my life. It was a dream come true. Sometimes I had to pinch myself. It was a special, special time for my family and me.

"I was able to live the dream, and then when it was over, go into my profession of teaching, which is what I had planned on doing with my life. It's been a pretty good life."

As he reflected on his pro career, Craig appreciated that he was part of the celebrity life, and that he got to meet people like Richard Nixon and many Hall of Fame players.

It takes a lot of luck and support to become a major-league baseball player, and Craig acknowledged his appreciation for the opportunities provided to him by the Twins.

"In particular, I'm thankful to the Calvin Griffith family, George Brophy, Jim Rantz, Tom Mee, and Herb Carneal, to name just a few. They were instrumental to helping me, a young college graduate, grow and mature into a professional athlete.

"Playing and being coached under the tutelage of Gene Mauch and Frank Quilici has allowed me to pass on my professional experiences as I teach my high-school players the finer points of the game of baseball.

"I learned from some of the best teachers in the game."

Craig and his wife have two grown children and reside in Apple Valley, Minnesota. Their son, Craig, was signed in the winter of 2001 to play arena league football.

Rich Reese

Bats: Left
Throws: Left
Height: 6' 3"
Weight: 185 lbs.
Born: September 29, 1941, in Ohio

YEAR	TEAM	LG	AVG	G	AB	R	H	2B	3B	HR	RBI	BB	K	OBP	SLG
1964	Min	AL	.000	10	7	0	0	0	0	0	0	0	1	.000	.000
1965	Min	AL	.286	14	7	0	2	1	0	0	0	2	2	.444	.429
1966	Min	AL	.000	3	2	0	0	0	0	0	0	1	2	.333	.000
1967	Min	AL	.248	95	101	13	25	5	0	4	20	8	17	.300	.416
1968	Min	AL	.259	126	332	40	86	15	2	4	28	18	36	.301	.352
1969	Min	AL	.322	132	419	52	135	24	4	16	69	23	57	.362	.513
1970	Min	AL	.261	153	501	63	131	15	5	10	56	48	70	.332	.371
1971	Min	AL	.219	120	329	40	72	8	3	10	39	20	35	.270	.353
1972	Min	AL	.218	132	197	23	43	3	2	5	26	25	27	.305	.330
1973	Det	AL	.137	59	102	10	14	1	0	2	4	7	17	.193	.206
1973	Min	AL	.174	22	23	7	4	1	1	1	3	6	6	.345	.435
			AVG	G	AB	R	H	2B	3B	HR	RBI	BB	K	OBP	SLG
			.253	866	2,020	248	512	73	17	52	245	158	270	.312	.348

It was August 3, 1969, and Baltimore pitcher Dave McNally was on a roll. He had won seventeen games in a row, tying a record. Now he had the lead against the Twins. The sacks were crowded when Rich Reese, left-handed pinch hitter, strode to the plate to face the Orioles' lefty.

Reese drove a shot to left-center over the fence at Metropolitan Stadium to propel the Twins to a 5-2 win over the Orioles. Rich would hit three pinch-hit grand slams in his career for a major-league record. He still holds that record alone in the American League. Two other players, both National Leaguers, have achieved the same mark to share the record.

It was heady stuff for the farm boy from Deshler, Ohio, who grew up following the Detroit Tigers and idolizing Al Kaline.

Reese signed with the Tigers in 1961. They sent him to Thomasville, Georgia, of the Georgia/Florida League, to play for the Tigers' minor-league affiliate. Rich moved up the same year to the Alabama/Florida League in Montgomery, Alabama.

The Twins drafted Reese off the Tigers' roster in the fall of 1962. This put him on the major-league forty-man roster; thus he went to 1963 spring training with the Twins. From there Rich was sent to Bismarck in the Northern League. He continued working his way through the minors with stops at Wilson and Charlotte, North Carolina, and AAA in Denver.

Reese played in short stints with the Twins in 1964, 1965, and 1966, totaling sixteen at-bats in the three years.

In 1965 Rich made the team out of spring training but was sent down when teams cut their rosters from twenty-eight to twenty-five players. He was recalled late in the season. Rich's fourteen game appearances in 1965 earned him a two-fifths share of the World Series payoff.

Reese's break came when he made the Twins roster in 1967 and appeared in ninety-five games. Early in his career, the slick-fielding first baseman was used as a defensive replacement and pinch hitter.

Rich explained his philosophy of pinch hitting. "Just be prepared, be ready and don't take too many pitches. Go up there hacking."

The 1968 season offered Reese even greater opportunity after Harmon Killebrew suffered a badly torn hamstring at the 1968 All-Star Game. The slugger's absence opened up more playing time for Rich, who took over for the injured star. After that All-Star break, Reese hit over .300 for the balance of the season, and he established himself as a valuable Twin and insurance for Killebrew.

That was the year of the expansion draft. The Twins decided to protect Reese in case Harmon didn't completely recover from his injury. Rich hadn't been on the protected list prior to Killebrew's being hurt.

Reese had his best season in 1969, batting .322 with sixteen home runs and sixty-nine RBIs. At year's end, Rich talked contract with Calvin Griffith, for those were before the days of sports agents.

"Son, you had a great year," the owner intoned. "Do it again and you'll be a bona fide big leaguer."

"I loved Calvin," Reese said. "He was a tough negotiator and had the image of being a tightwad, but I didn't hold it against him. He was just trying to make a bottom line. He had a business and a lot of family living off of him. I respected the man."

Reese's manager in Denver, Cal Ermer, replaced Sam Mele at the Twins helm in mid-1967.

"Cal Ermer was a great manager," Rich recalled. "He taught me a lot in one year about getting to the big leagues and staying there."

Rich also played for skipper Billy Martin. "He was a great baseball manager," Reese said. "But he had a Napoleon attitude. It was Billy's way or no way."

Under Ermer's tenure another Baltimore game stands out in Reese's memory. "Dave Boswell was pitching, we had a 8-2 lead and we blew it. They went ahead 9-8, and in the bottom of the ninth they brought in their closer, Moe Drabowsky.

"Cesar Tovar hit a topper off the plate and beat it out. Then I pinch hit. This was a Thursday afternoon, and everyone was down because we had blown a big lead. He threw me two breaking balls, and I pulled them both foul.

"Their pitching coach, Harry Brecheen, went out to talk to Drabowsky. The next pitch was a high fastball, and I hit it into the bullpen over Frank Robinson's head. We won 10-9. That game stands out to me because of the situation and the fact that 'you are never out of a game.'"

The Twins had many memorable games with Baltimore, including two A.L. Championship Series in 1969 and 1970. Unfortunately, the Twins were swept in both.

Rich remembered, "It was fate in 1969. Jim Perry pitched a great game in the first one. Mark Belanger hit the foul pole for a homer off Perry and then Baltimore tied it in the bottom of the ninth with Boog Powell's homerun. The Orioles won in twelve innings when Paul Blair bunted in the winning run."

One of Reese's teammates, pitcher Dave Boswell, also shared a vivid memory of that fateful game. "When Blair came up in the ninth, it got quiet. People don't realize it, but you can hear things pretty well on the field, your teammates, the players in the other dugout. But no one was saying anything.

"When Blair came to the plate, I knew something was up. I jumped to the first step of the dugout, so did Billy Martin. Our third baseman was back. There were two outs with a runner on third. Blair dragged a bunt down the third baseline and beat it out."

It was Boswell himself who climbed the hill the following day as the Twins suffered another tough defeat in extra innings.

Reese recalled, "The next day Boswell pitched a great game, too. We lost 1-0 in the eleventh inning. It was fate. They had Jim Palmer when we came home, and we lost convincingly. It was a three-of-five series then."

Reese's playing time diminished in 1971 and 1972, and his batting average dipped. He was sold to Detroit before the 1973 season. After only fifty-nine games, the Tigers released him, and the Twins picked him up again. He finished the season and his career with Minnesota that year.

Rich reflected on how baseball is different from his days in the big leagues. "The money has obviously changed. The respect for the game has changed. I cannot fathom, the way I grew up, that people make all this money and yet they have to be paid for autographs. They don't continue to build the fan base.

"It is obvious as fans of teams you can no longer identify with the roster inasmuch as free agency moves players every year.

"The owners and the players had better come together on some mutual ground. Free agency has gone too far. We have lost the loyalty of the fans to our teams.

"When I was young and rooted for the Tigers, the same players were consistently there. Today, players have the opportunity to get what the market bears. It is the wealthy owners who do not relate to bottom line responsibility.

"That is why Calvin had to get out, bless his soul; it was his only way of making a living. When I played, you couldn't go anywhere else. You had a contract."

Major-league baseball is a tough grind with ups and downs. Rich enjoyed "the camaraderie with your teammates, the fact that you were at the elite of the sport."

After his playing days ended, Rich started work as a salesman covering the Dakotas and Minnesota for Jim Beam Brands. Eventually he advanced up the company corporate ladder and moved to the home office in 1981. He is now president and chief executive officer of Jim Beam Brands and has been with them for twenty-six years.

Rich lives in the suburbs of Chicago with his wife, Marit, who was born in Brainerd, Minnesota.

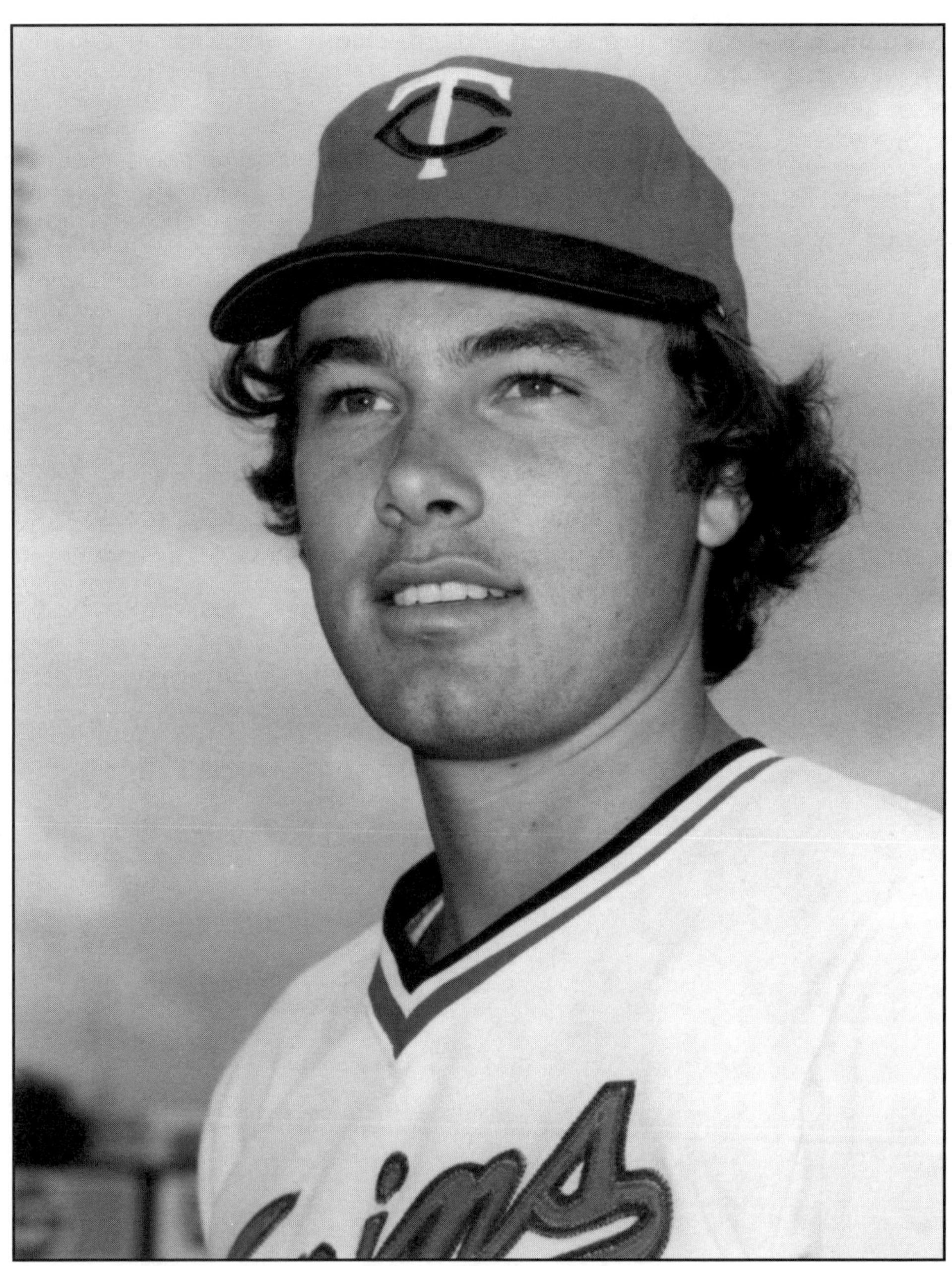

Gary Serum

Bats: Right
Throws: Right
Height: 6' 1"
Weight: 180 lbs.
Born: October 24, 1956, in North Dakota

YEAR	TEAM	LG	ERA	W	L	Sv	G	IP	H	R	ER	BB	K	AVG. A
1977	*Min*	*AL*	*4.37*	*0*	*0*	*0*	*8*	*22.2*	*22*	*11*	*11*	*10*	*14*	*.268*
1978	*Min*	*AL*	*4.10*	*9*	*9*	*1*	*34*	*184.1*	*188*	*88*	*84*	*44*	*80*	*.266*
1979	*Min*	*AL*	*6.61*	*1*	*3*	*0*	*20*	*64.0*	*93*	*47*	*47*	*20*	*31*	*.354*
			ERA	*W*	*L*	*Sv*	*G*	*IP*	*H*	*R*	*ER*	*BB*	*K*	*AVG. A*
			4.72	*10*	*12*	*1*	*62*	*271.0*	*303*	*146*	*142*	*74*	*125*	*.288*

Only three players have ever been signed out of a Twins open tryout camp and made it to the major leagues: Jerry Terrell, Charlie Walters, and Gary Serum.

Serum was eighteen years old in 1975, fresh from Alexandria (Minnesota) High School and the Minnesota State Baseball tournament. Twins Director of Scouting George Brophy saw him pitch in the tourney and suggested that Gary attend the Twins tryout camp.

Around 500 attended the open camp, including a teammate from Alexandria. Gary was number 388. He went through speed timings and other drills and was invited back for a second day. Gary pitched in a simulated game and impressed the Twins.

Later Serum considered that the scouts were looking for players at particular positions and that good pitchers were always in demand. The Twins signed the youngster from Alexandria and sent him to the their rookie team in Elizabethton, Tennessee, in the Appalachian League.

"I was eighteen years old, flew into Elizabethton, and pretty much had to fend for myself," Gary related. "There wasn't any housing or anything lined up for me. The team gave us $500 a month."

"We either had to find a couple of other teammates and share an apartment or find a family that wanted to take in a player. I stayed with a family."

The life of a young minor-league ball player could be exciting, but there was routine as well.

"On the road," Serum said, "the games got over at ten or eleven at night. We might go to a bar for an hour, then sleep in until 10:00 A.M. We'd get up and hang around the motel pool, play cards or maybe go to a movie if we had money. At 4:00 P.M. we'd get on the bus and go to the ballpark."

Rueben Nathe, a Twins farm hand in 1963, elaborated on the daily schedule during a homestand. "We got up and ate around 10:00 A.M. Then we'd have a couple of hours off until about 2:00 P.M., when we'd eat again."

"About three in the afternoon we'd go to the ball park for warm ups, batting practice, or running about three-thirty or four. The game was usually at seven or seven-thirty. When it was over, about eleven, we'd go eat again. Each day was pretty much the same."

The bus trips were often long, and the buses weren't always air-conditioned.

"But," Nathe added, "you do what you had to do if you wanted to play ball.

"I got $400.00 a month and some extras," Rube chuckled. "We got five dollars to be photographed for baseball cards."

The rookie league was well underway when Gary got there, and his pitching time was limited. Serum was sent back to Elizabethton in 1976 for more experience. About halfway through the season, he was moved up to Class A at Wisconsin Rapids.

Serum went to 1977 spring training in Orlando. Johnny Goryl, manager of the Twins' AA farm team in Orlando, suggested to Gary that, if he switched to becoming a relief pitcher, Goryl could put him on the AA team.

Gary jumped at the chance to move up a class. He started the year as a reliever with the Orlando club, but his stay in Florida proved short. In June of that season, Serum was sent up to AAA ball with the Twins affiliate in Tacoma, Washington.

Again, the assignment was of a brief duration. On July 17, Tacoma was on the road in Phoenix. As Gary and his roommate relaxed in their hotel room, the message light flashed on the phone.

Gary's roommate checked the message. He told Serum, "You better listen to this. It says, 'Holly to Tacoma, Serum to Oakland.'"

It took a moment for the meaning to sink in. The Minnesota Twins were in Oakland. He, Gary Serum, just twenty years old, was being called to the major leagues. Jeff Holly was being sent to the minors.

Serum went immediately to Oakland and the Twins' hotel. The first sight that greeted him was Rod Carew getting into a cab. When Serum entered the hotel, Tony Oliva met him and helped him make arrangements.

Gary was in awe. He was in the "show." He was playing with, and being mentored by, his childhood heroes.

He made his big-league debut on July 22, 1977, in the Seattle Kingdome in relief of Gregg Zahn. Used sparingly by the Twins that summer, Serum appeared in eight games and pitched just over twenty-two innings. He recorded no decisions and had an ERA of 4.37.

That was enough for an invite to the major-league camp in 1978 spring training. Serum was slated for long relief, but a slow start by the Twins and a nine-game losing streak had skipper Gene Mauch searching for an answer. He looked to Serum.

Sent out to the mound as a starter, the right-hander responded with a victory. He was in the starting rotation the rest of the season. Gary had some memorable games that summer, including a two-hit shutout against the Toronto Blue Jays, a July Fourth 4-1 win against the Milwaukee Brewers, and a Camera Day victory in Kansas City over Paul Splittorf.

"One hitter I really had trouble with was Ken Singleton," Gary said. "I remember one game he hit me for a double, single, and a home run. His fourth time up I just threw the ball into the dirt four times."

Serum finished the year 9-9 with a 4.11 ERA on a team that went 73-89. He appeared in thirty-four games, starting twenty-three of them.

Several factors led to a diminished role for Gary in 1979. Midway through the previous season, the Twins had signed closer Mike Marshall. Marshall was given a lot of work, pitching over 140 innings in 1979. Also, the Twins traded with California for right-handed pitcher Paul Hartzell. This bumped Gary from the rotation. Serum slipped to 1-3 with a 6.61 ERA in sixty-four innings.

It was back to the minors for the pitcher from Alexandria. In 1980 he was sent to the Toledo (Ohio) Mudhens in Class AAA. A highlight there was a visit from M*A*S*H* actor Jamie Farr.

Serum played for Tom Kelly and the Orlando Twins in 1981 with Gary Gaetti and Tim Laudner. They had a great year. Serum broke the Orlando record with twenty saves.

But Serum was assigned to Toledo again in 1982. He was to meet another player for breakfast when he reached that Ohio city. He pulled up in the Air Stream trailer with which he traveled and was met at the restaurant by a news-bearing player.

Gary had been traded, along with Roy Smalley, to the New York Yankees. He reported to their AAA affiliate in Columbus, Ohio, where he had a great 9-1 season.

Spring 1983 brought Serum to the Yankees' camp in Ft. Lauderdale. He didn't have an impressive spring training, however, and a new director of player personnel for the Yankees used the spring session as his primary evaluation tool.

When Gary received word that he was being sent back to AA ball, he decided to call an end to his baseball career and return to Minnesota.

Serum has since worked in sales, selling cars, insurance, and advertising. For the last ten years, he has been the owner of Serum's Restaurant in Anoka, Minnesota. He currently resides in nearby Champlin with his wife, Lori.

The player Roy Smalley dubbed as "Truth" misses the ambiance of places like Yankee Stadium and Fenway Park. He doesn't miss pitching against those powerful East Coast teams and riding in busses en route to minor-league parks.

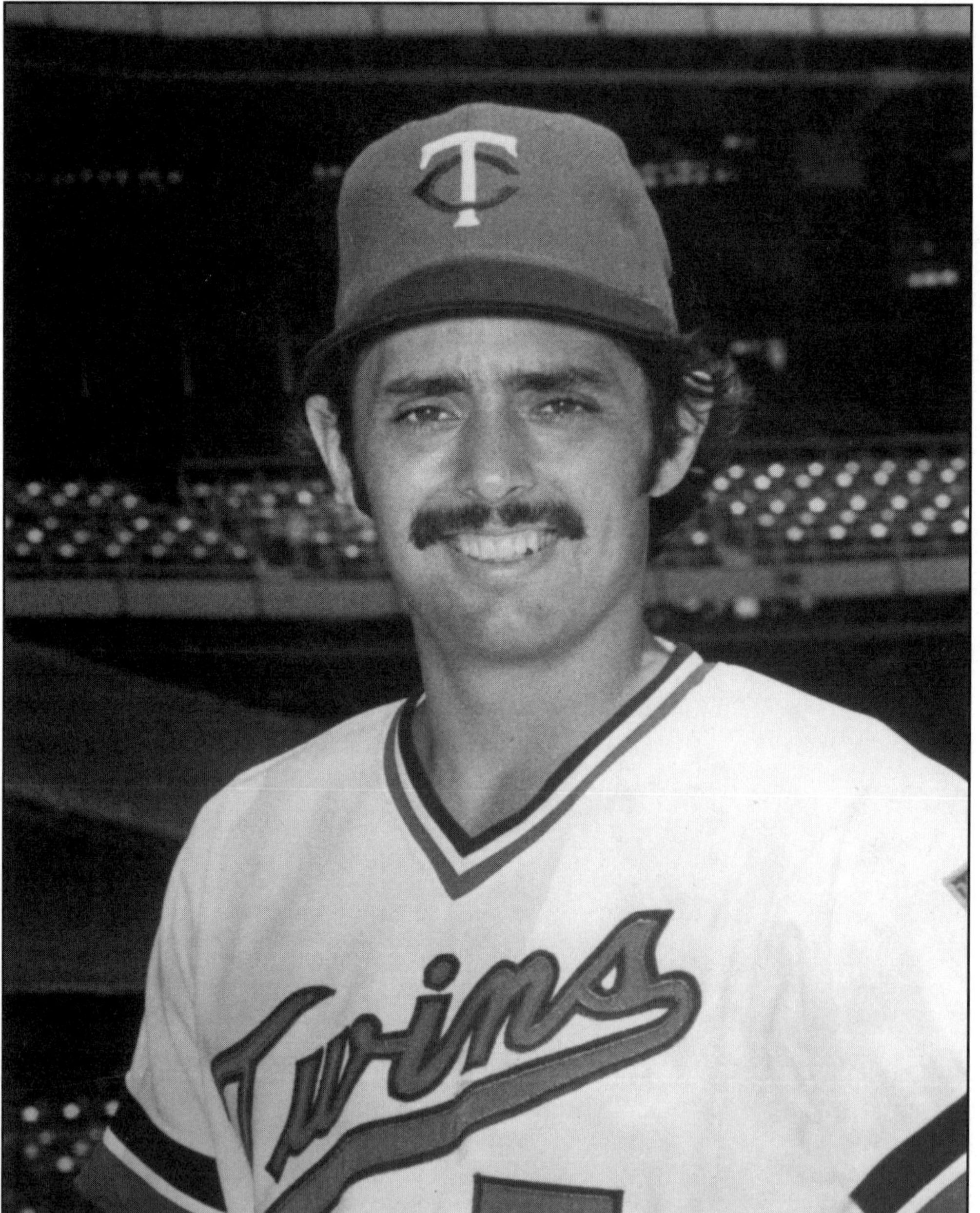
Twins

Roy Smalley

Bats: Right
Throws: Right
Height: 6' 1"
Weight: 185 lbs.
Born: October 25, 1952, in California

YEAR	TEAM	LG	AVG	G	AB	R	H	2B	3B	HR	RBI	BB	K	OBP	SLG
1975	*Tex*	*AL*	*.228*	*78*	*250*	*22*	*57*	*8*	*0*	*3*	*33*	*30*	*42*	*.309*	*.296*
1976	*Tex*	*AL*	*.225*	*41*	*129*	*15*	*29*	*2*	*0*	*1*	*8*	*29*	*27*	*.363*	*.264*
1976	*Min*	*AL*	*.271*	*103*	*384*	*46*	*104*	*16*	*3*	*2*	*36*	*47*	*79*	*.353*	*.344*
1977	*Min*	*AL*	*.231*	*150*	*584*	*93*	*135*	*21*	*5*	*6*	*56*	*74*	*89*	*.316*	*.315*
1978	*Min*	*AL*	*.273*	*158*	*586*	*80*	*160*	*31*	*3*	*19*	*77*	*85*	*70*	*.362*	*.433*
1979	*Min*	*AL*	*.271*	*162*	*621*	*94*	*168*	*28*	*3*	*24*	*95*	*80*	*80*	*.353*	*.441*
1980	*Min*	*AL*	*.278*	*133*	*486*	*64*	*135*	*24*	*1*	*12*	*63*	*65*	*63*	*.359*	*.405*
1981	*Min*	*AL*	*.263*	*56*	*167*	*24*	*44*	*7*	*1*	*7*	*22*	*31*	*24*	*.375*	*.443*
1982	*Min*	*AL*	*.154*	*4*	*13*	*2*	*2*	*1*	*0*	*0*	*0*	*3*	*4*	*.313*	*.231*
1982	*NYA*	*AL*	*.257*	*142*	*486*	*55*	*125*	*14*	*2*	*20*	*67*	*68*	*100*	*.346*	*.418*
1983	*NYA*	*AL*	*.275*	*130*	*451*	*70*	*124*	*24*	*1*	*18*	*62*	*58*	*68*	*.357*	*.452*
1984	*NYA*	*AL*	*.239*	*67*	*209*	*17*	*50*	*8*	*1*	*7*	*26*	*15*	*35*	*.286*	*.388*
1984	*ChA*	*AL*	*.170*	*47*	*135*	*15*	*23*	*4*	*0*	*4*	*13*	*22*	*30*	*.285*	*.289*
1985	*Min*	*AL*	*.258*	*129*	*388*	*57*	*100*	*20*	*0*	*12*	*45*	*60*	*65*	*.357*	*.402*
1986	*Min*	*AL*	*.246*	*143*	*459*	*59*	*113*	*20*	*4*	*20*	*57*	*68*	*80*	*.342*	*.438*
1987	*Min*	*AL*	*.275*	*110*	*309*	*32*	*85*	*16*	*1*	*8*	*34*	*36*	*52*	*.352*	*.411*
			AVG	*G*	*AB*	*R*	*H*	*2B*	*3B*	*HR*	*RBI*	*BB*	*K*	*OBP*	*SLG*
			.257	*1.653*	*5.657*	*745*	*1,454*	*244*	*25*	*163*	*694*	*771*	*908*	*.345*	*.395*

The young Californian always dreamed of being a pro baseball player. He certainly had the bloodlines for it. Roy Smalley's father, also Roy, played for ten years in the major leagues with the Cubs, Braves, and Phillies.

His mother's brother, Uncle Gene, Gene Mauch, was also a pro player and one of the finest baseball managerial minds of his time.

Roy attended high school at Westchester, a Los Angeles suburb, graduating in 1970. He spent one year playing ball at a junior college before moving on to the University of Southern California on a baseball scholarship.

Smalley had great years at U.S.C. In both 1972 and 1973, the Trojans won the College World Series. The 1973 victory came at the expense of the Dave Winfield-led Minnesota Gophers.

In January of 1974, Roy was the number-one pick in the draft. He was selected by the Texas Rangers and sent to play AA ball in Pittsfield, Massachusetts.

Smalley was a switch-hitting shortstop. He was a natural right-handed hitter who, under his father's guidance, had begun to also swing from the left side when he was fourteen.

Roy's move to AAA Spokane in 1975 was a short stay. About a month and a half into the season, the Rangers called him to the major-league club. He got 250 at-bats his rookie year and hit .228.

Two months into his second season with the Rangers, Smalley, Mike Cubbage, Bill Singer, and Jim Gideon were traded to the Twins for Bert Blyleven and Danny Thompson.

The trade united Roy with his uncle, Gene Mauch, who was in his first year as manager of the Twins. Smalley found that there were difficulties playing for a relative that other players didn't have to face.

"It was harder playing for my uncle, but it was worth it. He was the best manager I ever played for. I had fifteen managers in my thirteen years in the big leagues, and he was the best I ever saw by far. He was the smartest and best prepared.

"But it was tough for me. There were two things. There was a built-in reason for people to be derogatory towards me, and he adopted the stance that he wasn't going to be very promoting of me, positively or negatively.

"He was a terrific promoter of his players. He was very proud of his players, and I never got the benefit of that.

"Having my uncle as a manager was a double-edged sword."

1977 was a tough year for Roy in Minnesota. He hit only .231 while playing in 150 games. The cries of nepotism from Minnesota fans mounted and extended into Roy's slow start in 1978.

Then one game at Metropolitan Stadium against Detroit seemed to turn things around. "The first half of the year the fans had been really, really on me. Then all of a sudden, I caught fire, and I was hitting pretty well and playing good shortstop.

"It was a beautiful, sunny Sunday afternoon. There were a lot of people in the stands. The score was 1-1 in the bottom of the eighth, and we had a couple of guys on.

"John Hiller was the Tigers' closer. They brought him in to pitch to me. He got two quick strikes, and I hit a 0 and 2 pitch for a three-run home run; it essentially won the ball game. We had a three-run lead with a half inning to go, and Mike Marshall coming in from the bullpen.

"I can remember rounding third base and coming down the line toward home plate. I looked up into the stands that were jammed in all three decks with people. They were giving a standing ovation; they were cheering, and I thought, 'How sweet this is. It's finally over.'"

Roy continued the torrid hitting of the second half of 1978 into the first half of the next season. His play earned him a starting spot on the American League's 1978 All-Star Team as the fans voted him onto the squad. Smalley wound up hitting .271 for the year with career highs in home runs (twenty-four) and RBIs (ninety-five).

Smalley had a couple more consistent years for the Twins and then suffered an injury during the strike-shortened 1981 season. He batted only 167 times.

Just into the 1982 season, April 10, Roy and Gary Serum were traded to the New York Yankees for Ron Davis, Paul Boris, and Greg Gagne. Roy recalled, "It was difficult for me personally and for my wife. We had a young son." Christine Smalley, Roy's wife, is a native Minnesotan.

"New York is a tough place to play, but it was a great experience. I had two really good years there, '82 and '83. It got crazy in '84, and I asked to be traded."

Smalley rapped twenty homers for the Yankees his first year there and eighteen the next. But in 1984 his average dipped to .239, and the Yankees granted his desire to be traded. Roy was sent to the White Sox, but, at season's end, he was traded back to the Twins.

"It was a terrific stroke of good fortune for me," Roy explained. "Not only did I get to be in a World Series, but we were back home where we had spent most of our time as a family."

Roy was a valuable role player for the 1987 world champions. He played some infield, hit as a D.H., and hit .275 in 110 games. When the season was over, the Twins exercised an option they had, and returned Roy to the White Sox.

After spring training, the White Sox decided to go with younger, less expensive players, and Roy was cut. He had chances to catch on with other teams. But the Sox were still responsible for two more years of pay.

Roy decided to retire and let the Sox pay him. "It was kind of like free career guidance. I was going to get paid for two years whether I played or not. I was thirty-five years old, had played for thirteen years, and my family was growing up. If I had caught on with other teams, I would have had to move my family again.

"I liked the competition and trying to be good at what I consider to be the hardest thing to do in sport. I loved hitting, learning how to hit and trying to get better at it.

"Golf is the closest thing I can relate it to. When you hit the ball long, well and straight, it's a great feeling. One hundred times that is what it felt like to me to hit a baseball successfully in the big leagues."

After baseball Roy has worked mostly as a stock broker and investment advisor. Dain Rauscher employs Smalley. He ran the International Special Olympics that were held in Minnesota in 1991 and has worked in other pursuits, including a stint as a baseball analyst for ESPN. But he primarily has worked in financial businesses.

Roy and Christine Smalley live in the Twin Cities. They have a twenty-year-old son in college and seventeen-year-old twin daughters in high school.

Greg Thayer

Bats: Right
Throws: Right
Height: 5' 11"
Weight: 182 lbs.
Born: October 23, 1949, in Iowa

YEAR	TEAM	LG	ERA	W	L	Sv	G	IP	H	R	ER	BB	K	AVG. A
1978	*Min*	*AL*	*3.80*	*1*	*1*	*0*	*20*	*45.0*	*40*	*19*	*19*	*30*	*30*	*.258*
			ERA	*W*	*L*	*Sv*	*G*	*IP*	*H*	*R*	*ER*	*BB*	*K*	*AVG. A*
			3.80	*1*	*1*	*0*	*20*	*45.0*	*40*	*19*	*19*	*30*	*30*	*.258*

Greg Thayer was born in Cedar Rapids, Iowa, on October 23, 1949. He was raised in Minnesota and had a brief moment in the sun of major-league baseball.

When he was ten years old, Greg's family moved to Forest Lake, Minnesota. A few years later they relocated in St. Cloud, Minnesota. At St. Cloud Technical High School, Thayer excelled for the Tigers in football, basketball, and baseball.

One of his high school football coaches, Bill Frantti, described him as an athlete with abundant poise. "Greg had a great arm and was a strong, silent, confident competitor," Frantti said.

Thayer entered St. Cloud State University in the fall of 1968. He quarterbacked the Huskies football team for three years and pitched for the baseball team as well. In the spring of 1971, after his junior year, Greg signed with the San Francisco Giants. He spent two years in the minors and was released by the Giants.

Thayer returned to St. Cloud and then joined his brother, who was playing amateur baseball in Fargo, North Dakota. Their team won the state tournament and went on to defeat the South Dakota champions in a three-game series. Greg pitched well and was noticed by a Twins scout, who signed him to a contract.

For the next three seasons—1975, 1976, and 1977—Thayer pitched for three Twins minor-league clubs: AA Orlando and AAA Tacoma, Washington, and Toledo, Ohio.

Greg went to 1978 spring training with the Twins and made the club as a relief pitcher. His fastball was clocked in the eighties, but his screwball became his out pitch.

Thayer made his debut in the big leagues on April 7, 1978. He was playing for the team he had grown up watching as a kid. It was the team of his boyhood hero, Harmon Killebrew.

Unfortunately, it wasn't a long career in the majors. Greg pitched in twenty games for the Twins in 1978. He won one game and lost one. His ERA was a very respectable 3.80.

He remembers his victory as the highlight of his career. It came in long relief, three-plus innings against the Orioles. The Twins were trailing when Thayer entered the contest. The team rallied on a big hit by Rod Carew to claim victory over the Orioles.

Thayer is gratified that he was with the Twins long enough to visit every ballpark in the league. The Green Monster in Fenway and the monuments in center field of Yankee Stadium are permanently pressed in his memory.

Greg was sent back to the minor leagues at about the middle of the 1978 season. Two factors led to his demotion. The Twins had acquired Mike Marshall, a stellar relief pitcher known for his screwball, the same type of pitch Greg threw. Manager Gene Mauch had worked previously with Marshall.

Also, Greg suffered from control problems. His innings-to-walks ratio just wasn't good enough at thirty walks in forty-five innings.

Thayer remembered, "I was more a thrower than a pitcher."

His only regret was not being able to improve his control so that he might have stayed in the big leagues longer.

Greg spent the next season back in the Twins farm system, but it became apparent to him that he wasn't in the big club's plans for the future. He asked for a trade after the season.

The Twins obliged and sent him to the Cubs. Unfortunately, Thayer's father became ill and ultimately died during spring training. Greg missed most of training and was released by the Cubs. He hooked on with the Toronto Blue Jays and spent time in their farm system before retiring after the 1980 season.

Thayer, who had obtained a marketing degree from St. Cloud State University, returned to the St. Cloud area. He has worked in advertising and sales while living in Sauk Rapids with his wife, Chris, and their two children, a son and a daughter.

But he'll never forget the thrill of playing for the Twins, Greg related. "I got paid for doing something I loved."

Bill Zepp

Bats: Right
Throws: Right
Height: 6' 2"
Weight: 185 lbs.
Born: July 22, 1946, in Michigan

YEAR	TEAM	LG	ERA	W	L	Sv	G	IP	H	R	ER	BB	K	AVG. A
1969	Min	AL	6.75	0	0	0	4	5.1	6	7	4	4	2	.286
1970	Min	AL	3.22	9	4	2	43	151.0	154	63	54	51	64	.266
1971	Det	AL	5.12	1	1	2	16	31.2	41	20	18	17	15	.328
			ERA	W	L	Sv	G	IP	H	R	ER	BB	K	AVG. A
			3.64	10	5	4	63	188.0	201	90	76	72	81	.278

Bill Zepp shined for one year, 1970, as a pitcher for the Twins. Then, a year later it was all over, and Zepp was working for Chrysler Corporation. He's an excellent example of never taking anything for granted and being prepared for whatever the future holds.

A native of the Detroit area, Zepp attended Redford High School and graduated in 1963. He went on to the University of Michigan, where he earned both a bachelor's and a master's degree in Business Administration and Marketing.

The right-handed pitcher played baseball at Michigan. "I didn't play all that well in college," Zepp related, "and I wasn't drafted after I graduated. That's why I stayed and got my master's. But I kept playing baseball in sandlots and amateur ball after I graduated. I was getting better. Since a pro team hadn't selected me, I called scouts that had followed me before.

"A scout from Minnesota, Frank Franchi, decided I was worth a try."

In 1968, Zepp was sent to the Twins farm club at Wisconsin Rapids in the Midwest League. He moved up to Red Springs, North Carolina, the next season, but spent most of the year at Charlotte before joining the Twins at the end of the year.

Zepp commented on one of the less-than-glamorous aspects of the life of a minor-league ball player. "There were very long bus trips, and I didn't sleep very well on the bus. A couple of our trips were nine to ten hours. It was tiring and long, but it was what you had to do to get to the big leagues."

A couple days after he joined the Twins in 1969, Zepp made his debut in relief as he mopped up a blowout game.

"Every kid grew up either wanting to play with his hometown team or the Yankees," Zepp said. "I happened not to like the Yankees when I was growing up. My first game was in the old Yankee Stadium. That was a big thrill."

Zepp made the Twins out of 1970 spring training. He appeared in forty-three games, starting twenty, for the Western Division Champs.

Which was his most memorable game? "I pitched against the Tigers on Al Kaline Day. I was a native Detroiter and grew up following Kaline's career," Zepp related.

"As luck would have it, I was in the starting rotation when he had his recognition day in Tiger Stadium, and it was my turn to pitch. I went eight and one-third innings and we won 4-3. Kaline was 1-4 against me that day."

Another highlight was a shutout Zepp hurled against the Chicago White Sox.

Bill was 9-4 with a 3.22 ERA in 151 innings for the Twins in 1970. He also racked up a couple of saves and threw in two games in the American League Championship Series against Baltimore. But Bill wanted to be traded. Specifically, he wanted to go to Detroit.

"There were some personal things I had to get straightened out," Zepp explained. He hoped that being closer to home and near both his and his wife's families would help him achieve that.

The Twins traded Zepp to Detroit on March 29, 1971, for outfielder Mike Adams and pitcher Art Clifford. Bill appeared in sixteen games with the Tigers and then was sent to their minor-league team in Toledo, Ohio. While playing for the Mudhens, Bill injured his arm. "I hurt my elbow and couldn't pitch anymore. They couldn't do the surgery to repair it like they can today."

Zepp was philosophical about his career-ending injury. "You have to understand that that's one of the risks. If you don't get a sore arm at some point, you're pretty lucky. My experience in college had proved to me how tenuous your position can be.

"Everybody is a superstar in high school. I hadn't done so well in college. Then I got it back again and had the major-league career. But I knew it could be temporary. It turned out that it was."

Fortunately for Zepp, he had prepared for life without baseball. He had his degrees and had also participated in a major-league program to prepare for the days after baseball.

"In spring training of 1969, Marvin Miller of the Player's Association came around and gave a talk to the players about union benefits. One of the things he talked about was their off-season employment program," said Zepp.

"You needed to work in the off-season back then because you needed the money. A secondary reason was to get a career going so that you'd have something to fall back on."

Zepp presented himself as an excellent candidate for the program, and Miller wrote a letter of introduction for Bill to several corporations. Many responded, including Chrysler, and Bill went into their training program. He began to work for Chrysler for two to three months in the winter during breaks from baseball.

"I did that for three years until the sore arm ended my baseball career," Zepp said. "I had a foot in the door and went to work full time for Chrysler. I was trained for marketing and have done that pretty much ever since I've been there.

"Baseball was my whole life from a kid growing up through the major leagues. Wow! I got to do what I really liked to do. I was fortunate to be good enough at it to keep on and have a real nice career, albeit kind of short.

"But an awful lot of people never get a chance to go as far as I did. I was lucky to be able to play in the major leagues."

Zepp worked with Chrysler into the spring of 2001. On February 5, he received a retirement package that led to his leaving Daimler-Chrysler at the end of February after a thirty-one-year career in marketing.

Bill and his wife, Cheryl, live in the Detroit suburb of Plymouth. They have a daughter, twenty-seven, and a son, twenty-two.

Juan Berenguer

Bats: Right
Throws: Right
Height: 5' 11"
Weight: 186 lbs.
Born: November 30, 1954, in Panama

YEAR	TEAM	LG	ERA	W	L	Sv	G	IP	H	R	ER	BB	K	AVG. A
1978	NYN	NL	8.31	0	2	0	5	13.0	17	12	12	11	8	.327
1979	NYN	NL	2.93	1	1	0	5	30.2	28	13	10	12	25	.252
1980	NYN	NL	5.79	0	1	0	6	9.1	9	9	6	10	7	.250
1981	KC	AL	8.69	0	4	0	8	19.2	22	21	19	16	20	.289
1981	Tor	AL	4.31	2	9	0	12	71.0	62	41	34	35	29	.235
1982	Det	AL	6.75	0	0	0	2	6.2	5	5	5	9	8	.200
1983	Det	AL	3.14	9	5	1	37	157.2	110	58	55	71	129	.193
1984	Det	AL	3.48	11	10	0	31	168.1	146	75	65	79	118	.232
1985	Det	AL	5.59	5	6	0	31	95.0	96	67	59	48	82	.259
1986	SF	NL	2.70	2	3	4	46	73.1	64	23	22	44	72	.242
1987	Min	AL	3.94	8	1	4	47	112.0	100	51	49	47	110	.238
1988	Min	AL	3.96	8	4	2	57	100.0	74	44	44	61	99	.207
1989	Min	AL	3.48	9	3	3	56	106.0	96	44	41	47	93	.246
1990	Min	AL	3.41	8	5	0	51	100.1	85	43	38	58	77	.232
1991	Atl	NL	2.24	0	3	17	49	64.1	43	18	16	20	53	.189
1992	Atl	NL	5.13	3	1	1	28	33.1	35	22	19	16	19	.269
1992	KC	AL	5.64	1	4	0	19	44.2	42	30	28	20	26	.247
			ERA	W	L	Sv	G	IP	H	R	ER	BB	K	AVG. A
			3.90	67	62	32	490	1,205.1	1,034	576	522	604	975	.232

Juan Berenguer toed the rubber in Game 2 of the 1987 American League Championship Series against Detroit, his former team. The husky Panamanian glared in for the sign, his shaggy, dark-black hair flowing beneath his cap, his drooping mustache hiding his upper lip.

Then the right-hander reared back and fired a ninety-eight-MPH fastball past the Tiger batter for strike three. Juan pumped his fist, drew an imaginary pistol from his belt, and made a shooting motion with his hand in the direction of the Tiger dugout and his former manager, Sparky Anderson.

The Metrodome crowd screamed approval as Juan, "Señor Smoke," nailed down a 6-3 win for Twins starter Bert Blyleven in their team's quest for the pennant.

Berenguer said he wasn't trying to show anyone up that day. He was just having a good time and doing his best. Juan had spent four years playing for the Tigers and was anxious to do well against many of the same guys with whom he had played.

The 1987 American League Championship Series was a highlight of Juan's four-year career with the Twins. He appeared in four games and pitched six innings, earning a save while giving up just one run. Berenguer surrendered only one hit and walked three while fanning six Tigers.

Juan looked intimidating on the mound. He was broad shouldered, hairy, and had a blazing fastball that he liked to throw inside.

Bob Brenly, his catcher with the San Francisco Giants, said of Berenguer's appearance, "If I pulled up in front of a restaurant, and he came out to park my car, I'd eat somewhere else."

Juan never gave much thought to his appearance. "I just wanted to do my job and get out of there. A lot of people are scared to pitch inside today. I liked to."

Berenguer threw consistently in the low nineties and was just wild enough to keep hitters from digging in too deep against him. His fastball was his out pitch, and he also developed an effective forkball to set up his strikeouts.

Berenguer loved playing for the 1987 Twins. His role was mostly as a set-up man for the closer, first Jeff Reardon, and later Rick Aguilera.

"The Twins were hungry to win," Juan remembered. "Bert Blyleven kept up good spirit on the team. He relaxed us."

Sometimes things got too relaxed. Blyleven liked to sneak up on sleeping players on plane trips and cut off their ties. Berenguer soon came up with a remedy for Bert's prank. He purchased cheap clip-on ties and substituted them for his good ties when he wanted to ward off Blyleven's scissors attacks.

Berenguer contributed to amusing relaxation for the ball club and the public when he and several other Twins produced a music video called the "Berenguer Boogie." It came out in connection with the 1987 World Series.

Berenguer appeared in three games in the 1987 Series and suffered a loss in his only decision.

A native of Panama, Juan was a high-school pitcher when an early-morning visitor came by the family's home one day. Juan's mother told the man to leave; it was too early to be bothering a young student. Nino Escalera explained that he was a scout for the New York Mets and had come to offer her son a contract to play baseball.

Berenguer toiled in the Mets farm system starting in 1975, pitching in Wausau, Wisconsin; Jackson, Mississippi; and Tidewater, Virginia. His major-league debut with the Mets came on August 17, 1978. He played for the New Yorkers parts of the next two seasons before dividing 1981 between Kansas City and Toronto.

Juan signed as a free agent with Detroit in 1982 and got in a couple games for the Tigers that year. But he really found a home in Detroit the next three years, winning twenty-five games, mostly as a starter. In 1984 the Tigers played in the ALCS and the World Series. However, Berenguer didn't take the mound during the 1984 postseason. That fact later helped to fuel Juan's desire to excel against his former skipper, Sparky Anderson, in the 1987 ALCS.

The Tigers traded Berenguer in 1986 to San Francisco, where he pitched in forty-six games. After the season, again as a free agent, Juan signed with the Twins to become part of the magical 1987 season under skipper Tom Kelly.

Juan pitched for two renowned managers, Tom Kelly and Sparky Anderson.

"Sparky was too strict," Berenguer recalled. "Everything was his way. If you made a mistake, you were out. They called him 'Mr. Hook.'

"Tom Kelly made you more relaxed. If you got hit hard one day, he'd say, 'Be ready, I might need you tomorrow.' You felt like you got more chances with him."

Berenguer, like most good pitchers, learned with experience. At first he was a "thrower" and just let the fastball go. Later, through the tutelage of Detroit pitching coach Roger Craig, he developed his split finger and worked more on his slider. He began to hit the corners more consistently with his fastball as well.

During his career Juan started, pitched middle relief, was set-up man and sometimes closed. He yearned for the chance to become a team's main closer.

After the 1990 season, the opportunity to become a closer with the Atlanta Braves beckoned, and Juan left Minnesota for Atlanta. He earned seventeen saves for the Braves and compiled a 2.24 ERA, the best of his career.

But 1991 led to the advent of Todd Woehrle as Atlanta's main finisher, and Juan's innings dropped. In 1992 he joined the Kansas City Royals for his final season.

Since retiring, Juan has lived in Eden Prairie, Minnesota, and has operated baseball clinics, not just locally, but with an emphasis in Mexico and Panama.

"Señor Smoke" found another way to keep in touch with the sport he loves after retiring from the "bigs." He played some independent minor-league baseball in Austin, Minnesota, on a team coached by former Brave and Twin Greg Olson. Playing only in home games, he enjoyed the experience and stayed for an hour after the games, talking with fans and signing autographs.

Juan misses the friendships made in the big leagues and, of course, the money. But he emphasized that it wasn't always fun and easy.

"Baseball is hard for family and players," Juan said. "You don't get to see your family much and you miss things your kids do in school."

Back in 1990, Juan had speculated about life after baseball. He had anticipated that he might move his family to Orlando, Florida, and open a business. It was too cold to remain permanently in Minnesota, in his opinion.

Juan must have adjusted to the North since then. He lives with his wife, Denise, and their family in Eden Prairie. They have a daughter, Jody, who's twenty, and two sons, Christopher and Andrew, ninth and eighth graders. Both boys play baseball and hockey. Now their dad, a Panamanian who thinks eighty-eight degrees is a nice temperature, proudly takes his seat alongside the frozen rinks of Minnesota arenas to watch his sons play.

Twins
28

Bert Blyleven

Bats: Right
Throws: Right
Height: 6' 3"
Weight: 200 lbs.
Born: April 6, 1951, in the Netherlands

YEAR	TEAM	LG	ERA	W	L	Sv	G	IP	H	R	ER	BB	K	AVG. A
1970	Min	AL	3.18	10	9	0	27	164.0	143	66	58	47	135	.232
1971	Min	AL	2.81	16	15	0	38	278.1	267	95	87	59	224	.255
1972	Min	AL	2.73	17	17	0	39	287.1	247	93	87	69	228	.233
1973	Min	AL	2.52	20	17	0	40	325.0	296	109	91	67	258	.242
1974	Min	AL	2.66	17	17	0	37	281.0	244	99	83	77	249	.233
1975	Min	AL	3.00	15	10	0	35	275.2	219	104	92	84	233	.219
1976	Min	AL	3.12	4	5	0	12	95.1	101	39	33	35	75	.283
1976	Tex	AL	2.76	9	11	0	24	202.1	182	67	62	46	144	.242
1977	Tex	AL	2.72	14	12	0	30	234.2	181	81	71	69	182	.214
1978	Pit	NL	3.03	14	10	0	34	243.2	217	94	82	66	182	.235
1979	Pit	NL	3.60	12	5	0	37	237.1	238	102	95	92	172	.265
1980	Pit	NL	3.82	8	13	0	34	216.2	219	102	92	59	168	.262
1981	Cle	AL	2.88	11	7	0	20	159.1	145	52	51	40	107	.245
1982	Cle	AL	4.87	2	2	0	4	20.1	16	14	11	11	19	.211
1983	Cle	AL	3.91	7	10	0	24	156.1	160	74	68	44	123	.267
1984	Cle	AL	2.87	19	7	0	33	245.0	204	86	78	74	170	.224
1985	Cle	AL	3.26	9	11	0	23	179.2	163	76	65	49	129	.240
1985	Min	AL	3.00	8	5	0	14	114.0	101	45	38	26	77	.237
1986	Min	AL	4.01	17	14	0	36	271.2	262	134	121	58	215	.250
1987	Min	AL	4.01	15	12	0	37	267.0	249	132	119	101	196	.249
1988	Min	AL	5.43	10	17	0	33	207.1	240	128	125	51	145	.294
1989	Cal	AL	2.73	17	5	0	33	241.0	225	76	73	44	131	.248
1990	Cal	AL	5.24	8	7	0	23	134.0	163	85	78	25	69	.303
1992	Cal	AL	4.74	8	12	0	25	133.0	150	76	70	29	70	.285
			ERA	W	L	Sv	G	IP	H	R	ER	BB	K	AVG. A
			3.31	287	250	0	692	4,970	4,632	2,029	1,830	1,322	3,701	.247

Bert Blyleven was just nineteen years old when he took the mound for the first time in his major-league career. It was June 5, 1970. Dressed in a Minnesota Twins uniform, he faced hard-hitting outfielder Lee May of the Washington Senators.

Bert was anxious: first game, first big-league hitter. He wanted to start well, maybe even get a strikeout. May belted the ball out of the ballpark. But that was all the Senators could muster that day. Blyleven and the Twins won 2-1.

The rookie's auspicious beginning foretold a career that would lead to baseball stardom. Even though Blyleven had a tendency to give up frequent home runs, he chalked up an impressive number of wins. He notched 287 victories in twenty-three years in the major leagues. His 149 wins for Minnesota are the most of any Twins right-handed pitcher.

Blyleven was born to Dutch parents in 1951. The family of five immigrated into North America when Bert was two; his father had learned that Canada was seeking strong young men to work on farms in western provinces.

The Blylevens spent three and one-half years in Canada before Bert's father got the urge to move again. The elder Blyleven went to California to establish himself and, three months later, sent for his family. A powerful man, he worked in a shop straightening car bumpers in the days before machines did the work.

As southern Californians, the Blylevens became big fans of the Los Angeles Dodgers. Young Bert's hero was the great Dodger left-hander Sandy Koufax, who possessed a magnificent curveball.

His father also admired Koufax. When he heard the lefty advise boys not to throw curveballs until they were fourteen or fifteen years old, he forbade Bert from experimenting with the pitch.

It wasn't until after his junior year in high school that the budding hurler began developing what would become his trademark, a devastating curveball. Where some pitchers' curves move inches, the break in Blyleven's measured in feet. When at its best, Bert's curve went from shoulder to ankle, a drop from two to seven o'clock.

The Californian was just out of high school and nineteen years old when he was drafted in the third round and signed to a contract by Twins scout Jesse Flores. Before he'd turned twenty, Bert was in the regular rotation of the Minnesota Twins, had notched ten victories, and was named the *Sporting News* American League Rookie Pitcher of the Year for 1970.

For six straight years, Bert recorded over 200 strikeouts per season, including five years with more than fifteen wins. Despite his great success, when it came time to talk contract after the 1975 season, Blyleven was offered a twenty-percent cut in pay by Twins owner Calvin Griffith. Known well for a conservative pocket book, Griffith had begun to feel the effects of operating a small-market team in a changing baseball economy.

Blyleven never actually negotiated his contract with the owner. He recalled that Calvin basically just said, "This is it. Take it or leave it."

With the advent of free agency, Bert made it clear that he would become a free agent and not sign with the Twins when his contract expired. In June of 1976, he was traded to the Texas Rangers for Bill Singer, Roy Smalley, Mike Cubbage, Jim Gideon, and $250,000.

One of Blyleven's most memorable games occurred September 22, 1977. Pitching for the Rangers, he faced Los Angeles in the Angels' home stadium. Bert shut down L.A. to record his only no-hitter. His parents and family were in attendance.

Blyleven was traded to the Pittsburgh Pirates for Al Oliver and Nelson Norman on December 8, 1977. By 1979, the Pirates were a powerhouse team with great pitching and hitting. They won their division. The next honor they claimed was the National League pennant. Finally, aided by a Blyleven victory, the Pirates ended the 1979 campaign in triumph as World Series champions.

But Bert became disgruntled with manager Chuck Tanner's use of his pitchers. The strategy of going to the bullpen in close games rankled a man like Bert, who wanted to finish what he started whenever possible.

The pitcher announced his intention to retire unless he was traded. The Pirates placed Blyleven on the disqualified list after April 30, 1980. Bert agreed to rejoin the team on May 13. On December 9, 1980, he was traded to Cleveland in a six-player deal.

The right-hander was sidelined with an elbow injury for most of 1982. He couldn't regain his customary form the next year, but rebounded to 19-7 with a 2.87 ERA in 1984. However, Cleveland seemed destined to continue playing bad baseball, and Bert Blyleven missed Minnesota, where a new owner was moving the Twins in a more promising direction.

Bert was traded back to the Twins in 1985. The Minnesota team was building around a nucleus of coming stars like Kirby Puckett, Kent Hrbek, and Gary Gaetti.

The Twins hadn't gelled yet in 1986 and finished in last place. At the close of the 1986 season at Fan Appreciation Day ceremonies, Bert made a bold prediction to the Twins' faithful. He sensed a tremendous chemistry developing among the Twins players and believed in the direction that manager Tom Kelly was taking the team. Bert told the fans that the Twins, cellar dwellers in 1986, would win a pennant in 1987.

He was right. The Twins did an about-face to win the 1987 American League pennant—and, eventually, the World Series.

In the meantime, Bert was chalking up many victories, his strikeout totals were on the rise, but he was giving up many homers. Although the Metrodome is a hitter's park, Blyleven refused to blame it for his dramatic increase in allowing home runs.

Blyleven had surrendered fifty homers, a major-league record, in 1986. In 1987 he gave up a league leading forty-six round trippers. He discounted the significance of his homers-surrendered mark; indeed, other statistics attested to Blyleven's success. He won thirty-two games in 1986 and 1987, and his strikeout totals continued to mount. Also, it helped that in 1986, forty-two of the fifty home runs Blyleven gave up were solo shots. In one game he surrendered five home runs, all solo, yet won the game.

Blyleven said, "Maybe the ball was juiced, maybe my arm was juiced, or I hung too many balls. I knew I had a team behind me that could score runs. Sometimes I'd throw a pitch, and, when it was hit, I'd think it was going to the warning track. When it kept going over the fence, I'd be shocked."

So, while Blyleven's ERA rose, his victory total did the same. He was aided by a team that averaged five or six runs a game.

Blyleven did his part. He won fifteen games for the division-winning Twins. He followed that success with outstanding post-season pitching. Bert won two games against Detroit in the A.L. Championship Series.

The World Series championship of 1987 was the highlight of Blyleven's Twins career. He won Game 2 at the Metrodome against the St. Louis Cardinals and was overwhelmed by the support given the Twins by fans in the Upper Midwest.

After a mediocre season in 1988, the Twins traded Bert home to Los Angeles, where he finished his career with the Angels. The year 1989 was another banner year for the former Twins star. He won seventeen games with a 2.73 ERA and five shutouts. He finished the 1980s as the active career leader in shutouts and was second only to Nolan Ryan among active players in strike-outs.

Bert was well known for his curveball and strikeouts. But his fastball consistently clocked in the high eighties and low nineties. He didn't consider either to be his "strikeout" pitch. He felt each pitch helped set up the other.

Pranks and jokes were another big part of Blyleven's notoriety. Cutting off half of someone's tie with a scissors, shaving cream in the face, and going to great lengths to execute the perfect hotfoot were all part of his legend.

Mike Kingery, a native of Atwater, Minnesota, who played for the Kansas City Royals, related how Royals star George Brett and Bert tried to outdo each other in the prank department. During one game when Bert wasn't pitching, he made his way into the Kansas City players' clubhouse, where he cut the toes out of Brett's socks. Brett retaliated by cutting the legs off Blyleven's pants.

When asked what it was liked to face Blyleven, Kingery said that the first time he faced the right-hander was in the Metrodome, a day after he had gone four-for-four during Atwater Night at the Dome.

"I had never been so dominated by a pitcher," Mike explained. "I couldn't catch up with his fastball, and I couldn't touch his curveball. He struck me out three times. His curveball was among the best I've ever seen."

Bert Blyleven's life in pro baseball spanned twenty-three years. Baseball changed during that time. He cited pitching as one of the areas in which baseball has undergone considerable alterations over the years. Starting hurlers are no longer expected to go the distance. Teams have added middle relievers and closers to their pitching arsenals.

Blyleven witnessed other significant changes, too. The advent of free agency, an explosion in salary contracts, expansion and movement of franchises, and changes in strategy and in attitude were among the most prominent.

Bert noted, "In the 1970s you didn't talk to the opposing players before the game. Baseball was a war, and we were taught to dislike the enemy. Teams mostly developed their own players, and they came up through the system. Free agency changed that. The loyalty players had to one team and one group of players changed."

Bert faced plenty of tough hitters in his career. Pitching in both leagues through the 1970s and 1980s, he faced Brett, Tony Gwynn, Rod Carew, Dave Winfield, Henry Aaron, and many others who are, or are destined to be, in the Baseball Hall of Fame.

But when asked who was the toughest hitter he ever faced, Blyleven answered that whoever was holding a bat was tough.

"I didn't doubt my ability or the ability of the hitters I faced. Before each game, I looked at the lineup card. I knew each team had two or three guys that could beat me if I threw a bad pitch."

It's evident that Bert Blyleven still loves the game. He said, "Baseball motivated me and allowed me to fulfill a dream. It helped me to learn sportsmanship, hard work, desire and dedication. It helped me to know what it takes to be the best.

"Baseball was a dream come true, a fantasyland where I had a lot of fun. I loved putting on the uniform every day. It was a battle, and I miss it."

The former Twins right-hander certainly has Hall of Fame statistics himself. Bert is ninth all-time in career shutouts (sixty), third in strikeouts (3,701), thirteenth in innings pitched, eighth in starts, twenty-second in wins (287) and thirty-first in ERA (3.31). Plus, he finished 242 games. He posted double-digit victory seasons seventeen times.

In his Twins career Bert had 345 starts, 149 wins, a 3.28 ERA and still holds the club records for strikeouts (2,035), shutouts (twenty-nine), and complete games (141).

Blyleven became a broadcaster for the Minnesota Twins telecasts in 1995. He currently lives in Fort Myers, Florida, with his second wife, Gayle, two stepsons and a seventeen-year-old son by his first marriage. He has three other children, ages eighteen, twenty-five, and twenty-eight.

Bert would love to return to the field someday, perhaps as a pitching coach. He misses the competition and the battle. Above all, he misses standing on the mound with a ball in his hand, glaring at a hitter who is about to see a curveball drop out of the sky and cross the strike zone at his ankles.

Randy Bush

Bats: Left
Throws: Left
Height: 6' 1"
Weight: 186 lbs.
Born: October 5, 1958, in Delaware

YEAR	TEAM	LG	AVG	G	AB	R	H	2B	3B	HR	RBI	BB	K	OBP	SLG
1982	*Min*	*AL*	*.244*	*55*	*119*	*13*	*29*	*6*	*1*	*4*	*13*	*8*	*28*	*.305*	*.412*
1983	*Min*	*AL*	*.249*	*124*	*373*	*43*	*93*	*24*	*3*	*11*	*56*	*34*	*51*	*.323*	*.418*
1984	*Min*	*AL*	*.222*	*113*	*311*	*46*	*69*	*17*	*1*	*11*	*43*	*31*	*60*	*.292*	*.289*
1985	*Min*	*AL*	*.239*	*97*	*234*	*26*	*56*	*13*	*3*	*10*	*35*	*24*	*30*	*.321*	*.449*
1986	*Min*	*AL*	*.269*	*130*	*357*	*50*	*96*	*19*	*7*	*7*	*45*	*39*	*63*	*.347*	*.420*
1987	*Min*	*AL*	*.253*	*122*	*293*	*46*	*74*	*10*	*2*	*11*	*46*	*43*	*49*	*.349*	*.413*
1988	*Min*	*AL*	*.261*	*136*	*394*	*51*	*103*	*20*	*3*	*14*	*51*	*58*	*49*	*.365*	*.434*
1989	*Min*	*AL*	*.263*	*141*	*391*	*60*	*103*	*17*	*4*	*14*	*54*	*48*	*73*	*.347*	*.435*
1990	*Min*	*AL*	*.243*	*73*	*181*	*17*	*44*	*8*	*0*	*6*	*18*	*21*	*27*	*.338*	*.387*
1991	*Min*	*AL*	*.303*	*93*	*165*	*21*	*50*	*10*	*1*	*6*	*23*	*24*	*25*	*.401*	*.485*
1992	*Min*	*AL*	*.214*	*100*	*182*	*14*	*39*	*8*	*1*	*2*	*22*	*11*	*37*	*.263*	*.302*
1993	*Min*	*AL*	*.156*	*35*	*45*	*1*	*7*	*2*	*0*	*0*	*3*	*7*	*13*	*.269*	*.200*
			AVG	*G*	*AB*	*R*	*H*	*2B*	*3B*	*HR*	*RBI*	*BB*	*K*	*OBP*	*SLG*
			.251	*1,219*	*3,045*	*388*	*763*	*154*	*26*	*96*	*409*	*348*	*505*	*.334*	*.413*

Randy Bush didn't grow up idolizing major-league baseball players like a lot of kids. He was raised in Florida, and his heroes were Miami Dolphin football players.

But it became obvious that Randy had exceptional skills as a baseball player. He attended Miami Dade Community College and then went to the University of New Orleans on a baseball scholarship. While at New Orleans, he played well enough to earn big-league attention.

The Minnesota Twins drafted Bush in the second round in 1979. For the next few years he played in the Twins minor-league system, first in Orlando, Florida, and then in Toledo, Ohio.

Randy was part of the Twins Class of 1982 that formed the nucleus of two World Series champions. Kent Hrbek, Tim Laudner, Gary Gaetti, and Frank Viola were just a few of the players who came up with Bush.

Tom Kelly likes to put players in positions where they can succeed. He used Randy Bush wisely. Bush was a left-handed batter with power who spelled time as a right fielder and DH. He was also very valuable coming off the bench as a pinch hitter.

Bush excelled in the role of pinch hitter. During the Twins' 1991 pennant drive, he had a stretch of seven pinch-hits in a row, including a couple off Dennis Eckersley, then the game's premier reliever.

Randy tied an American League record with two consecutive pinch-hit home runs in 1986. As a rookie in 1982, he delivered a ninth-inning single to spoil an impending no-hitter by Toronto's Tom Clancey.

Battling pitchers late in the game was one of the things Bush liked most about major-league baseball. To be a good pinch hitter, Randy said, "You have to be competitive and want to be up there. You have to be prepared physically and mentally."

Bush was a big part of the 1987 and 1991 world championship teams. While both were great accomplishments, the 1987 season was special to Randy because it was the first and unexpected by most fans.

When the team returned from Detroit after winning the pennant, it was greeted by over 50,000 in the Metrodome. Bush remembered, "It was one of the greatest things I've ever seen. It was a very emotional moment."

Personal highlights for Randy in the two World Series were a bases-loaded double in 1987, and a pinch-hit against the Braves in 1991.

But beyond personal accomplishments, the most important part of Randy's World Series games was the simple fact that the Twins won. The team victory was more important to him than anything else.

In twelve seasons with the Twins, Bush hit double figures in home runs six times. This is particularly impressive considering that Randy never topped 400 at-bats in his Twins career, averaging 253 a year. His .303 batting average in 1991 marked his best percentage year.

Bush entered the Twins organization while Calvin Griffith was the owner. Randy respected Griffith as a great man who was a very good evaluator of talent.

But another Twins official has had a lasting effect on Bush's life as well, his former skipper, Tom Kelly. Randy was released in June of 1993 when Kelly called him into his office and told him his baseball career with the Twins was over.

Bush, acknowledging that Kelly was usually pretty accurate in his talent assessments, decided it would be best to retire from major league baseball.

He went back to New Orleans, his wife, Cathy's, hometown, and in one and one-half years, he finished a degree in finance. For a year, in 1998, Bush was minor league hitting instructor for the Chicago Cubs.

Then, in 1999, the position of head baseball coach opened up at his alma mater, the University of New Orleans. Randy's former college coach, now New Orleans athletic director, suggested he apply. Bush was hired.

While the former Twin tries to be himself in coaching, he admits the Kelly influence. "Tom Kelly was a great leader. Leadership can't be taught. A great deal that I do, I learned from him. He's shaped my coaching in ways I don't always realize."

In Bush's first year of coaching, his team won the Sunbelt Conference and qualified for the NCAA Regionals.

"Baseball has been a tremendous part of my life," Bush related. "It's influenced and shaped my life. I developed long lasting friendships through it."

Randy and Cathy Bush live in the New Orleans suburb of Algiers with their two sons: Ryan, a junior in high school, and Jason, a freshman.

Jim Eisenreich

Bats: Left
Throws: Left
Height: 5' 11"
Weight: 200 lbs.
Born: April 18, 1959, in Minnesota

YEAR	TEAM	LG	AVG	G	AB	R	H	2B	3B	HR	RBI	BB	K	OBP	SLG
1982	Min	AL	.303	34	99	10	30	6	0	2	9	11	13	.378	.424
1983	Min	AL	.286	2	7	1	2	1	0	0	0	1	1	.375	.429
1984	Min	AL	.219	12	32	1	7	1	0	0	3	2	4	.250	.250
1987	KC	AL	.238	44	105	10	25	8	2	4	21	7	13	.278	.467
1988	KC	AL	.218	82	202	26	44	8	1	1	19	6	31	.236	.282
1989	KC	AL	.293	134	475	64	139	33	7	9	59	37	44	.341	.448
1990	KC	AL	.280	142	496	61	139	29	7	5	51	42	51	.335	.397
1991	KC	AL	.301	135	375	47	113	22	3	2	47	20	35	.333	.392
1992	KC	AL	.269	113	353	31	95	13	3	2	28	24	36	.313	.340
1993	Phi	NL	.318	153	362	51	115	17	4	7	54	26	36	.363	.445
1994	Phi	NL	.300	104	290	42	87	15	4	4	43	33	31	.371	.421
1995	Phi	NL	.316	129	377	46	119	22	2	10	55	38	44	.375	.464
1996	Phi	NL	.361	113	338	45	122	24	3	3	41	31	32	.413	.476
1997	Fla	NL	.280	120	293	36	82	19	1	2	34	30	28	.345	.372
1998	Fla	NL	.250	30	64	9	16	1	0	1	7	4	14	.294	.313
1998	LA	NL	.197	75	127	12	25	2	2	0	6	12	22	.266	.244
			AVG	G	AB	R	H	2B	3B	HR	RBI	BB	K	OBP	SLG
			.290	1422	3995	492	1160	221	39	52	477	324	435	.341	.404

Jim Eisenreich was part of the renowned Twins Class of 1982. The group included future stars such as Kent Hrbek, Tim Laudner, and Gary Gaetti.

Eventually the Class of 1982 would play in two World Series and bring championships and glory to Minnesota. Jim Eisenreich played in two World Series as well, but not for the Twins.

The youth from St. Cloud would achieve a measure of glory and stardom himself in major-league baseball. But the route he took wasn't as smooth as that of his 1982 Twins teammates. If fact, in 1984 it looked like his pro career was over.

Eisenreich was born April 18, 1959, in St. Cloud, Minnesota. He grew up watching his heroes Harmon Killebrew, Tony Oliva, and Rod Carew play for the Twins.

He attended St. Cloud Tech High School, where he played Tech "Tiger" baseball and hockey. After high school, he went on to St. Cloud State University and played baseball for the Huskies.

Bob Hegman, an infielder on Eisenreich's college team, was a touted pro prospect. When scouts came to watch him play, they noticed Eisenreich. The skinny, left-handed line-drive hitter with lightning speed made a strong impression. As a result, the Minnesota Twins drafted Jim in the sixteenth round in 1980, after his junior year.

Eisenreich was sent to Elizabethton, Tennessee, to play in the rookie league in the summer of 1980. The next year he moved up to Class A at Wisconsin Rapids. He was invited to 1982 spring training with the Twins, but wasn't expected to make the team.

However, he had fallen into a good situation. The Twins, under President Calvin Griffith, were in a money bind. They were rebuilding with good, young, relatively inexpensive players. Eisenreich had an impressive spring and made the team.

It was a dream come true for the young Minnesotan. When the brand-new Metrodome opened for its first game in April 1982, the starting Twins center fielder was Jim Eisenreich.

He had a great first month, batting .303 in April. One of the fondest memories of his Twins career came during an afternoon game at the Dome. Attendance was sparse that day and, when he hit his first big-league home run, Jim was able to pick out his mom, dad, and sister in the stands as he circled the bases.

Then it all came crashing down. Since boyhood, Jim had exhibited occasional facial tics and spasms. Under the pressure and spotlight of major-league baseball, they began to get worse. Fans and other players began to notice.

During the previous winter and in spring training, Jim had felt an increase in anxiety and the spasms that accompanied it. The condition overwhelmed him as the 1982 season unfolded.

"On a road trip to Boston in early May, the tics and anxiety became unbearable," Jim said. "The fans were taunting me, I guess, but I didn't hear them. Other pressures became too much. The fans didn't affect me."

He had to leave the game. Some thought it was a case of nerves or that the big leagues were too much for Jim. Eisenreich knew it was something more. He knew that something was wrong, but he had no idea what it was. His emotions went up and down, and he didn't know why. Jim came to believe that he wasn't normal. He couldn't bear to stand in the outfield, where he felt exposed to the world.

Doctors eventually diagnosed Tourette Syndrome, a neurological disorder in which victims exhibit facial or body spasms and, sometimes, uncontrollable verbal outbursts. They prescribed medication, but treatment seemed unsuccessful. After aborted attempts at playing for the Twins in 1983 and 1984, his battle with Tourette forced Jim to retire from major-league baseball.

He went back home to St. Cloud. For the next two summers, he played amateur ball, a Minnesota tradition. He played for Boudreaus in St. Cloud, not knowing or caring if he would ever play big-league ball again. Jim Eisenreich just wanted to live a normal life.

Through medication and the love and support of his family, Jim improved. He grew in self-esteem. In small-town ballparks around central Minnesota, line drives continued to pop off his bat like mini-missiles.

Meanwhile, Bob Hegman, his old teammate with the St. Cloud State Huskies, was a Kansas City Royals executive. His own major-league career had lasted one inning in the field. But Bob's front office career was proving more successful.

He heard that Jim was controlling his Tourette, and that he could still play baseball. Hegman asked Jim if he wanted to give it another try. In 1987, Jim found himself at Kansas City's AA affiliate in Memphis.

Hitting .382 about midway through the season, Jim was called up to the Royals. For the next couple of years, he was used mostly as a DH and pinch hitter, since he was better able to control his Tourette's when not in the field.

But by 1989, Jim was playing all three outfield positions and batting .293 with twenty-seven stolen bases. He was named Royals Player of the Year that season. He played three more years in Kansas City before signing as a free agent with Philadelphia after the 1992 campaign.

The Phillies years were high points in Jim's career. He hit over .300 in each of his four seasons in Philadelphia. The next season, 1993, was a dream. The Phillies were a great team. They had fun and, as Jim related, "We had one plan, to beat the other team." The dream took Jim and his club all the way to the 1993 World Series, which the Phillies lost to Toronto.

Eisenreich hit .316 as the Phillies regular right fielder in 1995. The following year grew more outstanding as Jim, at the age of thirty-seven, batted for a .361 average.

Eisenreich joined the Florida Marlins in 1997. Their owner opened his pocketbook and assembled a team for one purpose: to win a championship in one year. Eisenreich hit .280 in 120 games as an outfielder, first baseman and pinch hitter. He gained a World Series Champion ring as the Marlins were successful in their quest.

The next season the Marlins owner, having met his goal, lowered his high payroll by dumping players in a fire sale. Jim was traded to Los Angeles in May. After a disappointing .197 average in seventy-nine games, Eisenreich retired when the season drew to a close.

Since leaving major-league baseball, Jim has lived near Kansas City with his wife of ten years, Leann, and their three children, ages nine, six, and two. Fishing and golfing occupy some of his time, but another passion is the Jim Eisenreich Foundation for Children with Tourette.

Jim Eisenreich came a long way since the days when he was forced to leave the Twins outfield in frustration and despair. Through determination and support, he managed to play all or part of sixteen years in the major leagues, be part of a World Series championship and hit .290 lifetime.

Some called him a role player. Jim didn't mind the sobriquet.

"My calling in life was not to be a superstar ballplayer," Eisenreich said in a phone interview. "I have another job to do: to be a quality player, help my team win and show kids who have Tourette what they can accomplish."

Gary Gaetti

Bats: Right
Throws: Right
Height: 6' 0"
Weight: 200 lbs.
Born: August 19, 1958, in Illinois

YEAR	TEAM	LG	AVG	G	AB	R	H	2B	3B	HR	RBI	BB	K	OBP	SLG
1981	Min	AL	.192	9	26	4	5	0	0	2	3	0	6	.192	.423
1982	Min	AL	.230	145	508	59	117	25	4	25	84	37	107	.280	.443
1983	Min	AL	.245	157	584	81	143	30	3	21	78	54	121	.309	.414
1984	Min	AL	.262	162	588	55	154	29	4	5	65	44	81	.315	.350
1985	Min	AL	.246	160	560	71	138	31	0	20	63	37	89	.301	.409
1986	Min	AL	.287	157	596	91	171	34	1	34	108	52	108	.347	.518
1987	Min	AL	.257	154	584	95	150	36	2	31	109	37	92	.303	.485
1988	Min	AL	.301	133	468	66	141	29	2	28	88	36	85	.353	.551
1989	Min	AL	.251	130	498	63	125	11	4	19	75	25	87	.286	.404
1990	Min	AL	.229	154	577	61	132	27	5	16	85	36	101	.274	.376
1991	Cal	AL	.246	152	586	58	144	22	1	18	66	33	104	.293	.379
1992	Cal	AL	.226	130	456	41	103	13	2	12	48	21	79	.267	.342
1993	Cal	AL	.180	20	50	3	9	2	0	0	4	5	12	.250	.220
1993	KC	AL	.256	82	281	37	72	18	1	14	46	16	75	.309	.477
1994	KC	AL	.287	90	327	53	94	15	3	12	57	19	63	.328	.462
1995	KC	AL	.261	137	514	76	134	27	0	35	96	47	91	.329	.518
1996	StL	NL	.274	141	522	71	143	27	4	23	80	35	97	.326	.473
1997	StL	NL	.251	148	502	63	126	24	1	17	69	36	88	.305	.404
1998	StL	NL	.265	91	306	39	81	23	1	11	43	31	39	.339	.454
1998	ChN	NL	.320	37	128	21	41	11	0	8	27	12	23	.397	.594
1999	ChC	NL	.204	113	280	22	57	9	1	9	46	21	51	.260	.339
			AVG	G	AB	R	H	2B	3B	HR	RBI	BB	K	OBP	SLG
			.255	2,507	8,951	1,130	2,280	433	39	360	1,341	634	1,602	.308	.434

The left-handed Cardinal hitter bounced the ball sharply toward the hole between short and third. Third baseman Gary Gaetti moved to his left, cut the ball off and snapped the white sphere across the diamond to Kent Hrbek.

An instant later, Hrbek and Gaetti met joyously at the mound with pitcher Jeff Reardon. In another instant they were joined by their jubilant teammates as a pile of elated humanity converged on the mound. They were World Series champions for the first time.

No matter what Gary Gaetti has done since, no matter what other teams he has played for, or other roads he has journeyed, the image of Gaetti's throw from that moment in the 1987 World Series finale is frozen in Minnesota sports history. Because of that, Gary Gaetti will always be a Minnesota Twin.

A native of Centralia, Illinois, Gaetti graduated there in 1976. He went to Northwest Missouri State for a year, then to Lakeland Junior College and returned to Missouri for a third year.

The Minnesota Twins drafted Gary in 1979 in the first round of the draft's secondary phase. He was sent to the Twins rookie team at Elizabethton, Tennessee.

In 1980, the young shortstop was at Wisconsin Rapids in the Midwest League. Gary won the home run championship of the Class A league. He moved up to Orlando in 1981. In September, he was called up to the Twins.

Gaetti made his major-league debut against the Texas Rangers in Metropolitan Stadium on September 20, 1981. In his first at-bat, Gary drove a Charlie Hough knuckleball over the fence.

Gaetti was a full-time Twin in 1982, joining Kent Hrbek, Randy Bush, Frank Viola, Tim Laudner, and Tom Brunansky as the nucleus of a future championship team.

But they sure didn't look like champions in the beginning. They were young and still learning how to be professional ball players under their manager, Billy Gardner. Did they see the possibility of greatness in their team?

"No, not really," Gaetti chuckled. "That team lost 102 games. So I'd have to say no, we weren't thinking of that, we were just trying to learn how to play major-league baseball and compete. We had so many rookies on our team, we really didn't know what we were doing. We played ball, but we were getting abused."

But they kept improving. They won seventy games in 1983. Then, in 1984, Kirby Puckett joined the Twins. The team actually made a run at the pennant before losing down the stretch to finish 82-82. Gary Gaetti had become the Twins' third baseman in 1982, when John Castino was moved to second.

While many of his team's performances were forgettable, Gaetti remembers fondly some personal moments.

"The first regular season game at the Metrodome in 1982 against Seattle, I hit two home runs. Sandwiched in between, I tried for an inside-the-parker and got thrown out at the plate."

Gary's batting average improved, but his power numbers were inconsistent. His glove work was exceptional and kept getting better. The team slumped below .500 for the next two years, winning seventy-seven and then seventy-one games. But more pieces to the puzzle were being added. Dan Gladden, Bert Blyleven, and closer Jeff Reardon were in place by 1987.

In 1987, for the second year in a row, Gary hit over thirty home runs and drove in over 100 runs. Many times in his career, Gary would lead the league's fielders in putouts, assists, and double plays. In 1986, he won the first of three consecutive Gold Gloves at third base. In 1987, Gary set a Twins third-base record with a .973 fielding percentage.

The Twins won the American League West title in 1987, winning just eighty-five games. They were big underdogs in the League Championship Series against the Detroit Tigers.

But it was to be the Twins' year. Gary became the first player to ever hit two home runs in his first two at-bats of postseason play. He was the LCS Most Valuable Player, batting .300.

Gary hit .259 in the World Series against St. Louis with a homer and four RBIs. The Twins were undefeated in the Metrodome in the postseason. They also had an excellent regular season mark at home.

"I always liked the Metrodome," Gaetti related. "It was fast, kinda sterile for a while, but when the crowds were large, it was awesome. The best home field advantage ever, with the ceiling and the lights and the baggie.

"I guess we pretty much adopted it as our favorite place to play. It wasn't a great baseball stadium compared to some that have been built, but it was ours and we took advantage of playing there.

"It's a lot better now than it was. They got some bugs worked out and the clubhouse is a lot nicer. It just looks better now."

While he was excelling with both the glove and the bat, offense still had the biggest appeal to Gary.

"You always think about winning the game by driving in the winning run. There's a lot of satisfaction in that. The offensive part of the game is more dramatic.

"On defense, you're just doing your job. On offense, when you give the other team a 'walk off' you win the game and it's over."

Gary had his best year in 1988. At .301 he had the highest batting average of his career while popping twenty-eight home runs and eighty-eight RBIs. The team never reached the heights of the year before. They won ninety-one games, but they finished in second place, thirteen games out.

Gaetti underwent another change. He became a born-again Christian.

"It didn't change the way I played," Gary explained. "It was more a personal lifestyle change. It didn't affect me on the field. I just couldn't spew foul things out like I did before and act certain ways.

"It tempered my person a little bit. I still played hard. I was still coming back from a knee injury in '88. I don't think a lot of people realize that.

"I blew out my knee and it took awhile to come back from that. A lot of people blamed a drop-off in my performance on my Christianity, but there's a lot of other things. My knee didn't feel right for about a year."

Gary's numbers did decline the next couple of seasons. Still, in 1989 he hit nineteen home runs and had seventy-five RBIs, and he was named to the 1989 All-Star Team. At the game, he ignited a minor controversy when he wrote "Jesus is Lord" on his batting glove and showed it to a cameraman.

While he struggled a little more on the field, his newfound Christianity also led to changes with some of his friendships in the locker room. After his average dipped to .229 in 1990, Gaetti signed with the California Angels and left the Minnesota Twins.

"I felt like I got a lot better contract offer. Plus there were personal things I felt, like with me being born again, and I felt a strain that's hard to describe. I felt like maybe I needed a change.

"I can look back on it now and say that financially it was a great decision, but baseball career-wise, it was probably the worst decision I ever made.

"But you learn. I had a chance to meet a whole lot of new people. You never know what would have happened if I had stayed in Minnesota. Obviously, I missed out on the '91 World Series team.

"It might have been a really bad decision, but there were a lot of positives that came out of it, too. There were a few years after that I wanted to come back and play for the Twins. They weren't interested."

Gaetti's numbers didn't rebound with the Angels, so he moved on to Kansas City. In 1995, he hit thirty-five homers and ninety-six RBIs.

In 1996 Gaetti was in St. Louis, where he had two solid years with the Cardinals before going to the Cubs during the 1998 season. In blowout games, Gaetti even pitched a couple of innings. Gary slumped to .204 in 1999 and retired after playing in five games in the 2000 season for Boston.

Gaetti had played twenty years in the big leagues and popped 360 homers. He had been a World Series champion.

"Baseball was my life for a lot of years. It was a good life," Gary said. "I played organized baseball since I was five years old. You train to do a certain thing and you just do it. It was a nice lifestyle. Financially it provided a lot.

"It was a lot of hard work. People don't realize how much hard work. It's not all that glamorous. A lot of hard work and dedication go into the time on the field.

"It's hard on families, too. I have a son in college now that I hardly ever saw play baseball," Gary continued. "I bet I saw him play organized games about ten times.

"There were many ups and downs, but I don't think a day went by in baseball where you didn't have a real good laugh or something really funny didn't happen at the ballpark. That's what I liked the best."

Gaetti has two sons. He lives with his second wife, Donna, in suburban New Orleans, Louisiana. He enjoys hunting, fishing, and life in the outdoors.

Dan Gladden

Bats: Right
Throws: Right
Height: 5' 11"
Weight: 180 lbs.
Born: July 7, 1957, in California

YEAR	TEAM	LG	AVG	G	AB	R	H	2B	3B	HR	RBI	BB	K	OBP	SLG
1983	*SF*	*NL*	*.222*	*18*	*63*	*6*	*14*	*2*	*0*	*1*	*9*	*5*	*11*	*.275*	*.302*
1984	*SF*	*NL*	*.351*	*86*	*342*	*71*	*120*	*17*	*2*	*4*	*31*	*33*	*37*	*.410*	*.447*
1985	*SF*	*NL*	*.243*	*142*	*502*	*64*	*122*	*15*	*8*	*7*	*41*	*40*	*78*	*.307*	*.347*
1986	*SF*	*NL*	*.276*	*102*	*351*	*55*	*97*	*16*	*1*	*4*	*29*	*39*	*59*	*.357*	*.362*
1987	*Min*	*AL*	*.249*	*121*	*438*	*69*	*109*	*21*	*2*	*8*	*38*	*38*	*72*	*.312*	*.361*
1988	*Min*	*AL*	*.269*	*141*	*576*	*91*	*155*	*32*	*6*	*11*	*62*	*46*	*74*	*.325*	*.403*
1989	*Min*	*AL*	*.295*	*121*	*461*	*69*	*136*	*23*	*3*	*8*	*46*	*23*	*53*	*.331*	*.410*
1990	*Min*	*AL*	*.275*	*136*	*534*	*64*	*147*	*27*	*6*	*5*	*40*	*26*	*67*	*.314*	*.376*
1991	*Min*	*AL*	*.247*	*126*	*461*	*65*	*114*	*14*	*9*	*6*	*52*	*36*	*60*	*.306*	*.356*
1992	*Det*	*AL*	*.254*	*113*	*417*	*57*	*106*	*20*	*1*	*7*	*42*	*30*	*64*	*.304*	*.357*
1993	*Det*	*AL*	*.267*	*91*	*356*	*52*	*95*	*16*	*2*	*13*	*56*	*21*	*50*	*.312*	*.433*
			AVG	*G*	*AB*	*R*	*H*	*2B*	*3B*	*HR*	*RBI*	*BB*	*K*	*OBP*	*SLG*
			.270	*1,197*	*4,501*	*663*	*1,215*	*203*	*40*	*74*	*446*	*337*	*625*	*.324*	*.382*

The four Gladden brothers of Cupertino, California, loved to play baseball. Young Dan admired the players who competed hard at the game, men like Pete Rose, Chris Spiers, and—even though he hated the Dodgers—Davey Lopes.

Gladden termed the way he played "controlled aggression. I played hard." At first, it didn't look like the boy from the Bay Area would get a chance. Dan was not drafted by any major-league team after he left Fresno (California) State College.

Dan called several teams in 1979 and got a tryout with the minor-league Fresno Giants. He had always been an infielder, but, after four or five days of tryout drills, the Giants said they were looking for outfielders. Gladden said he'd be glad to play outfield. He was signed to a contract with the Fresno team.

Gladden moved up the professional ladder, from A ball in Fresno, to AA in Shreveport, Louisiana, and to AAA in Phoenix. The San Francisco Giants called him up from Phoenix in September 1983.

Dan started 1984 back in Arizona. He was smashing the ball at a .397 clip when an injury to the Giants' Jack Clark brought Gladden to the big club in June.

The speedy outfielder continued his torrid hitting, batting .351 for the Giants in 342 at-bats. He was named to the *Topps* and *Baseball Digest* All-Rookie teams in 1984. For the next two seasons he played outfield regularly for San Francisco.

Three Giant outfielders, including Gladden, had various surgeries prior to the 1987 season. Concerned that they might have a shortage of healthy outfielders, the Giants moved to bolster their contingent by adding several.

Spring training found that the three injured players had healed satisfactorily and six others were competing for their jobs. The glut made some expendable. Gladden was traded to the Twins on March 31, 1987. The Twins sent Jose Dominguez, Bryan Hickerson, and Ray Velasquez for Gladden and pitcher David Blakely.

"I had no clue about Minnesota," Dan recalled regarding the trade.

Dan Gladden proved to be a spark the Twins needed. An intense competitor who gave the Minnesotans an excellent glove in left field, he was key to both the 1987 and 1991 world championship seasons.

Gladden's uniform testified to his intense play; it was always dirty. This prompted Kent Hrbek to call him "Wrench."

"He said I looked like some mechanic guy," Gladden explained.

In Game 1 of the 1987 Series, Dan drilled a grand-slam home run to help pace the Twins to a 10-1 victory. He was also a big part of one of the greatest-ever World Series victories in 1991.

Game 7 of the 1991 Series was scoreless in the bottom of the tenth. Twins hurler Jack Morris had pitched a masterful ten innings. Gladden led off the bottom of the inning with a double by blooping the ball into short left and hustling for two. Chuck Knoblauch bunted him to third base. Two intentional walks brought up Gene Larkin, who drove a hit to left, scoring Dan with the world championship run.

When asked to name his career highlights, Dan recalled, "Celebrating after we clinched the pennant in Texas in 1987, and scoring the winning run in the 1991 Series."

Gladden signed as a free agent with Detroit after the 1992 season. His playing time declined over two years and, with a strike looming in 1994, Dan left the United States to play in Japan for the Yomiuri Giants of the Japanese Central League.

"I had always been a union rep and involved in union meetings, and I had a pretty good idea what was coming down with free agency, and there was a good opportunity in Japan," he recalled.

Gladden spent one year in the "Land of the Rising Sun," then returned to the United States. From 1996 to 1998, he worked as an advance scout for the Colorado Rockies. He became a minor-league roving instructor for San Francisco in 1999.

Dan's lifetime batting average was .270 with 203 doubles, forty triples, seventy-four home runs, 446 RBIs and 221 stolen bases in 1,197 games.

He began a new career as a Twins broadcaster, taking Herb Carneal's place for all road games, in 2000.

"I owe everything I have to baseball," Dan reflected, "my education, foundation, my house, the way I live. Baseball was what I played, from when I was a kid with my brothers throughout my life."

What does he miss about playing the game that was such a part of his life? "The people you meet and the competition," Dan replied.

Dan, his wife, Janice, and their daughters, Ashley and Whitney, live in Eden Prairie, Minnesota.

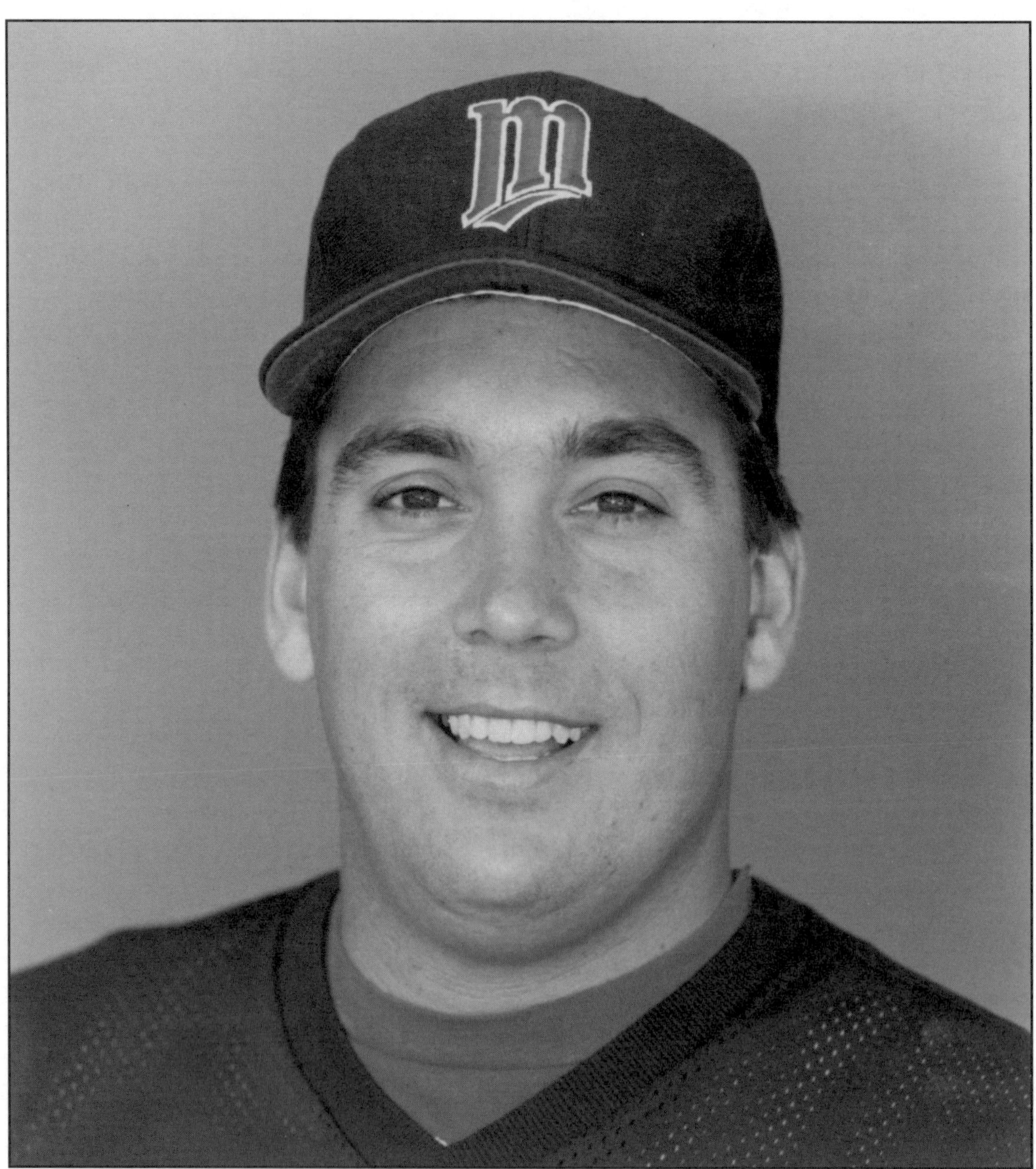

Kent Hrbek

Bats: Left
Throws: Right
Height: 6' 4"
Weight: 260 lbs.
Born: May 21, 1960, in Minnesota

YEAR	TEAM	LG	AVG	G	AB	R	H	2B	3B	HR	RBI	BB	K	OBP	SLG
1981	Min	AL	.239	24	67	5	16	5	0	1	7	5	9	.301	.358
1982	Min	AL	.301	140	532	82	160	21	4	23	92	54	80	.363	.485
1983	Min	AL	.297	141	515	75	153	41	5	16	84	57	71	.366	.489
1984	Min	AL	.311	149	559	80	174	31	3	27	107	65	87	.383	.522
1985	Min	AL	.278	158	593	78	165	31	2	21	93	67	87	.351	.444
1986	Min	AL	.267	149	550	85	147	27	1	29	91	71	81	.353	.478
1987	Min	AL	.285	143	477	85	136	20	1	34	90	84	60	.389	.545
1988	Min	AL	.312	143	510	75	159	31	0	25	76	67	54	.387	.520
1989	Min	AL	.272	109	375	59	102	17	0	25	84	53	35	.360	.517
1990	Min	AL	.287	143	492	61	141	26	0	22	79	69	45	.377	.474
1991	Min	AL	.284	132	462	72	131	20	1	20	89	67	48	.373	.461
1992	Min	AL	.244	112	394	52	96	20	0	15	58	71	56	.357	.409
1993	Min	AL	.242	123	392	60	95	11	1	25	83	71	57	.357	.467
1994	Min	AL	.270	81	274	34	74	11	0	10	53	37	28	.353	.420
			AVG	G	AB	R	H	2B	3B	HR	RBI	BB	K	OBP	SLG
			.282	1747	6192	903	1749	312	18	293	1086	838	798	.367	.481

Kent Hrbek played the game of baseball the way it should be played, hard but fun. He was a big kid who attracted the attention of Twins scouts with prodigious belts for his Bloomington American Legion team.

Growing up near old Metropolitan Stadium, Hrbek could see its lights glow as they illuminated the night sky. He enjoyed taking in games and watching his hero, Tony Oliva.

The Twins drafted Hrbek in the seventeenth round of the free agent draft after the 1978 Legion tournament. He played at Elizabethton, Tennessee, and then Wisconsin Rapids, before being assigned to Visalia, California, the Twins Class A affiliate, in 1981.

Hrbek tore up the California League, hitting .380 with twenty-seven homers and 112 RBIs. He was called up to the Twins on August 24, 1981.

In his first game, played at Yankee Stadium, Hrbek ripped a twelfth-inning home run to give his team a 3-2 triumph over the Yanks.

The next season Kent made the Twins out of 1982 spring training. He continued the promise shown the year before as he smacked twenty-three home runs with ninety-two RBIs while hitting .301. He attracted attention early that season with a twenty-three-game hitting streak. Hrbek went on that season to be named to the 1982 All-Star squad. He finished runner-up to Cal Ripken in Rookie-of-the-Year balloting.

Kent and his young teammates—Gary Gaetti, Tom Brunansky, Frank Viola, Randy Bush and others—struggled through some tough seasons as a team. They won only sixty games in 1982; through 1986, they finished well under .500 most years.

The exception was 1984, when the Twins finished 81-81. They made a run at the Western Division title before fading down the stretch.

But the team was maturing, and Hrbek's numbers stayed solid. The burly first baseman was surprisingly nimble in the field. His soft hands and quick feet made him one of the game's elite first sackers.

Kent grew increasingly disciplined as a hitter, sometimes sacrificing batting average for power. He set club records in 1987 with twenty home runs in the Metrodome and a .996 fielding percentage at first base.

The Twins finished twenty games under .500 for sixth place in 1986. But the players who had become full-time Twins in 1982 had struggled together and gelled. They surprised the world in 1987 by winning the American League pennant.

The highlight of Kent's Twins life was "coming home from Detroit to see 60,000 people cheering and waiting for us in the Metrodome" after winning the pennant.

The 1987 series was a tense, back-and-forth affair. The Twins won the first two games at home, then lost three at St. Louis. On October 24, they came home to the Metrodome and fell behind 5-2. Then Hrbek belted a grand-slam homer to lead the Twins to an 11-5 comeback victory and knot the Series at three apiece going in the final game.

A lot of players have spent sleepless nights before Game 7 of a World Series. Kent Hrbek got a call from a duck-hunting buddy who told him the ducks were flying at a favorite spot near Litchfield, sixty-five miles west of Minneapolis.

Kent spent the morning of the biggest game in his life in a duck blind.

"You're nuts," his friends, the Piepenburgs, told him.

"Hey, it's just a game," he replied.

He admitted that he was too excited and couldn't sleep anyway. He also said, according to Doug Piepenburg, "Tom Kelly would kill me if he knew."

After a successful hunt, he took some pictures with the Piepenburg kids and headed back to Minneapolis to play baseball.

The Twins won Game 7 by a score of 4-2. Hrbek recorded the final put-out on a throw across the diamond from Gary Gaetti.

Over seven years, Kent kept putting up big numbers for the Twins. Ten times in his thirteen full seasons he hit over twenty home runs to rank second on the Twins' all-time list. Only Harmon Killebrew has hit more than Kent's 293 round trippers.

The Twins captured a second World Series championship in 1991. One of the highlights of Game 2, played in Minnesota, occurred at first base.

The Atlanta Braves' Ron Gant singled to left. The throw from the outfield skipped past the outfielder and was fielded by the pitcher, Kevin Tapani. Tapani alertly gunned a throw across the diamond as Gant went back to the bag standing up. Gant stumbled, his leg came up, and he came off the base. The umpire called Ron out. It looked, to viewers, like Kent may have pushed Gant's leg off the bag.

"No," Hrbek commented, "he just stumbled, and I kept the tag on him. If he had slid, he would have been safe."

Over the next few years, injuries took their toll, and Hrbek did not top 400 at-bats again. He also missed spending time with his family, along with golfing, hunting, and fishing. He retired after the 1994 season to "enjoy what I had been missing."

"Baseball got me where I am today," Hrbek reflected. "It was something I did as a kid. I loved all sports. Baseball meant everything, as far as my life is concerned. It set my family up well and made me comfortable."

On the Twins all-time leader board, Hrbek is second to Killebrew in homers, RBIs, and walks. His number, 14, was retired on August 13, 1995.

Kent lives in the Twin Cities with his wife, Jeanne, and their eight-year-old daughter. He appears in some local television commercials, but mostly Kent is doing what he said he retired to do: be with his family, golf, hunt and fish.

Jerry Koosman

Bats: Right
Throws: Left
Height: 6' 2"
Weight: 205 lbs.
Born: December 23, 1942, in Minnesota

YEAR	TEAM	LG	ERA	W	L	Sv	G	IP	H	R	ER	BB	K	AVG. A
1967	NYN	NL	6.04	0	2	0	9	22.1	22	17	15	19	11	.259
1968	NYN	NL	2.08	19	12	0	35	263.2	221	72	61	69	178	.228
1969	NYN	NL	2.28	17	9	0	32	241.0	187	66	61	68	180	.216
1970	NYN	NL	3.14	12	7	0	30	212.0	189	87	74	71	118	.237
1971	NYN	NL	3.04	6	11	0	26	165.2	160	66	56	51	96	.256
1972	NYN	NL	4.14	11	12	1	34	163.0	155	81	75	52	147	.250
1973	NYN	NL	2.84	14	15	0	35	263.0	234	93	83	76	156	.242
1974	NYN	NL	3.36	15	11	0	35	265.0	258	113	99	85	188	.257
1975	NYN	NL	3.42	14	13	2	36	239.2	234	106	91	98	173	.261
1976	NYN	NL	2.69	21	10	0	34	247.1	205	81	74	66	200	.226
1977	NYN	NL	3.49	8	20	0	32	226.2	195	102	88	81	192	.232
1978	NYN	NL	3.75	3	15	2	38	235.1	221	110	98	84	160	.255
1979	Min	AL	3.38	20	13	0	37	263.2	268	108	99	83	157	.268
1980	Min	AL	4.03	16	13	2	38	243.1	252	119	109	69	149	.272
1981	Min	AL	4.20	3	9	5	19	94.1	98	49	44	34	55	.272
1981	ChA	AL	3.33	1	4	0	8	27.0	27	10	10	7	21	.260
1982	ChA	AL	3.84	11	7	3	42	173.1	194	81	74	38	88	.287
1983	ChA	AL	4.77	11	7	2	37	169.2	176	96	90	53	90	.266
1984	Phi	NL	3.25	14	15	0	36	224.0	232	95	81	60	137	.267
1985	Phi	NL	4.62	6	4	0	19	99.1	107	56	51	34	60	.276
			ERA	W	L	Sv	G	IP	H	R	ER	BB	K	AVG. A
			3.36	222	209	17	612	3,839.1	3,635	1,608	1,433	1,198	2,556	.252

Jerry Koosman was one of the most dominating pitchers in major-league baseball from the late 1960s into the 1980s. The left-hander from Appleton, Minnesota, reached double figures in wins nine times during that span. Twice he won twenty or more games.

Koosman attended Morris (Minnesota) Agriculture School in 1960, then spent a year the University of Minnesota, Morris. He went to Wahpeton State School of Science in North Dakota for one year.

Jerry entered the United States Army in October 1962, and played on the Army baseball team in El Paso, Texas. A scout for the New York Mets watched Koosman pitch and signed him to a contract on August 28, 1964.

Jerry pitched in the Mets' farm system in 1965 in Greenville, South Carolina. The final two weeks of the season, he played for Williamsport, Pennsylvania.

Jerry moved up quickly. In 1966 he pitched in Auburn, New York. In 1967, he made it to the Mets' major-league club for the first month as a relief pitcher. Then he was sent down to the AAA club in Jacksonville, Florida, where he was a starter.

Jerry was called up to the big club for the last month of that season. He stayed with the New York Mets for more than a decade until he was traded to the Twins.

He made the Mets' opening-day roster in 1968, but got in only nine games that year. In his rookie year, Koosman became the Mets' left-handed ace. Not only was he named National League Rookie Pitcher of the Year, but he was also runner-up to Johnny Bench for the N.L. Rookie of the Year honor. He lost out on that honor by only one-half vote; a Chicago writer split his ballot.

Jerry broke three Met club rookie records, all set by Tom Seaver the year before, with his nineteen wins, seven shutouts, and a 2.08 ERA. But Jerry also struck out sixty-two times in ninety-one at-bats, the most by a N.L. pitcher since 1900.

Later in his career Koosman became a hitting pitcher, but as he explained, "In pro ball you don't get to take much batting practice. Ten pitchers get about twenty minutes, and much of that time is spent bunting." But, he said, "I loved to hit."

Seaver and Koosman became one of baseball's top pitching duos the next season, 1969. It was a glorious year for the Mets as they swept through the playoffs and into the World Series after finishing ninth the year before.

Jerry won seventeen games during the season, but the 1969 World Series proved to be one of the biggest events of his career. He won two games against Baltimore, the first and last contests in the Mets' quest for the 1969 championship.

Through most of the 1970s, Seaver and Koosman mowed down opposing hitters, winning another pennant in 1973. Jerry overcame two sub-par seasons. In 1971, arm problems dropped his record to 6-11. Then, in 1973, his 2.84 ERA garnered him only a hard luck 14-15 record.

His best year with the Mets was 21-10 in 1976. Then the Mets began to decline. Seaver was traded away in 1977, and Koosman followed with seasons of 8-20 and 3-15.

"We were bad," Jerry remembered. "The Mets couldn't throw anybody out, field, hit, or score runs. We were an AA caliber team in the major leagues."

After the 1978 season, realizing that the Mets were not improving, Jerry tried to force a trade to the Minnesota Twins. On December 12, his wish came true.

He had really enjoyed playing in the Big Apple. "New York fans take sports very seriously," Jerry remembered. "They are avid fans."

Jerry bounced back in 1979 with the Twins. He went 20-13 with a 3.38 ERA for a team that compiled an 82-80 record. Koosman enjoyed playing for Calvin Griffith.

"Calvin was fun to play for," he said. "He treated his players fine."

The next year, 1980, was a good year for Koosman; he went 16-13. He was traded to the Chicago White Sox after nineteen games in 1981. Koosman pitched two more full seasons with the Sox before heading back to the National League in 1984 with the Phillies. Each season brought double-digit victory totals.

Jerry dropped to 6-4 for Philadelphia in an injury-plagued 1985 season. He hurt his knee working out, had surgery, and then tried to come back too quickly and re-injured his knee. He ended up retiring following the 1985 campaign.

Jerry Koosman was known as a control pitcher. In his career, he walked only 1,198 batters in 3,839 innings to average less than one free pass for every three innings.

"Concentration, steady mechanics, and practice," were key. "Or maybe," he joked, "throwing corn cobs and rocks at birds on highline wires around Morris."

Reflecting upon his career, Jerry said, "It was the highlight of my life. It was an opportunity to play against the best, and to know you were beating, or getting beat, by the best." He added that he enjoyed traveling, but there wasn't much time to see a lot.

When asked what he missed about major-league baseball, Koosman responded, "Playing on the field, everything else they can have. I miss pitching and the competition."

For the last ten years, Koosman has owned an engineering company in Hudson, Wisconsin, where he also lives.

Gene Larkin

Bats: Both
Throws: Right
Height: 6' 3"
Weight: 195 lbs.
Born: October 24, 1962, in New York

YEAR	TEAM	LG	AVG	G	AB	R	H	2B	3B	HR	RBI	BB	K	OBP	SLG
1987	*Min*	*AL*	*.266*	*85*	*233*	*23*	*62*	*11*	*2*	*4*	*28*	*25*	*31*	*.340*	*.382*
1988	*Min*	*AL*	*.267*	*149*	*505*	*56*	*135*	*30*	*2*	*8*	*70*	*68*	*55*	*.368*	*.382*
1989	*Min*	*AL*	*.267*	*136*	*446*	*61*	*119*	*25*	*1*	*6*	*46*	*54*	*57*	*.353*	*.368*
1990	*Min*	*AL*	*.269*	*119*	*401*	*46*	*108*	*26*	*4*	*5*	*42*	*42*	*55*	*.343*	*.392*
1991	*Min*	*AL*	*.286*	*98*	*255*	*34*	*73*	*14*	*1*	*2*	*19*	*30*	*21*	*.361*	*.373*
1992	*Min*	*AL*	*.246*	*115*	*337*	*38*	*83*	*18*	*1*	*6*	*42*	*28*	*43*	*.308*	*.359*
1993	*Min*	*AL*	*.264*	*56*	*144*	*17*	*38*	*7*	*1*	*1*	*19*	*21*	*16*	*.357*	*.347*
			AVG	*G*	*AB*	*R*	*H*	*2B*	*3B*	*HR*	*RBI*	*BB*	*K*	*OBP*	*SLG*
			.266	*758*	*2,321*	*275*	*618*	*131*	*12*	*32*	*266*	*268*	*278*	*.348*	*.374*

It must have been like a dream come true for a boy from North Bellmore, New York, to play baseball at Columbia University. Especially if he was a Yankee baseball fan, like Gene Larkin.

Larkin grew up watching the exploits of a fine Yankee center fielder, Bobby Murcer. But he was following in the footsteps of another Yankee legend, the immortal "Iron Man," Lou Gehrig, who had also played first base at Columbia.

Gene went on to surpass all of the great Gehrig's school batting records, including batting average and home runs. Larkin was drafted out of Columbia in 1984 in the twentieth round.

The Twins sent Larkin to Elizabethton, Tennessee, to play a short season of rookie ball in the Appalachian League. Gene played a full season of A ball at Visalia, California, in 1985. The next year he moved up to a full AA season at Orlando, Florida.

Larkin did well in the minors, never hitting below .302, and his rewards came soon. He played just one month of AAA ball for Portland in 1987, before being called up to the Twins. The call-up was great timing, as the team was en route to its first world championship.

"Eighty-seven was special because I was a rookie. Your dream is not only to get to the big leagues, but once you get there, to play in the World Series. I accomplished that in one year.

"To me it was phenomenal just to be in the right place at the right time. I learned a great deal about how to play the game at a professional level. Tom Kelly was a big help to me in how I approached the game.

"Kelly relates to everyone very well. He knows the game is very, very tough. He knows everyone's strengths and weaknesses, and tries to put players in positions where they can succeed. He uses his whole roster and understands that the game gets very mentally tiring.

"He uses his bench wisely. Kelly knows who his superstars are and might ride them a little bit. He doesn't let his players get too high or too low.

"When you give Kelly players with the ability to compete, his managerial skills are second to none on the field. He's never gotten the accolades he deserves, even though he won two World Series, because he manages a Midwestern team in a small market."

For the next three years, the switch-hitter was remarkably consistent. As a first baseman, right fielder, and pinch hitter, he batted over 400 times each year, hitting .267 twice and .269 once.

Glory struck again in 1991 as the Twins made another World Series appearance. Larkin will always be known for his dramatic tenth inning hit, which plated the game- and series-winning run in the final game.

"Ninety-one was very special," Gene said, "because of that one hit in Game 7. Every October people bring that hit up, so some way it'll always be remembered."

The series against the Braves was tied three games apiece. After nine and one-half innings, the final game remained scoreless. Dan Gladden led off the bottom of the tenth with a double. Chuck Knoblauch sacrificed him to third. Puckett and Hrbek were intentionally walked to fill the bases with just one out.

Jarvis Brown, who had pinch run for Chili Davis two innings earlier, was due up. Right-hander Olejandro Pena was on the hill for Atlanta. Larkin explained the setting.

"It was a perfect situation. I was a contact hitter, and in that situation you just want to put the ball in play. Preferably you want to hit a fly ball and not strike out or hit into a double play.

"I had watched Pena pitch the whole series, and predominantly his best pitch was a fastball. He liked to get ahead of the hitters with a high fastball. He threw it high and away. I just had to put a decent swing on the ball and hit the ball in the outfield.

"The outfield was playing in. Outside of the situation being very nerve-wracking, it was a situation that a lot of hitters should succeed in, because both the outfield and infield are in.

"You just wanna put the ball in play and the chances of succeeding are very strong."

Larkin, batting left against the right-handed pitcher, drove the ball to left over the outfielder's head to score Gladden. The Twins had won another World Series championship. Gene's hit is immortalized in baseball records.

For Larkin, who started playing the game when he was six years old under his dad's tutelage, it was the greatest moment of his career.

"Getting to the big leagues was my greatest moment. But that hit was my biggest moment in the big leagues," Gene commented.

"It was always a dream to get to the big leagues. I didn't have the greatest ability in the world, but I had a terrific work ethic.

"I think baseball is very special. Number one, it's a team game that doesn't depend on how big you are, or how strong you are or how smart you are. It combines a lot of different ingredients. You have to have a lot of instinct, mental prowess as a ballplayer. You might not be the smartest guy off the field, but there are a lot of guys who are very, very baseball smart," Larkin continued.

"I just thought it was very intriguing to combine all that into one game, the defense, the hitting, the pitching, the specialties of the role player, the pinch hitting, the relief pitching.

"It's a very special game. I'm biased, but hitting a baseball, a round ball with a round bat, has to be one of the, if not the, most difficult things to do in sports. It's a great physical and mental game."

The Twins released Larkin during the last week of 1994 spring training. He had opportunities to catch on with other major-league teams, but, he said, "I just felt it was very special I had played my entire career, seven years, with just one team. I played on two World Series teams. I played with a terrific manager and a great group of guys.

"I didn't want to move my family and sit on the bench behind some guy on some team that I didn't have any allegiance to. I wanted to say I played my whole career with the Minnesota Twins. I wanted to reside the rest of my life in Minnesota."

Larkin reflected on what he liked about baseball. "I really enjoyed competing at that level. I enjoyed preparing myself every day to play at a major-league level. I was a role player and didn't play every day. I knew I wasn't going to start every day, but I took pride that, when I was called upon, I'd be physically and mentally ready to play.

"The game is more of a business than a game now. To get twenty-five guys together on the same page for six months is quite an accomplishment. We did that. We competed and put on a good show. I'm very proud that I was on a team that did that. I came along at a terrific time."

For the last six years, Gene has put his economics degree to work in the Twin Cities area, doing insurance and financial planning.

Gene and Kathleen have been married thirteen years and have two children: a daughter, nine, and a son, seven. They reside in Eden Prairie, Minnesota.

Tim Laudner

Bats: Right
Throws: Right
Height: 6' 3"
Weight: 212 lbs.
Born: June 7, 1958, in Iowa

YEAR	TEAM	LG	AVG	G	AB	R	H	2B	3B	HR	RBI	BB	K	OBP	SLG
1981	Min	AL	.163	14	43	4	7	2	0	2	5	3	17	.234	.349
1982	Min	AL	.255	93	306	37	78	19	1	7	33	34	74	.328	.392
1983	Min	AL	.185	62	168	20	31	9	0	6	18	15	49	.250	.345
1984	Min	AL	.206	87	262	31	54	16	1	10	35	18	78	.258	.389
1985	Min	AL	.238	72	164	16	39	5	0	7	19	12	45	.292	.396
1986	Min	AL	.244	76	193	21	47	10	0	10	29	24	56	.333	.451
1987	Min	AL	.191	113	288	30	55	7	1	16	43	23	80	.252	.389
1988	Min	AL	.251	117	375	38	94	18	1	13	54	36	89	.316	.408
1989	Min	AL	.222	100	239	24	53	11	1	6	27	25	65	.293	.351
			AVG	G	AB	R	H	2B	3B	HR	RBI	BB	K	OBP	SLG
			.225	734	2,038	221	458	97	5	77	263	190	553	.292	.391

It was a moment Tim Laudner never expected. He was standing shoulder to shoulder with twenty-five guys, being introduced to play in a World Series game. Soon he would be part of a world championship baseball team.

"Providing," Tim commented, "the area, state, and region with one of the greatest presents ever."

Laudner was born in Mason City, Iowa, and lived in the small town of Rockford, Iowa, until he was seven. In 1965 the Laudner family moved to Minnesota, where Tim attended school in the Osseo district.

Tim grew up playing sports like a lot of kids. He liked to play baseball. While professional baseball players didn't occupy much of his attention, he did admire Boston outfielder Fred Lynn. Mostly, he just played sandlot ball with his buddies.

Laudner laments that kids don't play ball on their own the way they did when he was young. "There are very few opportunities for kids to go and do things on their own, so they don't because it's easier not to. They wait for someone to say, 'You have to do this, and they have to do that.'

"From a baseball standpoint, baseball is the most skilled and probably the hardest sport to master because you have to throw the ball, you have to catch the ball, and the hardest thing is to hit the ball. What ten-year old wants to do that? What ten-year old, what fifteen-year old, wants to set themselves up for that kind of failure? It's easier to do something else."

Tim graduated from Park Center (Minnesota) High School in 1976 and attended the University of Missouri. A catcher, he was taken in the third round of baseball's amateur draft of 1979 by the Minnesota Twins.

After a player's third year of college, he can elect to pursue a pro career or return to college. Tim reported to the Twins farm club in Orlando, Florida. Over the next few years, Laudner played in Orlando, then in Visalia (California) for Tom Kelly, and in AAA Toledo (Ohio). Tim was Southern League MVP at Orlando in 1981. He hit .284 with forty-two home runs to earn a late-season promotion to the Twins.

Laudner made his major-league debut a memorable one. It came on August 28, 1981, against Detroit pitcher Dave Rozema. In his first big-league at-bat, Tim ripped a homer over the Metropolitan Stadium fence. He cracked another one the next day against lefty Dan Shatzader.

Tim was starting catcher for the Twins in 1982. His former Orlando teammates Gary Gaetti, Kent Hrbek, Frank Viola, and Randy Bush joined him on the Twins squad.

The Twins struggled for the next several years. In 1983 Tim's former Orlando skipper, Tom Kelly, was named third-base coach. Their best finish was 81-81 in 1984. Minnesota sagged to 71-91 in 1986 and finished sixth. From 1983 until 1987, Tim shared catching duties with Dave Engle and Mark Salas.

The hopes and dreams of the "Class of '82" came true in 1987, Kelly's first full year at the Twins helm. The team that had struggled together for so long finally won it all. Laudner started most games that year and appeared in 113.

In the second game of the World Series, Tim smacked a home run against Cardinal reliever Lee Tunnell. After the series, the Cardinals released Tunnell. Tim laughingly commented that most players he hit homers off seemed to get released.

Laudner remembered about Tunnell, "Funny thing was, Lee was a heck of a nice guy. I found that out because, in spring training of 1988, I wasn't playing and I went down to the bullpen.

"Unbeknownst to me, they had brought some guys in from our minor-league camp in case we ran out of pitching. Lee Tunnell had been released by the Cardinals and was with them. He sat down next to me and said, 'I thought you were going to have a steak dinner waiting here for me.'

"I said, 'Whadda ya mean?' and he said, 'I'm Lee Tunnell.' I said, 'Oh, how ya doin?' and he said, 'Don't worry about it, man.'" Tunnell played briefly for the Twins in 1989.

The year after the Twins won the 1987 World Series, Tim played in 117 games, the most in his career. Skipper Tom Kelly named him to the 1988 All-Star squad, along with Twins teammates Jeff Reardon, Frank Viola, Kirby Puckett, and Gary Gaetti. Laudner doubled in his only at-bat.

Tim remembered the All-Star Game as very nice. He felt extremely honored to have been picked by Kelly. But how he and his teammates reacted to receiving an individual honor there revealed the depth of their feelings of team unity.

Laudner noted, "The day of the game we went down for breakfast, the five of us and our wives. At the breakfast, major-league baseball awarded us with our All-Star rings. Everybody else in line was very proud and very appreciative and put on their rings. We had already been wearing our World Series rings, so we just stuck the All-Star rings in our pockets.

"Accomplishing something in a team sport is much more satisfying than accomplishing something individually. But the game was nice."

Laudner hit .251 in 375 at-bats in 1988 before dipping to .222 the following season. He was still a relatively young player, thirty-one years old, when he announced his retirement prior to the 1990 campaign.

"I'd had enough," he recalled. "There's a lot more to it. But I just wanted to spend more time with my family. Basically, I'd gotten a heck of a lot more out of my career than I'd ever anticipated.

"Quite truthfully, I think as a ball player you go out there and try to do your best, but the Twins were getting close to the realization that I couldn't play a lick." Tim chuckled, "You can only stay ahead of 'em for so long, and they were getting on to me."

For the last ten years, Tim has operated a subcontracting business and lived in Medina, Minnesota. He misses the opportunity to compete in major-league baseball, but golf and competitive target shooting provide outlets for him.

Tim enjoyed the camaraderie and the extraordinary people with whom he had an opportunity to advance in the sport. Being able to share something very special with them, a true team championship, held deep significance for him.

"I appreciated the people I met along the way and the things I learned along the way," Laudner said.

"I think one of the most important things was that I feel good about what we in turn gave back to the game of baseball as a group. I only hope that the players today treat the game with the respect and dignity that it deserves.

"I hope that the people who came before us—Oliva, Allison, Killebrew, Mincher, Reese, Uhlaender, those people who played into the late seventies—I hope they look upon us as a group of people that, yes, did indeed treat the game with some respect and some dignity and took care of the game and made it better for those who came behind us."

Tim lives in Medina with his wife of twenty years, Tammy, and their two children: Sam, fourteen, and Sarah, ten.

Kirby Puckett

Bats: Right
Throws: Right
Height: 5' 9"
Weight: 223 lbs.
Born: March 14, 1961, in Illinois

YEAR	TEAM	LG	AVG	G	AB	R	H	2B	3B	HR	RBI	BB	K	OBP	SLG
1984	*Min*	*AL*	*.296*	*128*	*557*	*63*	*165*	*12*	*5*	*0*	*31*	*16*	*69*	*.320*	*.336*
1985	*Min*	*AL*	*.288*	*161*	*691*	*80*	*199*	*29*	*13*	*4*	*74*	*41*	*87*	*.330*	*.385*
1986	*Min*	*AL*	*.328*	*161*	*680*	*119*	*223*	*37*	*6*	*31*	*96*	*34*	*99*	*.366*	*.537*
1987	*Min*	*AL*	*.332*	*157*	*624*	*96*	*207*	*32*	*5*	*28*	*99*	*32*	*91*	*.367*	*.534*
1988	*Min*	*AL*	*.356*	*158*	*657*	*109*	*234*	*42*	*5*	*24*	*121*	*23*	*83*	*.375*	*.545*
1989	*Min*	*AL*	*.339*	*159*	*635*	*75*	*215*	*45*	*4*	*9*	*85*	*41*	*59*	*.379*	*.465*
1990	*Min*	*AL*	*.298*	*146*	*551*	*82*	*164*	*40*	*3*	*12*	*80*	*57*	*73*	*.365*	*.446*
1991	*Min*	*AL*	*.319*	*152*	*611*	*92*	*195*	*29*	*6*	*15*	*89*	*31*	*78*	*.352*	*.460*
1992	*Min*	*AL*	*.329*	*160*	*639*	*104*	*210*	*38*	*4*	*19*	*110*	*44*	*97*	*.374*	*.490*
1993	*Min*	*AL*	*.296*	*156*	*622*	*89*	*184*	*39*	*3*	*22*	*89*	*47*	*93*	*.349*	*.474*
1994	*Min*	*AL*	*.317*	*108*	*439*	*79*	*139*	*32*	*3*	*20*	*112*	*28*	*47*	*.362*	*.540*
1995	*Min*	*AL*	*.314*	*137*	*538*	*83*	*169*	*39*	*0*	*23*	*99*	*56*	*89*	*.379*	*.515*
			AVG	*G*	*AB*	*R*	*H*	*2B*	*3B*	*HR*	*RBI*	*BB*	*K*	*OBP*	*SLG*
			.3181	*783*	*7,244*	*1,071*	*2,304*	*414*	*57*	*207*	*1,085*	*450*	*965*	*.360*	*.477*

It was a spine-tingling matchup in the 1991 World Series. Charlie Leibrandt, Atlanta Braves left-hander, peered from the mound at the short, stocky, muscular hitter standing at the plate. The din in the Metrodome defied belief as over 50,000 voices roared the batter's name: "KIRBY, KIRBY!"

Leibrandt swung into his windup and fired. Kirby Puckett lifted his front leg slightly and then ripped at the pitch. The ball shot deep to left-center, rocketing into the stands.

The next thing millions heard was the voice of a television broadcaster shouting, "And we'll see you tomorrow night!"

Kirby Puckett, the young man from Chicago, had just ended Game 6 of the 1991 World Series with one of the most dramatic home runs in World Series history. The Twins and Braves would meet the next night in the deciding Game 7.

Kirby Puckett's story is one about which young athletes dream. Born in the projects of Chicago in 1962, Puckett became what many believe to be the greatest Twin ever.

In his twelve years with the team, Puckett built a career that led to glory at Cooperstown. He was voted into the Baseball Hall of Fame, on the first ballot, on January 16, 2001.

"It's one of the proudest moments in my life," he said. "I always had a goal to be a ballplayer. I didn't know I'd make the Hall of Fame."

He credits much of his success to the athletes with whom he played. "I was fortunate to be with great players, a great manager, Tom Kelly, and a great organization. I don't miss the games so much as I miss the camaraderie."

He achieved Twins career records in five categories: hits, doubles, total bases, at-bats, and runs. He was a ten-time American League All-Star. Six times Puckett was awarded a Gold Glove as the league's best defensive center fielder. Five times his hitting was rewarded with a Silver Slugger Award.

The odds against him were enormous for more than the usual reasons aspiring athletes face. It's tough to come out of the projects with your head on straight, but Kirby did. He played baseball almost every day through the summers, went to school and stayed out of trouble.

When asked what it was like growing up in Chicago, Kirby replied, "It was hard, but I had to be very strong. The police called the projects 'the place where hope died.'" He was one of nine children.

Kirby went to Chicago Calumet High School, where he was named a High School All-American in 1979. At Triton Junior College in River Grove, Illinois, Kirby hit .472 and led Triton to the NJCAA finals in 1982.

Puckett didn't have the chiseled body of a classic athlete. When a pro scout came to watch his team play, the scout was looking at someone else. But it was the hard-working hustle of Kirby Puckett that won the Twins representative's attention.

In the first round of the January 1982 Free Agent Draft, the Minnesota Twins took the outfielder from Chicago. Kirby would spend his entire career in a Twins uniform. His play would directly correspond to the glory days of Minnesota baseball, as Puckett helped deliver two world championships.

His stay in the minor leagues was a short one. Kirby was sent to Elizabethton, Tennessee, to play rookie ball, and then to Visalia in the California League. Spring of 1984 found Puckett with Toledo, Ohio, in AAA ball. But he lasted just a month with the Mudhens before getting the call to the Twins.

On May 7, 1984, Kirby, after a long taxi ride from the airport, arrived late and short of cab fare, for a game in Anaheim. Manager Billy Gardner told him to sit and watch and that the next night he'd lead off and play center field.

Kirby made his major-league debut against the California Angels on May 8. His first time up, he rapped a ball into the hole. The shortstop backhanded the ball and fired it across the diamond. In a bang-bang play at first, Kirby was out.

Puckett thought, "Man, in Triple A that would have been a hit."

But it was the only time he was retired that night. In his following at-bats, the rookie rapped out four hits for an auspicious start.

"I knew that first night, I could make in the big leagues," Kirby recalled.

He started out as a singles and doubles hitter. But new skipper Ray Miller decided to make him the number-three hitter in the lineup. Then batting coach Tony Oliva worked with Kirby to develop a front-leg kick. The technique helped him to stay back and then move forward with power. It worked well, and Kirby hit for power.

Many memorable games would follow in his twelve years in major-league baseball. Kirby lashed out six hits in six at-bats, slugging for fourteen total bases in one game at Milwaukee on August 30, 1987. The next day he went 4-5, engineering an amazing 10-11 streak.

Kirby described his amazing series. "I was in a slump coming into Milwaukee. I didn't take batting practice the first game. Tony Oliva just talked about hitting and the pitchers with me. I went 4-5.

"The next day coach Rick Stelmaszek was throwing to me and I knew just where the ball was going. I even hit one out of County Stadium. The first time I ever did that in batting practice. I went 6-6 that afternoon."

Kirby was known for his work ethic. He was often the first to arrive at the ballpark and the last to leave. For a 7:00 P.M. game, it was not unusual for Puckett to leave home by 2:00 P.M. to head to the park.

"I wanted to unwind, read my mail, and take extra hitting if I needed it," Kirby said.

Game 6 of the 1987 World Series saw Puckett go 4-4. Even so, it was four years later in Game 6 of the 1991 World Series that stamped Kirby Puckett's greatness firmly into the minds of millions of baseball fans.

The Twins had jumped ahead of the Braves two games to none while opening the World Series at the Metrodome. Then big trouble struck the Twins in Atlanta. They dropped three in a row.

The Twins returned home on the brink of disaster. One loss and the series would be over. Puckett told his teammates, "Jump on my back, and I'll carry you." He wasn't kidding.

The Twins took an early 2-0 lead in the first inning. In the second inning with a runner on base, the Braves' Ron Gant lofted a drive deep to left-center field. Kirby raced back to the Plexiglas fence and timed his leap perfectly. Gant's drive slapped into Kirby's glove, robbing him of an extra-base hit, and the Braves of at least one run.

Finally, in the bottom of the eleventh, Puckett's third hit of the game—the homer off Leibrandt—sent Twins fans home deliriously happy.

The next night Minnesota won its second baseball world championship with a thrilling 1-0 extra-inning victory. Kirby was World Series MVP.

Kirby Puckett continued to make baseball history for the Twins for the next four years as he excited crowds at bat and in the field. Then, baseball fans got a big scare at the end of the 1995 season, when Kirby was hit by a pitched ball near his left eye in the last series of the season.

Relief that the injury wouldn't end Kirby's playing days was short-lived. On March 28, 1996, during spring training in Fort Myers, Florida, Kirby awoke with blurred vision in his right eye. It was diagnosed as glaucoma, unrelated to his injury. Later that summer Puckett was forced to announce his retirement from active play because of irreversible damage to his right retina. He had planned to play through 2000.

As of spring 2001, Puckett was active in the Twins front office as an executive vice president, with responsibilities including team strategy, player evaluation and recruiting, and individual player instruction, while also working as an instructor in the minor-league system.

Kirby still is very involved in the community. He was awarded the 1996 Roberto Clemente Man of the Year Award by Major League Baseball for his outstanding community service as well as the Branch Rickey Award for his community involvement.

According to Kirby, major-league baseball was "like living a fairly tale life, a dream. It was all I thought it would be and more. I owe my life to baseball."

Many honors came his way, but the most special moment was "the world championships. Walkin' out on the field and seeing how all the hard work paid off."

Wherever he goes, Kirby is still the subject of adoration from fans who remember the smiling, determined ball player who made watching baseball fun and exciting in Minnesota. He was dedicated to winning but never forgot the fans.

The *Minneapolis Star-Tribune* named Puckett "Minnesota's Most Important Sports Figure of the Twentieth Century."

Kirby and his wife, Tonya, have two children, Catherine and Kirby, Jr. The family lives in Edina, Minnesota.

Paul Molitor

Bats: Right
Throws: Right
Height: 6' 0"
Weight: 195 lbs.
Born: August 22, 1956, in Minnesota

YEAR	TEAM	LG	AVG	G	AB	R	H	2B	3B	HR	RBI	BB	K	OBP	SLG
1978	Mil	AL	.273	125	521	73	142	26	4	6	45	19	54	.301	.372
1979	Mil	AL	.322	140	584	88	188	27	16	9	62	48	48	.372	.469
1980	Mil	AL	.304	111	450	81	137	29	2	9	37	48	48	.372	.438
1981	Mil	AL	.267	64	251	45	67	11	0	2	19	25	29	.341	.335
1982	Mil	AL	.302	160	666	136	201	26	8	19	71	69	93	.366	.450
1983	Mil	AL	.270	152	608	95	164	28	6	15	47	59	74	.333	.410
1984	Mil	AL	.217	13	46	3	10	1	0	0	6	2	8	.245	.239
1985	Mil	AL	.297	140	576	93	171	28	3	10	48	54	80	.356	.408
1986	Mil	AL	.281	105	437	62	123	24	6	9	55	40	81	.340	.426
1987	Mil	AL	.353	118	465	114	164	41	5	16	75	69	67	.438	.566
1988	Mil	AL	.312	154	609	115	190	34	6	13	60	71	54	.384	.452
1989	Mil	AL	.315	155	615	84	194	35	4	11	56	64	67	.379	.439
1990	Mil	AL	.285	103	418	64	119	27	6	12	45	37	51	.343	.464
1991	Mil	AL	.325	158	665	133	216	32	13	17	75	77	62	.399	.489
1992	Mil	AL	.320	158	609	89	195	36	7	12	89	73	66	.389	.461
1993	Tor	AL	.332	160	636	121	211	37	5	22	111	77	71	.402	.509
1994	Tor	AL	.341	115	454	86	155	30	4	14	75	55	48	.410	.518
1995	Tor	AL	.270	130	525	63	142	31	2	15	60	61	57	.350	.423
1996	Min	AL	.341	161	660	99	225	41	8	9	113	56	72	.390	.468
1997	Min	AL	.305	135	538	63	164	32	4	10	89	45	73	.351	.435
1998	Min	AL	.281	126	502	75	141	29	5	4	69	45	41	.335	.382
			AVG	G	AB	R	H	2B	3B	HR	RBI	BB	K	OBP	SLG
			.306	2,683	10,835	1,782	3,319	605	114	234	1,307	1,094	1,244	.369	.448

The score stood knotted at 1-1 in the bottom of the eighth inning. Sal Bando of the Milwaukee Brewers danced off third base. The Minnesota Twins pitcher Gary Serum faced a fellow native Minnesotan wearing a Brewers' uniform, Paul Molitor.

"Molitor's hands were so quick," Serum recalled, "it didn't work to pitch inside. He'd get around on it. If you went with a slider away, he'd go with the pitch. You just had to hit your spot and hope to get him out. Paul didn't hurt his .300 career batting average against me."

That day in Milwaukee, Paul Molitor used another of his weapons. With two outs and two strikes on him, he bunted down the third baseline. Third sacker Mike Cubbage charged and fired to first base, too late to get the speedy Molitor. Bando scored, and the Brewers won 2-1.

It was 1978, the rookie year in what was to be a stellar career for the man from St. Paul, Minnesota. Molitor, or "Molly," attended Cretin High School in St. Paul, where he played soccer, basketball, and baseball. Then he moved on to the University of Minnesota.

His accomplishments as a Gopher include being named an All-American by the *Sporting News*, and twice All Big Ten Conference. They placed Paul high in the draft. He was the third pick overall, Milwaukee's first, on draft day, June 7, 1977. After a brief tour in the minors at Burlington, Iowa, Paul made the Brewers in 1978.

An infielder, Molitor played second base and then moved to shortstop when Robin Yount was injured. Paul hit .273 in 1978 and was named the *Sporting News* American League Rookie of the Year.

Molly ripped the ball at a .322 clip the following season, mostly batting leadoff. He hit .304 in 1980 and was voted onto the All-Star squad as a second baseman, his first of seven All-Star selections.

In 1981 he was moved to center field, then to right after he had surgery to repair torn left ankle ligaments. Molitor was extremely versatile in the field. He was also plagued by injuries much of his career.

Paul had one of his most memorable seasons as a third baseman in 1982. In addition to hitting .302, he led the league with 136 runs scored, also a club record.

He socked three solo home runs in a 9-7 loss to Kansas City on May 12 of that year.

Paul helped to lead his team into the World Series against the St. Louis Cardinals. On October 12, 1982, he set a series record with five hits in one game, a 10-0 drubbing of the Cards. St. Louis eventually won the series.

Molitor missed most of 1984 when an injury to his elbow required surgery. But the following season he fought back to a .297 average and another trip to the All-Star Game. Molitor was named Milwaukee's Comeback Player of the Year.

From that point on in his career, Paul was used mostly as a designated hitter. His glove work was still exceptional, but the Brewers wanted to protect him from further injury.

In a career of exceptional seasons, 1987 shone bright. Joe DiMaggio's fifty-six-game hitting streak is one of baseball's most enduring records. Paul mounted a serious challenge until his streak ended at thirty-nine.

Another high point came when Molly stole three bases in one inning against the Oakland A's on July 26 of that season.

In spite of two trips to the disabled list that year, Molitor led the American League with 114 runs scored and forty-one doubles. His .353 batting average was good for second in the league.

Molly played fifteen years for the Brewers. Eight times in that span he hit over .300. But in 1993, he joined the Toronto Blue Jays as a free agent.

The year 1993 was a dream season for Paul. A .332 average, twenty-two home runs, and 111 RBIs led to a tremendous World Series. This time Molitor was on the winning side as the Blue Jays took the series in six games.

Paul was named Series MVP, deservedly so. He set six game World Series records for hits (twelve), runs (ten), triples (two), extra-base hits (six), and average (.500). He had six consecutive hits in the series.

After two great seasons in Canada, again topping .300 both years, Paul slumped to .270 in 1995.

Deciding it was time to come home and play for his hometown team, Molitor signed with the Twins. He rebounded with a sterling year. He hit a robust .341

with career highs in hits (225) and RBIs (113). Besides Paul, only Ty Cobb and Sam Rice have hit for over .300 after passing their fortieth birthdays.

Late in the year, at Kansas City, Paul reached a dramatic milestone when he rapped his 3,000th hit, a triple to right center. "My most memorable moment as a Twin was that hit," Paul related.

The next two seasons in Minnesota, Molitor continued to play well, mostly as a DH. Getting over 500 at-bats, he hit .305 and .281. Paul announced his retirement prior to the 1999 campaign.

It was a long career. Considering all the physical adversity, Paul felt fortunate to have played so long. "My most satisfaction," he said, "was to be able to play twenty-one years after having so many injuries early in my career."

Molitor's impressive career is likely to lead to the Baseball Hall of Fame. It included 3,319 hits and a .308 batting average. His fans will remember Molly as a man of remarkable skill who played with hustle and determination to rise above physical injury and adversity to star at the top level in his profession.

Paul's accomplishments are a recipe for enshrinement at Cooperstown. He is the only one to have over 500 doubles, 200 home runs and 500 stolen bases. No other player has over 3,000 hits, 200 home runs and 500 stolen bases.

Molitor is also the only player to have over a .300 career batting average, 200 home runs and 400 stolen bases. In the history of major-league baseball, Paul ranks eighth in total hits, fifteenth in runs scored, and tenth in total at-bats.

Most important, Molitor changed how the designated-hitter position could be played. Paul used a high batting average and speed, not just power. His play changed the position.

"Baseball gave me a chance to fulfill a boyhood dream and achieve a goal I was passionate about," Paul commented. "It also provided me with an opportunity to garner many life memories and produce lifelong friendships."

The Twins have employed Molitor as a bench coach since his retirement. He lives in Edina with his wife, Linda, and daughter, Blaire.

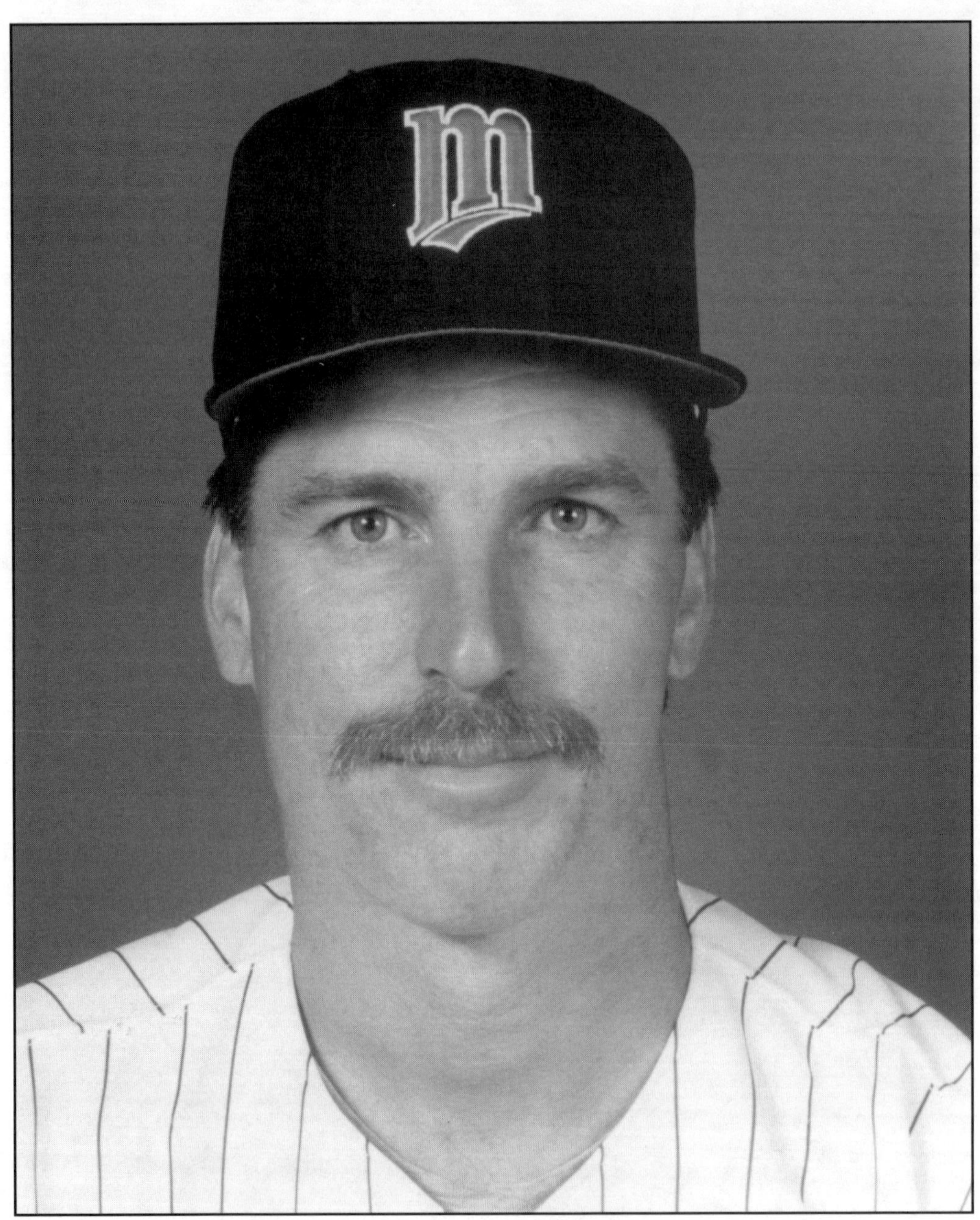

Jack Morris

Bats: Right
Throws: Right
Height: 6' 3"
Weight: 200 lbs.
Born: May 16, 1955, in Minnesota

YEAR	TEAM	LG	ERA	W	L	Sv	G	IP	H	R	ER	BB	K	AVG. A
1977	Det	AL	3.74	1	1	0	7	45.2	38	20	19	23	28	.235
1978	Det	AL	4.33	3	5	0	28	106.0	107	57	51	49	48	.268
1979	Det	AL	3.28	17	7	0	27	197.2	179	76	72	59	113	.244
1980	Det	AL	4.18	16	15	0	36	250.0	252	125	116	87	112	.263
1981	Det	AL	3.05	14	7	0	25	198.0	153	69	67	78	97	.218
1982	Det	AL	4.06	17	16	0	37	266.1	247	131	120	96	135	.247
1983	Det	AL	3.34	20	13	0	37	293.2	257	117	109	83	232	.233
1984	Det	AL	3.60	19	11	0	35	240.1	221	108	96	87	148	.241
1985	Det	AL	3.33	16	11	0	35	257.0	212	102	95	110	191	.225
1986	Det	AL	3.27	21	8	0	35	267.0	229	105	97	82	223	.229
1987	Det	AL	3.38	18	11	0	34	266.0	227	111	100	93	208	.228
1988	Det	AL	3.94	15	13	0	34	235.0	225	115	103	83	168	.251
1989	Det	AL	4.86	6	14	0	24	170.1	189	102	92	59	115	.283
1990	Det	AL	4.51	15	18	0	36	249.2	231	144	125	97	162	.242
1991	Min	AL	3.43	18	12	0	35	246.2	226	107	94	92	163	.245
1992	Tor	AL	4.04	21	6	0	34	240.2	222	114	108	80	132	.246
1993	Tor	AL	6.19	7	12	0	27	152.2	189	116	105	65	103	.302
1994	Cle	AL	5.60	10	6	0	23	141.1	163	96	88	67	100	.292
			ERA	W	L	Sv	G	IP	H	R	ER	BB	K	AVG. A
			3.90	254	186	0	549	3,824.0	3,567	1,815	1,657	1,390	2,478	.247

Game 7 of the 1991 World Series is burned indelibly in the minds of Minnesota baseball fans. Snapshots like frozen memories are etched in the past.

We see Gene Larkin slapping the ball to left, Dan Gladden racing home to score, and we remember Jack Morris.

Jack Morris, who pitched the masterful ten-inning shutout of the Braves. Morris, who confidently glared at Atlanta hitters as he slammed the door on their championship hopes.

It was even better that Morris was a hometown boy. Jack was from St. Paul, attended Highland Park High School and grew up watching Killebrew, Oliva, and Carew. However, it was pitchers like Tom Seaver, Nolan Ryan, and Steve Carleton who really captured his admiration.

After high school, Jack attended Brigham Young University. Following his third year there, the Detroit Tigers drafted him in 1976. They immediately sent Morris to AA ball in Montgomery, Alabama.

Jack pitched AAA for Evansville, Indiana, in 1977, until he was called up to the Tigers late in the year. Morris was used sparingly the next year, appearing in only twenty-eight games for the 1978 Tigers.

Then, for the next nine seasons, Jack was the Tigers' top winner. He was baseball's winningest pitcher for the 1980s. His durability and success were incredible. Using a fastball, split-finger fastball, and slider, Morris pitched in at least thirty-three games every year between 1980 and 1988, with the exception of strike-shortened 1981.

He gave up plenty of home runs. But most were with the bases empty, a statistic that marks the record of many a great pitcher.

Jack pitched into the seventh inning twenty-six straight times during the 1983 season. Going into the sixth inning is considered a "quality" start. He matched the date of the earliest-ever no-hitter when he threw a no-no at Chicago on April 7, 1984.

Morris won two games playing for Detroit in the World Series. He earned a victory in the American League Championship Series as well. He set a record in the 1984 Series for most putouts by a pitcher in a five-game series. Jack recorded five.

Morris wasn't as fortunate in the ALCS of 1987 when he lost to Bert Blyleven and the Twins, 6-3.

Morris is among Detroit's all-time leaders in a host of pitching categories, but he suffered a couple of sub-par years in 1989 and 1990, going 6-14 and 15-18. He decided it was time to move on, time to go home.

"I thought the Twins could win, and I was right," Morris commented. "And it was home."

Jack was a big part of the Twins success that year. His record was 18-12. He threw for 246.2 innings with a 3.43 ERA and represented the Twins in the All-Star Game. It was the fifth time the right-hander was named to the All-Star squad.

But his glory that year will be forever linked to the post season. Morris was the winning pitcher in Game 1 and Game 4 of the American Championship Series against Toronto. In Game 1 of the 1991 World Series, he beat Atlanta 5-2.

Then, with the series tied 3-3, Morris cried, "Let's get it on!" to his teammates and took the mound in Game 7 at the Metrodome before 55,118 screaming fans.

There were tense moments. In the sixth inning of a scoreless game, the Braves put runners on first and third with one out.

Morris got the dangerous Terry Pendleton to pop to shortstop Greg Gagne. Then Jack faced the tough Ron Gant. On a 3-2 pitch Morris froze Gant with a fastball on the outside corner for strike three.

Jack recalled, "I made a pretty good pitch, in a critical situation against a hitter I respected tremendously."

The scoreless duel between Morris and the Braves' John Smoltz rolled into the eighth inning. Atlanta's Lonny Smith looped a check-swing single to right to open the inning. Terry Pendleton doubled to left-center, sending Smith to third. Gant bounced out to Kent Hrbek at first with the runners holding.

Tom Kelly came out to talk to his pitcher. Morris was afraid his manager had come out to remove him. But Kelly merely suggested that David Justice be intentionally walked. Jack complied and pitched to Sid Bream with the sacks crowded.

Bream bounced to Hrbek, who threw home to Brian Harper for the force at the plate. Harper rifled back to Hrbek for the third out.

The Twins had their own bases-loaded threat in the bottom of the inning, but Hrbek lined into a double play to end it.

Morris related, "After the ninth inning, Kelly said, 'You did a good job. That's enough.'

"I said, 'No, it isn't. It's my game.'

"He said, 'Okay.' Kelly was just giving me a chance to take myself out if I wanted to."

One of the greatest games in World Series history was concluded in the bottom of the tenth inning when Gene Larkin drove home Dan Gladden to make the Twins the 1991 world champions. Winning hurler Jack Morris was named the MVP of the series. Sadly, it was to be the last game Jack Morris pitched as a Minnesota Twin.

Morris stated, "They had to keep their money for Kirby Puckett, and the team fell apart because of it. But that's business in baseball. I did what I had to do for my future. The Twins did what they felt was right for the community and the popularity of one player.

"I'm an old baseball man," Jack continued. "Offense sells tickets, but defense win championships. Pitching wins, but I'm a pitcher, and I'm biased. I'd still build an organization around pitching."

Morris signed with Toronto, where he shined again, finishing 21-6 in 1992. After dropping to 7-12 in 1993, Jack finished out his career with the Indians in 1994.

For ten years, Jack tried his hand at farming and ranching near Great Falls, Montana. Now he lives near New Richmond, Wisconsin, and is exploring other opportunities. He has two children, one in college, the other in high school in Michigan.

"Baseball was my life," said Morris. "It owned me and I breathed it for thirty-six years. Eighteen years in the big leagues pretty much controlled my adult life. There wasn't a whole lot of time to think about other things. Professional sports are very demanding of your time.

"A lot of players get married when they're young and don't have the maturity to understand relationships, I being one of them. I think the irony is that there is great popularity and demand on your time, and you don't have the time to dedicate everything to two different things.

"Obviously, the financial end keeps you going, but it's a very difficult lifestyle for families. Not that it can't work. You just need two strong people."

Jack misses the competition and camaraderie of major-league baseball. "I think all of us that play professional sports have a drive that is hard to explain. Competition is the only thing that satisfies us. There's really no other profession that any of us can get in to that replaces it. We all try to find ways to replace it or accept life.

"It all comes back to your upbringing and where you came from and who you know. It's kind of nice now for me to have a life again because baseball did consume me."

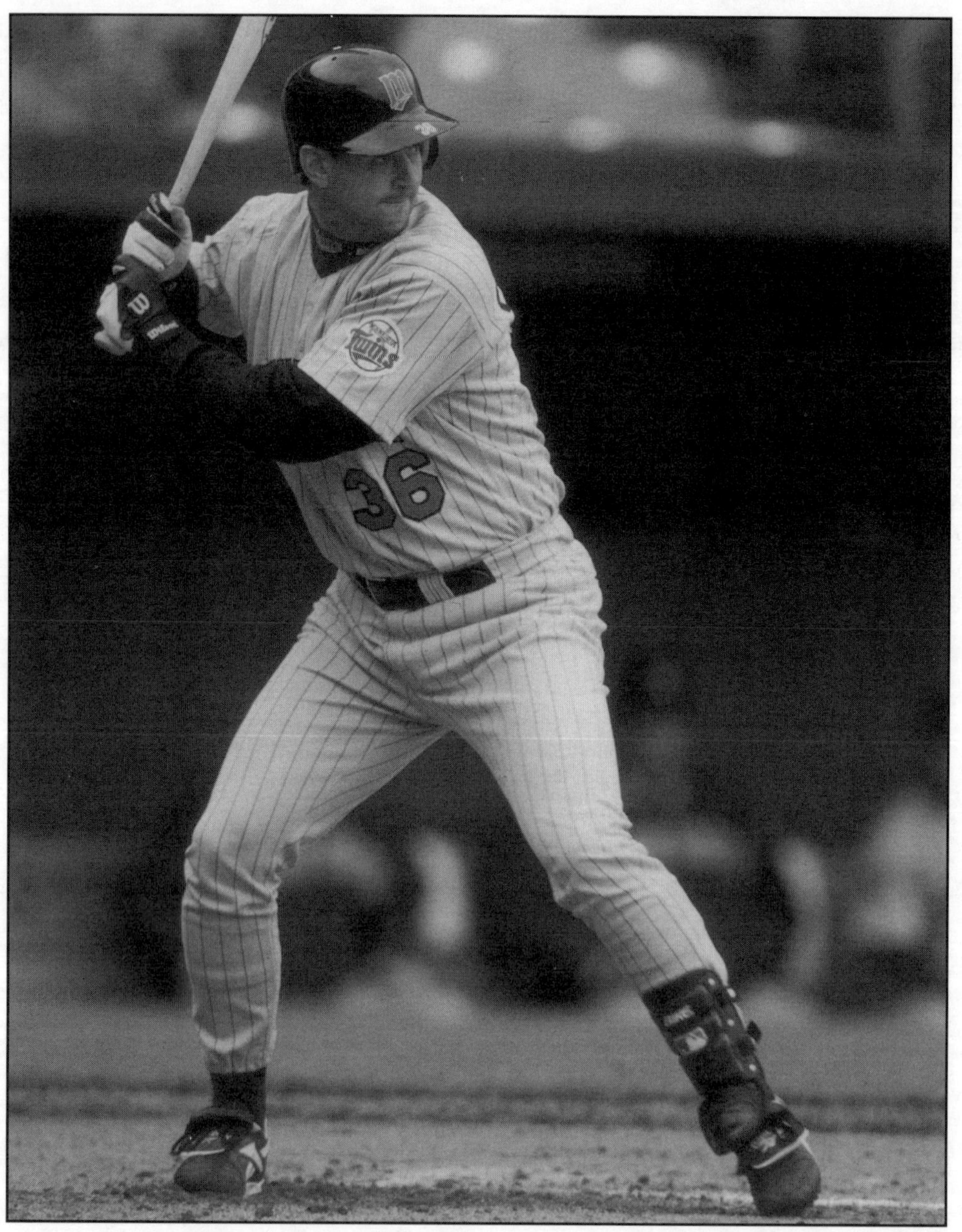
36
Twins

Terry Steinbach

Bats: Right
Throws: Right
Height: 6' 1"
Weight: 212 lbs.
Born: March 2, 1962, in Minnesota

YEAR	TEAM	LG	AVG	G	AB	R	H	2B	3B	HR	RBI	BB	K	OBP	SLG
1986	Oak	AL	.333	6	15	3	5	0	0	2	4	1	0	.375	.733
1987	Oak	AL	.284	122	391	66	111	16	3	16	56	32	66	.349	.463
1988	Oak	AL	.265	104	351	42	93	19	1	9	51	33	47	.334	.402
1989	Oak	AL	.273	130	454	37	124	13	1	7	42	30	66	.319	.352
1990	Oak	AL	.251	114	379	32	95	15	2	9	57	19	66	.291	.372
1991	Oak	AL	.274	129	456	50	125	31	1	6	67	22	70	.312	.386
1992	Oak	AL	.279	128	438	48	122	20	1	12	53	45	58	.345	.411
1993	Oak	AL	.285	104	389	47	111	19	1	10	43	25	65	.333	.416
1994	Oak	AL	.285	103	369	51	105	21	2	11	57	26	62	.327	.442
1995	Oak	AL	.278	114	406	43	113	26	1	15	65	25	74	.322	.458
1996	Oak	AL	.272	145	514	79	140	25	1	35	100	49	115	.342	.529
1997	Min	AL	.248	122	447	60	111	27	1	12	54	35	106	.302	.394
1998	Min	AL	.242	124	422	45	102	25	2	14	54	38	89	.310	.410
1999	Min	AL	.284	101	338	35	96	16	4	4	42	38	54	.358	.391
			AVG	G	AB	R	H	2B	3B	HR	RBI	BB	K	OBP	SLG
			.271	1,546	5,369	638	1,543	273	21	162	745	418	938	.326	.420

The setting was town team baseball, the summer of 2000. The Litchfield Blues took the field against the New Ulm Kaiserhoff. The usual crowd of fifty loyal Blues fans had swelled to nearly 500.

Litchfield hurler Jeff Wollin knew they hadn't all gathered to watch him pitch. The number-three hitter in the New Ulm lineup was no ordinary player. In fact, only one year earlier he had been facing the likes of Roger Clemens and Pedro Martinez in the major leagues. Love of baseball brought that batter, Terry Steinbach, and the hundreds of fans to Litchfield that night.

Terry and his brothers grew up in the baseball-crazy town of New Ulm, Minnesota. They played hard and often, not following major-league baseball closely, stars like Harmon Killebrew, Tony Oliva, and Rod Carew were inspirations to them.

"We were hard on bats, we needed lumber for our back yard," Terry remembered. "We'd try to get to bat days to build up our supply."

In high school at New Ulm, Terry played baseball and hockey and ran cross-country. The Cleveland Indians drafted Terry in the sixteenth round out of high school in 1980. He turned down their offer and instead attended the University of Minnesota.

Following his junior year, Steinbach was selected in the ninth round by the Oakland A's in the June 1983 draft. After the draft Terry was sent to Medford, Oregon, to play A ball. The next year he spent a full season in the minors in Madison, Wisconsin, followed by two years in AA in Huntsville, Alabama.

Steinbach was drafted as a third baseman. But when Oakland drafted a big, burly, third sacker off the Olympic team named Mark McGwire, Terry's future at the hot corner looked bleak. The A's had another phenom projected at first base. They asked Terry to try catching.

"I said, 'Yeah I'll try it,'" Terry related. "The rest is history, I guess.

"At first I was a little reluctant. I didn't know if it was where I wanted to be or needed to be. It took a lot of conversations at the major-league level even. Tony LaRussa; Dave Duncan, our pitching coach; and Renee Lacheman, our catching coach, really instilled in me the values and what's right about catching.

"Tony would say, 'I don't care how you hit today, you caught like crap. You called a bad game. If you keep calling bad games, we're gonna get you out of there, I don't care how you hit. Your job as a catcher is to be able to handle that stuff. I'd rather see you call a good game than get any hits.'

"That took a little bit to get used to, coming from a very offensive background."

Terry got used to his role and became a fine receiver. He agrees with Earl Battey's assertion that the catcher's position controls play.

"As catchers, we have to adjust to twelve different personalities. You usually have twelve pitchers on a team, and the bottom line is you gotta know what to do to these guys to get them to do what you want.

"One guy ya gotta pat on the rear, 'Hey, let's go.' Another guy you gotta get stern with, another guy you gotta be a jokester with. You find yourself almost like a shrink.

"Every day during batting practice, you kinda make your rounds and go from pitcher to pitcher. 'You did a good job yesterday.' 'Hey, don't worry about it, the guy got a home run, you just made a mistake. You threw a good pitch; you hung one pitch, he was just supposed to hit it out. We'll get 'em today.'

"You just find yourself literally going from pitcher to pitcher to make sure you have a good rapport with them. Your job every day catching is to make that guy on the mound have the best day he possibly can. When that's over, ya got the next guy and then the next guy.

"And when that's all done, don't forget to go up and knock in a few runs, either."

Terry was fortunate to have some tremendous pitchers to work with, including Dave Stewart, Dennis Eckersley, Bob Welch, Storm Davis, and Mike Moore with Oakland, and Brad Radke with the Twins.

The A's called him to the big club in September 1986. Steinbach homered in his first at-bat. He spent all of 1987 with Oakland and batted .284 with sixteen homers.

Despite hitting just .216 at the All-Star break in 1988, Steinbach was named to the American League squad. He silenced anyone who doubted the merits of his selection by smacking a homer in his first at-bat. He just missed a grand slam his next time up, getting a sacrifice fly. Terry's performance garnered him MVP honors in the 1988 All-Star Game.

Steinbach finished the season strong to boost his average to .265 for the year. He played in the 1989 All-Star Game and again in the 1993 edition.

Steinbach had a stellar ten-year career in Oakland, batting consistently in the .270s and .280s. Four times Terry helped lead the A's into postseason play. After reaching three World Series—1988, 1989, and 1990—Oakland suffered a playoff loss to Toronto in 1992.

The A's won the infamous "Earthquake Series" of 1989 against San Francisco. Terry had a great postseason that year. He had a homer and five RBIs in the League Championship Series against Toronto. He followed that up by hitting .364 in the World Series with seven RBIs and another home run.

When the quake hit at Candlestick, Terry remembered, the players didn't think they were in danger. They expected to start playing once the power came back on. A fan in one of the front rows had a portable TV. When the players saw the extent of the damage, they knew the game was off.

Steinbach shined during the 1996 campaign. He had career highs in home runs with thirty-five and drove in 100 runs while hitting a solid .272. But in December of 1996, Terry left Oakland and signed a free-agent contract with the Twins.

"They were making changes in Oakland at the time, manager Tony LaRussa was out, Art Howell was in," Terry explained. "The A's were going through new ownership and really didn't know what direction they were going.

"Personally, it was a nice change for me to be able to come back to Minnesota. We could get our kids acclimated to the schools and the area where we planned on raising them. That had a lot to do with it. For me, it was nice to get home to spend more time with my family than I could at Oakland.

"I also wanted the opportunity to play for Tom Kelly. It was a great experience to have been able to play for Tony LaRussa in Oakland and Tom Kelly in Minnesota.

"Tom Kelly was very sharp on the field," Steinbach continued. "He's never outmatched. His match-ups are always the way he wants them. Some teams miss their matchups and wind up with a left-handed pitcher facing a right-handed power hitter. T. K. was very good at not letting that happen.

"He knows the game; he understands it. T. K.'s biggest attribute is that he wants the players to play the game. He encourages the players to keep him out of it. If we pitch the way we should and catch the ball the way we should and knock in runs the way we're capable, then he doesn't have to get involved, and he'd prefer it that way.

"T. K. wants the players to go out and play. They're the ones who have the ability to do it; they're who people wanna see."

A highlight of Terry's Twins career was catching Eric Milton's no-hitter on September 11, 1999. He compared that day with a no-no he caught for Dave Stewart back in Oakland.

"Stewart was a mentor to me. He had a real good idea of how he wanted to pitch. He really taught me a lot about how to set up hitters. As we went on, I'd call a pitch, and he'd switch to a different one. We'd always communicate.

"It was kind of reversed when Eric pitched, he'd hardly shake anything. We got to the sixth inning, no-hitter, seventh inning, no-hitter. Well, shoot, eighth inning, we've only got six outs to go.

"Ya get to the ninth inning, I didn't want to screw it up. It was the most pressure I felt in my life in that game."

Terry retired from major-league baseball after the 1999 season, in which he hit .284. He lives in Corcoran, Minnesota, and dabbles in private baseball lessons.

Steinbach loves the outdoors and enjoys hunting and fishing. He stays involved in the game by doing some broadcasting of Twins games and helping out at spring training.

Terry and his wife, Mary, have three children. He's been devoting a lot of attention to family time, following the activities of their offspring. All three are involved in sports; their daughter plays softball and basketball, while their two sons play hockey and baseball.

Terry was asked what he would do when he retired. He replied, "I'm gonna see how long it takes to get bored. After the first year, I'm not close to coming up on the 'bored' word yet."

Baseball, however, will always be a big part of his life. "Baseball meant a lot to me. It was a major part of my life. People assume the obvious, the economics, the financial security, but there are intricacies of life that baseball taught me.

"The camaraderie of teammates, learning how to work together. Baseball taught me a lot of good work ethics. It taught me how to set goals. Tony LaRussa was huge: on every spring training we would set realistic goals. It can lead to success not only in baseball but in life. Those are lessons you can't buy or read about, you just have to experience them."

Terry misses a couple of things about baseball. The competitiveness jumps out at him. "The drive for perfection and the drive for excellence is something that I'll die with."

While coaching young kids, Terry has come to realize that everyone doesn't have the same drive or goals he did. "Let the kids be kids, and let them develop into who they're gonna be."

He also misses the camaraderie. "Having twenty-five guys who go to war together for six months, it's a marathon race, and you have to grind through the good and the bad."

And he just might keep playing town ball. "I was nervous at first, but I was impressed by the response. I had a good time."

After the game in Litchfield, he patiently signed autographs for young fans. It was a picture in time: a veteran major leaguer dressed in a town-ball uniform, making himself available for the future of the game.

Dave Winfield

Bats: Right
Throws: Right
Height: 6' 6"
Weight: 245 lbs.
Born: October 3, 1951, in Minnesota

YEAR	TEAM	LG	AVG	G	AB	R	H	2B	3B	HR	RBI	BB	K	OBP	SLG
1973	SD	NL	.277	56	141	9	39	4	1	3	12	12	19	.331	.383
1974	SD	NL	.265	145	498	57	132	18	4	20	75	40	96	.318	.438
1975	SD	NL	.267	143	509	74	136	20	2	15	76	69	82	.354	.403
1976	SD	NL	.283	137	492	81	139	26	4	13	69	65	78	.366	.431
1977	SD	NL	.275	157	615	104	169	29	7	25	92	58	75	.335	.467
1978	SD	NL	.308	158	587	88	181	30	5	24	97	55	81	.367	.499
1979	SD	NL	.308	159	597	97	184	27	10	34	118	85	71	.395	.558
1980	SD	NL	.276	162	558	89	154	25	6	20	87	79	83	.365	.450
1981	NYA	AL	.294	105	388	52	114	25	1	13	68	43	41	.360	.464
1982	NYA	AL	.280	140	539	84	151	24	8	37	106	45	64	.331	.560
1983	NYA	AL	.283	152	598	99	169	26	8	32	116	58	77	.345	.513
1984	NYA	AL	.340	141	567	106	193	34	4	19	100	53	71	.393	.515
1985	NYA	AL	.275	155	633	105	174	34	6	26	114	52	96	.328	.471
1986	NYA	AL	.262	154	565	90	148	31	5	24	104	77	106	.349	.462
1987	NYA	AL	.275	156	575	83	158	22	1	27	97	76	96	.358	.457
1988	NYA	AL	.322	149	559	96	180	37	2	25	107	69	88	.398	.530
1990	NYA	AL	.213	20	61	7	13	3	0	2	6	4	13	.269	.361
1990	Cal	AL	.275	112	414	63	114	18	2	19	72	48	68	.348	.466
1991	Cal	AL	.262	150	568	75	149	27	4	28	86	56	109	.326	.472
1992	Tor	AL	.290	156	583	92	169	33	3	26	108	82	89	.377	.491
1993	Min	AL	.271	143	547	72	148	27	2	21	76	45	106	.325	.442
1994	Min	AL	.252	77	294	35	74	15	3	10	43	31	51	.321	.425
1995	Cle	AL	.191	46	115	11	22	5	0	2	4	14	26	.285	.287
			AVG	G	AB	R	H	2B	3B	HR	RBI	BB	K	OBP	SLG
			.283	2,973	11,003	1,669	3,110	540	88	465	1,833	1,216	1,686	.353	.475

Bobby Thomson of the New York Giants delivered one of baseball's most famous home runs on October 3, 1951. It was the "Shot Heard Round the World" that propelled the Giants into the 1951 World Series.

In St. Paul, Minnesota, on that very day, Dave Winfield was born. His life would contain many memorable shots as well, for he is one of the most gifted athletes that Minnesota or any other state has ever produced.

Winfield became the second native Minnesotan elected to the Baseball Hall of Fame. His first-ballot vote into Cooperstown was announced on January 16, 2001. Minnesota's Charles "Chief" Bender was selected previously.

Winfield played twenty-two years of major league baseball. He clouted 465 home runs, ripped 3,110 hits and plated 1,833 runners. His career places him among the elite of baseball's power hitters.

But Dave's athletic gifts were so extraordinary that it would be interesting to see what would have evolved had he pursued careers in other sports.

Winfield gained attention as a baseball player at St. Paul's Central High School. He continued his education in his home state at the University of Minnesota, where he was a pitcher/outfielder for the Gophers' baseball team and a star on the basketball squad as well.

Dick Siebert had recruited Dave to play Gopher baseball. His college basketball career came almost by accident when Gopher hoops coach Bill Musselman spied the big guy playing intramural ball and urged him to come out for that team, too.

The teams excelled, aided by Winfield's considerable contributions. The Golden Gophers were Big Ten basketball champions in 1972; Winfield was a starter. The baseball Gophers earned their way into the 1973 College World Series (CWS) in Omaha. Winfield's superlative play on the diamond earned him Series MVP honors at Omaha and first-team college All-American honors.

In the semi-final game at the CWS, the Gophers faced the eventual champions, a University of Southern California team that contained the likes of Fred Lynn and future Twin Roy Smalley. The Gophers took a 7-0 lead into the ninth frame but lost after the Trojans rallied for eight runs that inning.

Winfield had some tough choices to consider when he completed his college career. Four teams in three sports drafted him. The Utah Stars of the ABA and the NBA's Atlanta Hawks sought him for basketball. The San Diego Padres wanted him to play baseball. The NFL's Minnesota Vikings drafted him in that sport, even though he had never played college football.

Dave decided to stay with baseball, a sport he'd loved from childhood. "When I was a kid it was baseball, baseball, baseball," Dave said. "I started playing baseball with my brother, Steve, when I was eight. We played at Oxford Playground near where we lived. I loved the game."

Picked fourth by the San Diego Padres in the 1973 free-agent draft, the six-foot, six-inch slugger bypassed minor-league ball and went straight to the majors.

In fifty-six games with the Padres, Winfield hit .273. He played with flair and style, competing hard in all facets of the game. Whether breaking up a double play, leaping to snare a would-be home run or displaying awesome offensive skills, he did it all.

Winfield played eight years for the Padres and hit 154 home runs with 626 RBIs. In 1979, his best year with San Diego, Dave hit .308 with thirty-four dingers and 118 RBIs.

A free agent after the 1980 season, Winfield signed a big contract with the New York Yankees. Greatness and controversy marked his nine-plus years in the Bronx.

Dave drove home 818 runners for the Yankees and hit 205 home runs. Six times he drove in more than 100 runs. He hit .340 in 1984. But he feuded with owner George Steinbrenner over payments the Yankees were to make to the Winfield Foundation, a charity for children.

Fans criticized Winfield for not being a leader in the mold of Yankee greats like DiMaggio, Mantle, Ruth, and Gehrig. While he had been the unmistakable star of the Padres, on the Yankees he was a member of a cast that thrived on controversy and ego, including Reggie Jackson.

Steinbrenner was unhappy that Winfield garnered merely one hit in the 1981 World Series. But Dave just kept playing hard. In 1988, his final full season with the Yankees, he hit .322 with twenty-five homers and 107 RBIs.

Problems with his back kept Dave on the shelf for the 1989 season, and he had trouble getting back in the swing in 1990. The Yanks traded him to the California Angels, where he popped forty-nine homers the next two years.

Winfield's free-agent signing with the Toronto Blue Jays in 1992 proved to be one of his best decisions. Dave led the Jays to their first World Series that same year. This time, the player once reviled for World Series futility became a hero.

Winfield used his Gold Glove to rob Atlanta hitters of extra bases. In Game 6, he won it all with his bat. That game was deadlocked at 2-2 in the top of the eleventh inning when Dave came to bat against Charlie Leibrandt. Runners were on first and second with two outs. Winfield smashed a double down the line to plate both runners in an eventual 4-3 victory. The Blue Jays were world champs.

The moment brought memories of his youth to the St. Paul slugger. "When I was a kid, like every other kid, I'm at the playground, it's almost dinnertime, so all of a sudden, it becomes the bottom of the ninth in the seventh game of the World Series. Your team is down by three. Full count . . . then bam!

"You hit a grand slam that wins it all. Okay, so mine was a double, a lousy double. But that hit, it just made everything right."

When asked if a particular game stood out in his memory, Dave responded, "The 1992 World Series was THE GAME. It's funny, but we (the Blue Jays) and our friends and family just knew from the beginning of the season that we were going to go all the way. There was no question. I've never experienced that before.

"I don't know if that happens all the time, with every team that wins, but that magical feeling was there from day one, from spring training actually."

The St. Paul boy came home in 1993. Dave had signed as a free agent in December 1992, to play with the Minnesota Twins. He was on the verge of 3,000 hits. Twins fans waited with eager anticipation.

Dave talked about his return to Minnesota. "Before I actually played, I was excited about coming home and playing in front of my family and friends. I was also excited about being teammates with my man, Kirby. But the 3,000th hit, at home, was by far the highlight of my Twins career."

The magic number arrived with the Twins playing Oakland on September 16, 1993, with Kirby Puckett on third base. Winfield rapped a hard ground ball into left field. As "his man" Kirby scored, Dave rounded first base and then accepted the adoration of Minnesota fans, who loudly cheered the accomplishment of hit number 3,000 and the career it represented.

Dave played with the Twins until August 31 of the next season. He was then traded to the Cleveland Indians to finish up the season. Used sparingly in 1995, he hit .191 in 115 at-bats and retired at the end of the year.

Mike Kingery, a major-league outfielder who played against Winfield, was amazed at Dave's ability. "He was an incredible athlete," Kingery recalled. "He ran hard, threw hard and hit hard. Winfield was a visually intimidating force. He was so aggressive. He'd stand at the plate and wave the bat, and it looked small in his hands.

"Winfield hit over 400 home runs, but I don't consider him a home-run hitter. He hit extremely hard line drives that went over the fence. He was a line-drive hitter."

Winfield elaborated. "Good hand-eye coordination is essential to being a good hitter. Also, reflexes and patience at the plate . . . my at-bats were among the longest lasting, an added bonus in those nationally televised games."

More than the playing, Dave fondly remembers the camaraderie and the humor. "The team virtually lived together for seven months or so. You form close friendships that, unfortunately, are subject to change every season.

"But you meet guys from all over the country; all over the world. You get to travel all over the country and Canada. It's a constant learning experience. There's always something to see."

Sometimes in sports, statistics can be misleading. In the case of Dave Winfield they tell a huge story. In twenty-two major-league seasons, Dave appeared in twelve straight All-Star games. He won seven Gold Gloves. Seven times Winfield finished in the top ten of MVP voting.

He hit at least twenty homers in fifteen seasons and drove in over 100 runs eight times. Winfield is one of only seven players who have 3,000 hits and 450 homeruns.

But statistics, while telling, are just facts. Dave Winfield, the player, with his arm, speed, defense, and power, could carry a team. Dave Winfield, the man, gave back to his community.

Winfield has won the Brian Piccolo Award for Humanitarian Service, the Branch Rickey Community Service Award, the Arete Award for courage in sports, and Major League Baseball's Roberto Clemente Man of the Year Award.

Dave started the David M. Winfield Foundation in 1977. The charitable organization continues to be one of his major interests.

What occupies most of Dave's time and attention today? "First and foremost," Dave said, "spending quality time with my family. After twenty-three-plus years of being on the road and extensive training in the off-season, it was good to just kick back and spend time with my wife, Tonya, who I met during the 1981 World Series (see, it wasn't all bad) and our 'Minnesota twins' David and Arielle.

"They were one year old when I stopped playing, now they're six and they're just getting some understanding of what daddy used to do. My son loves all sports. He's a first baseman, and already the number one home-run hitter in his league. Perhaps his sister will be his agent."

Los Angeles is home for Winfield, Tonya, and their children. As he remembers a great career, the Hall of Fame is most special.

"I didn't have an easy, smooth career. I worked hard, and it's a testament to the hard work that I put into it. It's a good day, man," Dave exulted upon learning the Hall vote totals, "a good day."

It was a great career.

Others

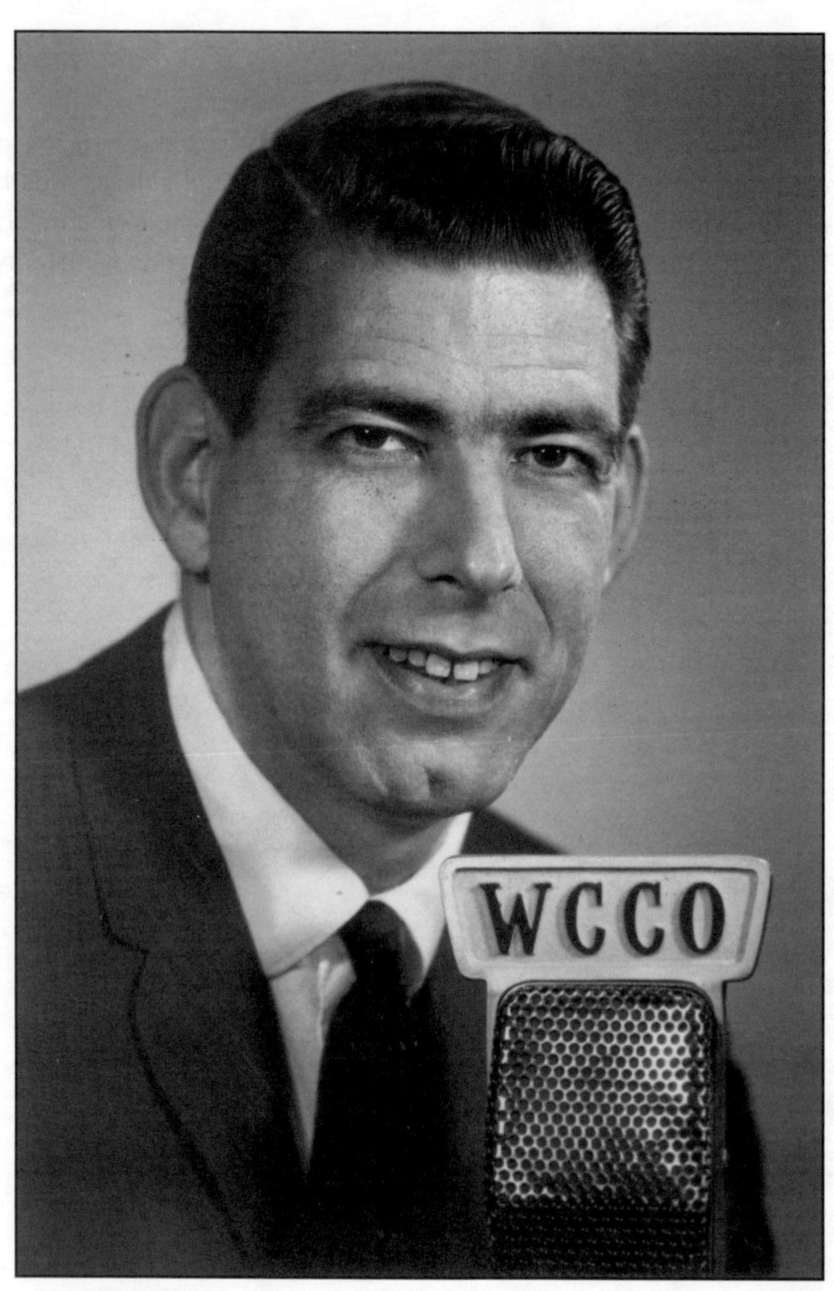
WCCO

Herb Carneal

"Good afternoon, everybaady." The signature introduction, with just the hint of a Southern accent, heralds another broadcast by a true Twins legend, Herb Carneal.

He never played pro baseball, but Herb had a special role. It was his task to make baseball vivid to millions of listeners over radio. "The Voice of the Minnesota Twins" has been the eyes of millions of baseball fans for thirty-nine of the Twins' forty seasons.

Carneal was born May 10, 1923, in Richmond, Virginia. He loved playing baseball and was a center fielder and a pitcher for the local American Legion team.

He listened to major-league games on a big-table model radio. Herb became enthralled with "the certain sound that goes with baseball" and the voices of announcers like Ernie Harwell and Mel Allen.

His father died when Herb was a young man. At age eighteen, Herb went to work for the local radio station in February of 1942. He did station breaks, weather, and emergency announcements.

Herb's first crack at covering sports came when the station's sports announcer got sick and couldn't do a boxing match. Young Carneal took over the assignment. It was the beginning of a long and distinguished career in sports broadcasting.

Carneal moved in 1945 to WSYR in Syracuse, New York, where he broadcast high school and college football. He also did major-league baseball recreations, making up games using dice. After a stop working for a station in Springfield, Massachusetts, Herb headed for Philadelphia, where he broadcast Athletics and Phillies games.

Then the Athletics moved to Kansas City, and Carneal received a job offer in Baltimore. This combination of events led him to leave Philadelphia in 1957 for the Chesapeake Bay. From 1957 through the 1961 season, he did Orioles play-by-play.

Carneal got his introduction to Minnesota in the fall of 1961, when he broadcast Minnesota Vikings football games for WCCO Radio. He was hired away from the Orioles for the 1962 baseball season and joined the Twins broadcast team of Ray Scott and Halsey Hall.

As an institution for a generation of baseball fans, Carneal is, in many respects, Minnesota Twins baseball. His style is plain and to the point. He lets the game tell the story and doesn't clutter his broadcasts with meaningless chatter.

Herb has many memories of his years in baseball, from when Halsey Hall started a fire in the booth with an errant cigar, to the action on the field. He broadcast three World Series and was especially fond of the 1987 victory, because it was the first Twins world championship.

Herb loved getting to know the Twins players over the years. He began many friendships in baseball that he nurtured later.

While the athletes played, he "got to know players, but you can't get too friendly. It might hurt objectivity."

The community outside of baseball is also important to Carneal. He found very enjoyable his appearance with the Rochester Symphony Orchestra, which included Herb's rendition of the immortal baseball poem, "Casey at the Bat."

In recent years, Carneal reduced his role with the Twins to doing the play-by-play of only their home games. The travel and night games on the road had become tedious for a man in his seventies.

The 2000 season brought a special sadness to Herb. His wife, Cathy, whom Herb termed "a terrific baseball wife," died after having a stroke while driving her car.

Herb lives in Edina. He has one daughter, Terri, who was an excellent golfer for the University of William and Mary.

The recent losing seasons can be wearing and make for long seasons, even for broadcasters. But Herb approaches the future with optimism. "There's always tomorrow, it's just a matter of advancing a runner and getting a hit at the right time. It's fun to win."

Herb Carneal is a winner. He entered the Baseball Hall of Fame in 1996, when he received the Ford C. Frick Award, which is baseball broadcasting's highest honor. Each year it's given to broadcasters who make major contributions to baseball and its fans.

But the people of the Upper Midwest didn't need an award to be convinced that Herb Carneal was a hall of famer. They already knew it.

Calvin Griffith and Clark Griffith

The Griffith family was one of baseball's great family dynasties. It started with Clark Griffith, the "Old Fox," a Hall-of-Fame player, manager, and owner.

Clark began his major-league career with the National League Chicago Colts (later Cubs) in 1893. His eight years in Chicago were the highlight of his playing career.

Griffith won his nickname by utilizing a six-pitch repertoire, a screwball (which he claimed to have invented), a quick-pitch delivery, and the ruse of hiding the ball in the plane of his body before delivering.

Clark also scuffed, scratched, cut and spit upon nearly every pitch. When the tactics became illegal in 1920, Clark helped lead the way to ban them.

He used his position as vice president of the league-protective Players' Association to lead the members in baseball's first strike in 1900. Griffith also used his labor position to help form the rival American Baseball League as he raided players from the National League.

Griffith became a player/manager with Chicago in the American circuit in 1901 and then with the New York Highlanders (later Yankees) and Cincinnati Reds.

Clark had the opportunity to manage and purchase equity in the Washington Senators in 1912. He continued buying equity until he wound up as majority owner with fifty-two percent.

Griffith placed himself in debt to make the purchase, a position from which he never strayed far and which often kept him at odds with his players.

Clark made notable contributions to the game. He was the first to actively recruit Cuban players and, in a strategic move, he developed the relief pitcher.

After he pitched his two star pitchers a combined 845 innings in 1904, they were much less effective the next year. Griffith began to personally finish games for them and made a career-high eighteen relief appearances in 1905. He helped to turn relief strategy into a great weapon.

Calvin's son, Clark Griffith II, traced the Griffith family history for this book.

"Clark Griffith has several brothers in California and Missouri. His wife, Addie Robertson, lived in Chicago with three sisters and a brother, Jim. They were all born in Scotland and came to America in the mid-1890s. Addie and Clark were married when Griffith was a pitcher for the White Sox," he said.

"Addie's brother Jim moved to Montreal about 1905. He got married to Jane and had seven children: Mildred, Calvin, Thelma, Bruce, Sherrard, and twin brothers Billy and Jimmy.

"Jim sold newspapers and had a small convenience-type store. Clark and Addie had no children and, to ease Jim's economic burden, offered to take in two of the children. Thelma and Calvin went to live in Washington. Shortly thereafter, about 1921, their father Jim died.

"Soon after that, they all moved to Washington. Bruce then died of rheumatic fever. Baseball became ingrained in the Griffiths. Mildred married the manager and shortstop for the Senators, Joe Cronin, who was later president of the American League. Thelma married Joe Haynes, a right-handed pitcher for Washington and Chicago.

"Sherrard played for ten years in the major leagues and was the minor-league director for the Twins through the 1960s. He died accidentally in 1969 after developing the Twins' minor-league system. Billy became the Twins' Director of Stadium Operations and Jimmy the Director of Concessions."

Calvin Griffith was groomed by his Uncle Clark to take his place. Young Calvin was a mascot and batboy for the Senators' pennant-winning teams of 1924 and 1925. He was educated at Staunton Military Academy and George Washington University, where he played basketball and baseball.

In 1935, Calvin was assigned by Clark to be treasurer and president of the Senators' Chattanooga, Tennessee, farm team. From 1938 to 1941 he was given those same jobs in Charlotte, North Carolina. Young Griffith also took a couple stints at managing while in Chattanooga and Charlotte.

Calvin's teams did well. Charlotte won a pennant and just missed two others. His teams produced major leaguers like Early Wynn and broke attendance records.

Uncle Clark called him back to Washington, D.C., in 1942 to become his chief assistant. Calvin began his tenure with Clark by operating the club's concessions at Griffith Stadium. His responsibilities grew to include negotiating radio and TV contracts and later player trades.

While in Charlotte, Calvin met and married Natalie Niven. They had three children: a son, Clark II, and two daughters, Corinne and Clare.

Clark Griffith died on October 27, 1955, and Calvin was named president of the Senators five days later. The Senators had been mired in the second division for nine straight years. They had also fallen far behind in developing young talent.

Calvin concentrated efforts on his farm system and in landing good young players. He also made some good trades, and attendance was on an upswing in the nation's capital.

Yet Calvin moved the Twins to Minnesota for the 1961 season. Clark II explained, "There was opportunity. He didn't see things working very well in Washington. He didn't like the location of the new stadium, didn't like the design, didn't like the economics of the District, and he thought that Minnesota was an absolutely wonderful place."

Calvin was right. For the next ten years, the Twins were among the leaders in the American League in attendance.

By 1965 the Twins were American League champions and playing in the World Series against the Los Angeles Dodgers. Calvin was named Major League Executive of the Year.

"Winning the pennant was Calvin's greatest thrill," Clark said. "Losing the World Series was his greatest disappointment."

As the years progressed, baseball changed. Free agency caused a dramatic change in the economics of the game as players' salaries skyrocketed.

Even before free agency, Griffith was notorious for his tight-fisted salary negotiations with his players. The public perception of him as a tightwad grew; however, his son noted, "He absolutely had no idea what the basis of that perception was. He thought he had to watch expenses, but in doing so, he lost track of asset value. This causes asset value to diminish because of failure to invest in the future."

A low point in Griffith's regime with the Twins came in September of 1978. Calvin's no-nonsense, off-the-cuff style caught up with him. In a speech before the Waseca (Minnesota) Lions Club, Griffith said, "Black people don't go to ball games, but they'll fill up a rassling ring and put up such a chant they'll scare you to death. We came to Minnesota because you've got good, hard-working white people here."

Responding to an uproar following his remarks, Calvin claimed he had been taken out of context. But damage was done. Among the fallout was star player Rod Carew's refusal to play for the Twins in response to Griffith's remarks.

Calvin survived the Waseca mess, but he couldn't keep up with the economic changes in the game, and in 1984 he sold the Twins to Carl Pohlad.

"He didn't have to lose the Twins. It was his choice," Clark II commented.

The former owner could take some pleasure in the fact that the Twins' world championship teams of 1987 and 1991 came largely from players put in place by the Griffith regime and Calvin's eye for talent.

Griffith's teams, in twenty-four seasons, were 1,930 and 1,887.

Clark Griffith II is now an attorney in Minneapolis and has made unsuccessful attempts to buy back his father's team.

Calvin died on October 20, 1999, at his winter home in Florida. He was eighty-seven years old. At his funeral, his former players, friends, family, and baseball dignitaries gathered to pay tribute and remember. They honored Calvin's memory by singing, "Take Me Out to the Ballgame" and "The Star-Spangled Banner."

Calvin Griffith has been called many things: an innovator, a visionary with an unfortunate knack to be his own worst enemy, tight-fisted and outspoken. To some, he was a dinosaur who tried to turn back baseball's clock; to others, he was a true baseball soldier. His legacy is Minnesota baseball.

Billy Martin

(**Author's Note:** The players and managers included in this book were all living when it was written. That was one of my qualifications for inclusion. After concluding my interviews, I decided to make one exception, Billy Martin.

After reviewing my conversations with the players, I was struck by how many refered to Billy. Many of the players cited the impact and accomplishments of Martin. He certainly had a great influence on Twins' baseball, and because of that, a brief description of his career seemed to be in order.)

Billy Martin, born in 1928, was from Berkeley, California. He started playing pro ball in 1946. Casey Stengel, his manager with the minor-league Oakland Oaks in 1948, grew to love his aggressive play and accepted him like the son he never had.

When Stengel became the Yankee skipper, he brought Billy to New York as his second baseman. Martin played to win. His team was one of great players like Mickey Mantle, Whitey Ford, Hank Bauer, and others. While Billy didn't have superstar ability, he provided a winning catalyst.

During his career in New York, the Yankees failed to win the pennant only once, when Billy was in the army in 1954. Martin hit .500 in the six-game World Series of 1953 and was named Series MVP. He set a World Series six-game record with twelve hits.

Martin's best season was 1956, when he made the All-Star team and set career marks with fifteen homers and seventy-five RBIs. On May 16, 1957, while his teammates were celebrating Billy's birthday at New York's Copacabana Club, a brawl broke out. Billy was blamed for being a bad influence on Mantle, Ford, and others. As a result, he was traded to Kansas City on June 15.

The brawl in New York was symbolic of Martin's playing and managerial career. Billy was an intense competitor both on and off the baseball field. Sometimes his bat did the talking, sometimes his fists.

Greg Matthews, a golf caddy for Billy in the 1960s, said, "Billy always wanted to win. I never saw a more fierce competitor on the golf course, and I caddied quite a few years, for a wide range of people, from sports personalities to business people to politicians."

On June 1, 1961, Billy was involved in the Twins' second trade in their brief history when the Twins dealt Billy Consolo to Milwaukee for him. Martin finished his playing career with the Twins in 1961 and hit .246. His career average was .257.

He stayed with the Twins' organization as a scout and then coach. Sam Mele, Twins manager in 1965, gave Billy much credit for helping his squad win the pennant.

After stints as a minor league manager, Billy took the Twins helm in 1969 and guided them to a Western Division crown with a record of 97-65. His .599 winning percentage is the best for any Minnesota manager.

But controversy followed Billy. He had a fist fight with his pitcher, Dave Boswell, publicly debated player moves, and started a pitcher, Bill Miller, in the playoffs against owner Calvin Griffith's wishes.

Griffith fired Martin after the season. Billy was extremely popular with Minnesota fans, and his dismissal was a public relations disaster for the Twins.

Martin went on to manage for many American League teams, including the Detroit Tigers, Texas Rangers, Oakland A's, and five different tenures with the New York Yankees.

Controversy continued to dog him. He got into a fight with a marshmallow salesman, kicked dirt on an umpire, almost came to blows with his own outfielder Reggie Jackson and engaged in frequent verbal sparring with Yankees' owner, George Steinbrenner.

But Billy was a great manager, and his teams were frequent winners. His 1977 Yankees were world champions. On July 23, 1988, the Yankees fired him for the fifth and final time. On December 25, 1989, Billy was killed in a car accident at the age of sixty-one.

Carl Pohlad

Carl Pohlad was born August 23, 1915, in West Des Moines, Iowa. He was the third of eight children. Carl attended West Des Moines High School, where he was an average student. But a lack of straight A's in school was not an accurate measure of young Pohlad's future success. Carl was an ambitious youth who became involved in business even before graduating from high school. After completing secondary school in Des Moines, Pohlad attended Gonzaga University in Washington State.

World War II interrupted his blossoming career as an entrepreneur. Pohlad went to Europe as part of the U.S. Army Infantry. He fought in combat in France, Germany, and Austria.

At the war's conclusion, Carl returned to Iowa for a short time before moving to Minneapolis in the 1940s. There he became involved in the banking business and, over a fifty-plus-year career, successfully created and expanded a number of important banking interests. Through hard work and shrewd dealings, Carl Pohlad became immensely successful.

Pohlad and his family have numerous investments as of spring 2001. They include bank-related service organizations, Marquette Banks, Pepsi Cola franchises, airline passenger and freight operations and—the acquisition that has brought Pohlad his greatest notoriety—ownership of the Minnesota Twins of the American Baseball League.

Carl assumed control of the Twins on September 7, 1984, after purchasing them from Calvin Griffith. The Twins were in danger of being sold and moved out of Minnesota. Pohlad bought them, in part, because of a deep sense of community responsibility and pride. He believed that it was important to keep professional baseball in Minnesota and build a winning team.

The Twins delivered World Series championships to their millions of fans in 1987 and 1991. Those were highlights of major-league sports for many in Minnesota.

As of spring 2000, Pohlad served on two of the most important ownership committees: the Major League Baseball Executive Council and the Player Relations

Committee Board of Directors. He was elected vice president of the American League.

For many decades, the business and civic communities of Minneapolis and St. Paul have looked to Carl Pohlad for leadership. He serves as president and director of Marquette Bancshares, chairman of the board of Mesaba Holdings, Inc., and director of Champion Air and Genmar Holdings, Inc.

His personal commitment to the Twin Cities and its people was evident when he helped a struggling young immigrant woman start a business in Bloomington. Her name: Leeann Chin.

Beyond his business interests, Pohlad has consistently believed in community involvement, particularly in activities that aid young people. He is a founding member of the Board of Directors of the Boys' Club and Girls' Club of Minneapolis.

Pohlad is also a member of the advisory council at Johns Hopkins Department of Orthopedic Surgery. He is a trustee of the Hugh O'Brian Youth Foundation and, since 1989, has been a member of the Horatio Alger Association of Distinguished Americans, which provides scholarships for graduating high-school seniors.

Pohlad's concern for his community is also apparent through his service as a board member of the Methodist Hospital and Health System and the Saddat Peace Foundation.

The Twins continue to be the Pohlad family's main passion. Carl's three sons all serve on the nine-member Twins Executive Board. He and his wife, Eloise, a passionate fan of her husband's team, resided in Edina as of spring 2001.

Opposite: Brent Urdahl (author's son), Jim Brant, Dave Boswell, and Don Mincher.

Appendix

1960s

Year	Team Record	Finish	Manager
1961	70-90	7	Lavagetto-Mele
1962	71-91	2	Mele
1963	91-70	3	Mele
1964	79-83	6	Mele
1965	102-60	1	Mele
1966	89-73	2	Mele
1967	91-71	2	Mele-Ermer
1968	79-83	7	Ermer
1969	97-65	1	Martin

1970s

Year	Team Record	Finish	Manager
1970	98-64	1	Rigney
1971	74-86	5	Rigney
1972	77-77	3	Rigney-Quilici
1973	81-81	3	Quilici
1974	82-80	3	Quilici
1975	76-83	4	Quilici
1976	85-77	3	Mauch
1977	84-77	4	Mauch
1978	73-89	4	Mauch
1979	82-80	4	Mauch

1980s

Year	Team Record	Finish	Manager
1980	77-84	3	Mauch-Goryl
1981	(1) 17-39	7	Goryl-Gardner
1981	(2) 24-29	4	Gardner
1982	60-102	7	Gardner
1983	70-92	5	Gardner
1984	81-81	2	Gardner
1985	77-85	4	Gardner-Miller
1986	71-91	6	Miller-Kelly
1987	85-77	1	Kelly
1988	91-71	2	Kelly
1989	80-82	5	Kelly

1990s

Year	Team Record	Finish	Manager
1990	74-88	7	Kelly
1991	95-67	1	Kelly
1992	90-72	2	Kelly
1993	71-91	5	Kelly
1994	53-60	4	Kelly
1995	56-88	5	Kelly
1996	78-84	4	Kelly
1997	68-94	4	Kelly
1998	70-92	4	Kelly
1999	63-97	5	Kelly
2000	69-93	5	Kelly

About the Author

Dean Urdahl is a native of Litchfield, Minnesota. He graduated from St. CLoud State University in 1971, and has taught American History in New London-Spicer (Minnesota) schools since that time.

Dean married Karen Frantti of St. Cloud, Minnesota, in 1971. They have three sons: Chad, sports editor of the *Owatonna People's Press*, and Brent and Troy, Spring 2001 graduates of Hamline University in St. Paul.

The Urdahls reside on a hobby farm in Meeker County. Dean's varied interests have led to involvement in many areas, including politics, education, government, sports, and writing. He has been a devoted fan of the Minnesota Twins since childhood.

Dean and Karen have derived much enjoyment watching their athletic sons compete in sports at the high school and college levels over the years. Dean is still an avid softball and basketball player, while Karen enjoys walking.

All members of the family have worked with Urdahl Paint Company, a business started by Dean's father Clarence fifty years ago. Dean has another book, *Lives Lived Large*, which features famous living Minnesotans, forthcoming from North Star Press. He is currently editing his novel on the Dakota Conflict.